The Hospitality Manager's Guide to Wines, Beers, and Spirits

Albert W. A. Schmid, CCP, CHE, CCE, CEC

Department of Hospitality Studies
Sullivan University, Louisville, KY

PEARSON
Prentice
Hall

Upper Saddle River, New Jersey 07458

Library of Congress Cataloging-in-Publication Data
Schmid, Albert W. A.
The hospitality manager's guide to wines, beers, and spirits / Albert
W. A. Schmid.
  p. cm.
Includes index.
  ISBN 0-13-091750-8
  1. Bartending. 2. Food service management. I. Title.
TX950.7.S36 2003
641.8′74—dc21

                     2003012103

Editor-in-Chief: Stephen Helba
Executive Editor: Vernon R. Anthony
Executive Assistant: Nancy Kesterson
Associate Editor: Marion Gottlieb
Editorial Assistant: Ann Brunner
Director of Manufacturing
  and Production : Bruce Johnson
Managing Editor: Mary Carnis
Production Liaison: Adele M. Kupchik
Creative Director: Cheryl Asherman
Design Coordinator: Christopher Weigand
Manufacturing Manager: Ilene Sanford
Manufacturing Buyer: Cathleen Petersen

Interior Design & Formatting: Pine Tree
  Composition, Inc.
Production Editor: Nicholas P. Angelides/
  Pine Tree Composition, Inc.
Cover Designer: Kevin Kall
Cover Image: Photodisk
Marketing Manager: Ryan DeGrote
Marketing Assistant: Elizabeth Farrell
Senior Marketing Coordinator: Adam Kloza
Printer/Binder: Phoenix Book Tech Park
Cover Printer: Phoenix Color Corp.

Pearson Education, Ltd.
Pearson Education Australia PTY. Limited
Pearson Education Singapore Pte. Ltd.
Pearson Education North Asia Ltd.

Pearson Education Canada, Ltd.
Pearson Educación de Mexico, S.A. de C.V.
Pearson Education–Japan
Pearson Education Malaysia, Pte. Ltd.

10 9 8 7 6 5 4 3 2 1
ISBN 0-13-091750-8

Contents

Visit us at www.prenhall.com/schmid

To my two muses, Thomas and Michael, for the time with me that you did not receive that I could finish this book. This book is in many ways yours; thank you.

Foreword

There is a simple axiom in journalism: "Reporting starts with what you know." It can be argued persuasively that the same is true in alcoholic beverage management, especially regarding wine. To be an effective restaurant beverage manager, knowledge of the product is absolutely essential. The ability to taste, understand, evaluate, and articulate your findings in a clear, easily understood manner is key to increasing wine and spirit sales and, ultimately, boosting profits for your establishment; and, as any owner or general manager will attest, a profit booster is worth his or her weight in, well, Cabernet Sauvignon.

The good news is that restaurant patrons throughout North America are increasingly more knowledgeable about wine (and spirits); the bad news is that the vast majority of people who do order wine in restaurants still have little to no knowledge about the wine. For most, red and white remain the primary distinguishing factors. Few can describe the general characteristics of, say, a Napa Valley Chardonnay or an Oregon Pinot Noir. Even fewer still have any knowledge whatsoever of the vast array of European wines on the market. What's more, the number of new labels from both established and "emerging" wine regions (both domestic and international) that come to market each year is staggering. Even for wine-savvy customers, keeping abreast of developments in the wine world is all but impossible.

This makes the role of a restaurant's wine and spirits manager all the more challenging. Whether a dedicated position or an add-on responsibility, to be an effective (i.e., profit-producing) beverage manager, the person in charge not only has to craft a wine/spirits list that fits the market position, food, and style of his/her establishment, but also has to taste and purchase the wines, receive and inventory shipments, track sales, calculate costs and profits, educate the waitstaff, and manage sales on the floor. It's a daunting task.

Unfortunately, the one key element that often gets short shrift (or neglected altogether) is staff training. Though most managers agree that training pays handsome dividends, finding the time to run meaningful education programs for front-of-the-house employees is—in the hectic day-to-day grind of the restaurant and hospitality industry—difficult, to say the least. What makes it even more difficult is the lack of concise, professional-oriented information. Though there has been a rash of wine (and spirits) books published in recent years geared to the general public, until quite recently, very little has been written exclusively for the restaurant professional. Of those currently in print, nearly all still read as though they were written for consumers, with little or no attention paid to the specific needs of the busy restaurant beverage manager.

The book you now hold in your hands is an exception to the rule. With *The Hospitality Manager's Guide to Wines, Beers, and Spirits*, Albert Schmid has crafted an educational tool that provides the reader in a concise, user-friendly format, the type of professional-level information he or she needs to be an effective beverage manager. His chapters on alcohol safety, mixology, alcohol service and cost control, marketing, purchasing, and storage provide invaluable information for seasoned as well as novice managers. The chapters on wine labels and bottle shapes, tasting, wine and food pairing, and the vineyard and winery offer a primer to the wine novice and can serve as an excellent outline for a basic staff wine training program.

The chapters on the specific wines themselves are arranged in categories ranging from light-bodied white wines to full-bodied red wines, with a separate chapter on sparkling, dessert, and fortified wines and aperitifs. This style rather than regional or varietal approach to wine grouping has become increasingly popular on wine lists. It provides both the beverage professional (and server) and the restaurant patron with a basic and easily understood departure point for discussing and selecting wines. The chapters on beer and spirits recognize the growing interest in specialty products in those categories and provide the necessary information for helping customers make informed beverage choices.

It is gratifying to see a wine, beer, and spirits management guide of this quality on the market. I highly recommended it for anyone with a professional interest in restaurant and hospitality beverage management.

Mark Vaughan
Editor and Publisher
Santé, the Magazine for Restaurant Professionals

Preface

What a treat, being able to write a book on a subject like wines, beers, and spirits. The subject is intriguing and has all the trappings of a wonderful dime-store novel: drama, tragedy, joy, celebration, and even sex!

The history of how man first discovered alcohol is very interesting: it was by accident. However, this accident sparked a question in the mind of early man that we take for granted today: where can I get more? During this time, man wanted to secure more alcohol, either beer or wine. This alcoholic beverage became sacred. So sacred that it was used in religious ceremony, and laws were written to maintain its purity.

The purity of alcohol has been one of the most important issues throughout time. People had many different tests to prove its purity to make sure that what they were getting was genuine.

Never has there been a better time to buy alcohol. Today, the question is not where to get alcohol or how pure the alcohol is, but what kind to get. Great imported wines from Australia cost, in many cases, less than California wine. Wine from Chile costs even less! And, the wine is good! Winemaking and the winemakers are just getting better and better.

Beer is also getting better, and there is more beer available than ever before. This beer is from all over the world. Frank Zappa once said, "You can't be a real country unless you have a beer and an airline—it helps if you have some kind of a football team, or some nuclear weapons, but at the very least you need a beer." There are very few countries that don't make beer. A store with a large selection will have a beer for everyone's tastes.

Spirits have gone through a renaissance. They used to be viewed as what your parents drank. Now we have designer spirits to go along with designer clothing. This is the age of super premium (or top-shelf) spirits. Most people are not drinking more, they are drinking better. We have traded quantity for quality.

Now more than ever it is important for the hospitality manager to know wines, beers, and spirits. Hospitality managers can help their business sell alcohol safely with great rewards. Hospitality managers need to understand this subject because their customers are more knowledgeable and savvy than ever before.

Over two years ago I started my journey of writing this book. As you begin your journey of studying this book and the subject of wines, beers, and spirits, I hope that for you, this is also just a beginning; or as Sir Winston Churchill said in a speech given at the Lord Mayor's luncheon, Mansion House, London,

November 10, 1942: "This is not the end. It is not even the beginning of the end. But it is, perhaps, the end of the beginning." I hope that this subject will become a lifelong interest. Enjoy this book, and good luck in your future as a hospitality manager.

Albert W. A. Schmid
CCP, CHE, CCE, CEC

Acknowledgments

The idea that a book can be written by one person without any help from other people is ridiculous. I would like to thank the following people for their direct or indirect contribution to this project in the following ways:

To Kerry Sommerville, CHE, CHA, Chairman, Hospitality Studies Department, Sullivan University, for copyediting, advice, support, and for writing the sections on alcohol law safety and cost control. To Dawn McGiffen, CHE, CHA, Instructor, Hospitality Studies Department, Sullivan University, for writing the section on marketing and selling; and to Eddie Maamry, CFBE, CHS, Instructor, Hospitality Studies Department, Sullivan University, for your support, advice, and help.

To my students, who inspire me to do the best job that I can do, thank you for all the help.

To "Computer Master" Bruns Warner, for advising me on the technical aspects of the computer, and especially for helping save the book from the shattered remains of a laptop and for advising me on Word 2000 and Word 97, which shaved countless hours off this project.

To the Rev. Dr. Thomas H. and Elizabeth Schmid, both of whom instilled the idea that that I could do it even if the odds were stacked against me, and for your thirty-five years of continued friendship. Also, to my sisters and brother—Gretchen, Rachel, and Bennett—thank you for all of your help and support.

To the Rev. Richard and Anita Wheatcroft, for proofreading and setting an early example of what it took to be a writer, and for your continued mentorship, support, and friendship.

To Steve Reed, for your friendship and your ear. Thank you for being someone that I could bounce ideas off of and for being a fellow writer, chef, and father who understood what I was going through.

To Dr. Newal Hunter, Dean of Education, Culinary and Hospitality Institute of Chicago, for your mentorship, for having the faith in me, and for leading me in the early years of teaching.

To Adam Segar, CHE, CCP, General Manager, of Thomas Keller's New York Restaurant for your advice and friendship.

To Chef Michael (Mik) Milster, CEC, CCE, CHE, CFBE, who shared his knowledge of wines, spirits, beers and the art and science of culinary art and teaching.

To Master Distillers Lincoln Henderson and Chris Morris of Brown-Forman Corporation, for advising and sharing their knowledge of distillation and distilled alcoholic beverages.

To Vern Anthony, Ann Brunner, Sue Kegler, Marion Gottlieb, Dave Garza, and the other people from Prentice Hall and Pearson Education, without whom this book would still be an idea. Thank you for taking a chance on me.

Sarah Labensky, CCP, for all of your mentorship, support, advice, and copy editing; thank you (which does not say enough).

To Scot Duvall, for friendly counsel.

To Ken and Scott Meier (the former owners) and Chris Piper (the current owner) of Meier's Cork and Bottle in Lincoln, Nebraska, for helping to support an expensive interest in the early, lean years and for showing me that "good wine" is not always expensive wine.

To Dr. Robert Johnston, Professor Emeritus of Biochemistry, University of Nebraska at Lincoln, for helping me understand the importance of and helping me obtain my "union card," and for your knowledge of the fermentation and distillation processes.

To Dr. Stephen Bhuler, Associate Professor of English, University of Nebraska at Lincoln, for encouraging me to write.

To Jennie Langham, one of my teachers from McDonna 15, in the New Orleans French Quarter, for making me write my first book 27 years ago, and for your continued friendship and support.

To Fran and George Seeley, Jonie Foote (formerly Chadwick), the late Joan Jopling, and the rest of my early editors, for your help and guidance early in my writing career; thank you.

To all of my good friends at Northwest Missouri State University in Maryville, thank you for the memories.

To President A. R. Sullivan, for having the continued vision for the school where I teach.

To Glenn Sullivan, Executive Vice President, Sullivan University, for being able to share stories of the love of home brewing, and for sharing your knowledge and perspective on all things fermented and distilled.

To Dr. Stephen Coppock, Executive Vice President/CEO, Sullivan University, for your inspiration and your good words every time I see you.

To Tammy M. Lubash, for early copy editing and advising on this project, and to Amy M. McMichael, CHE, for advising on this project.

To Ken Jarvis of Anne Aurundel Community College for your time spent reviewing my work.

To Keb Mo, Dave Matthews, Phil Collins, David Sandborn and Cheryl Crow, for writing and producing the wonderful music that I played in my office at home while I wrote. Thank you for the inspiration.

Chapter 1

A Brief History of Alcoholic Beverages

After reading this chapter, you will be able to:

❏ Identify key moments in the history of wine, beer, and spirits in the ancient world.
❏ Discuss wine's importance in the Greek and Roman civilizations.
❏ Identify key moments in French wine history.
❏ Discuss basic rules and regulations concerning wine production.
❏ Identify key moments in American winemaking history.
❏ Summarize the worldwide phylloxera crisis.
❏ Discuss the rise of microbreweries.
❏ Explain the effect of Prohibition on the alcohol industry.

It was not the subtle bouquet of wine, or a lingering aftertaste of violets and raspberries, that first caught the attention of our ancestors. It was, I'm afraid, its effect.

—Hugh Johnson, in *Vintage: The Story of Wine*

Introduction

Alcohol probably was discovered by accident about 6,000 to 7,000 years ago, but some estimates place this discovery as far back as 10,000 years ago. During this time people were hunting for wild game and gathering wild fruits and grains. At some point in time, early hunter-gatherer groups acquired the technology needed to store their food supplies. Storage over a period of time is key to the production of alcohol. If grapes were stored for an extended period of time, the natural yeast in the air or the yeast on the skins of the grapes would have converted the sugar in the fruit to alcohol and carbon dioxide. The carbon dioxide would have dispersed into the air, but the alcohol would have remained. Grain such as wheat or barley also could have been the first item from which alcohol was made. To convert the grain to alcohol, it needed to be exposed to water. The exposure to water allows the starch in the grain to convert to sugar, something that happens naturally during the growth process of grain. Storing the wet grain would allow time for the sugars to change to alcohol.

Imagine the surprise of someone experiencing the intoxicating effects of stored, fermented grapes or grains for the first time! This accident's affect on history is immeasurable; it may have been one factor in the switch from a hunter-gatherer subsistence base to one of cultivation.

Religion and Alcohol

Historically, wine has played an important role in many religious ceremonies. The early Roman Catholic bishops, priests, monks, and nuns were not only in charge of the religious ceremonies of the day, but many times they also were winemakers, brewers, and distillers. The early Roman Catholic Church was able to form a monopoly on the production of alcohol because the priests and monks were educated. Education meant literacy, which, in turn, meant the priests and monks could keep records of what they were doing. In addition, the Church had money and land, which they were able to use for research and production. The Church's ability to maintain the wine supply was very important because they needed to be sure wine would exist for the mass. The assurance of this "in-house" supply of wine for the ceremonies was important to the morale of people following and keeping a religious life as well.

The monks kept detailed notes on improvements to wine, beer, and spirits that they discovered or accidentally stumbled upon. The most famous of these accidental discoveries is credited to the Benedictine monk Dom Pierre Perignon. Even though most scholars on the subject agree that Dom Perignon did not invent sparkling wine, they do agree that he performed great volumes of research on the subject of sparkling wine. He designed the bottle that is still in use today

Figure 1.1   Many knights sought the Holy Grail, or the cup that the Christ and his disciples drank from during the Last Supper. According to legend Sir Galahad was the only knight pure enough to find the cup. [Dorling Kindersley Images]

and he began blending different grapes to make the "perfect juice" for wine production. Similar blends still can be found today in the repertoires of most champagne producers.

Over time the religious orders specialized their alcohol production, and specific groups became known for specific alcoholic products. The Christian Brothers Order is known for its brandy, and Benedictine is named after yet another religious order. The Trappist order of monks is known for their beers, which still are made to order. Many of these early orders distilled, brewed, and vinted products that were used by the early Church as both a medicine (for which it was not very effective) and to sterilize wounds (which it does rather well).

Wine is also used in Jewish ceremonies and celebrations, including Passover, weddings, and bris, or the circumcision ceremony. Kosher wines are produced for those who follow orthodox dietary rules. Some religions, however, totally ban the use or consumption of alcoholic beverages both from rituals and from the members' everyday life. These religions include Islam and some Protestant denominations.

Figure 1.2 This special cup is used to drink wine on the Shabbat Night during the *kiddush,* or Jewish Prayer. [Dorling Kindersley Images]

Wine

Wine has been around far longer than written records, but stories concerning wine have been handed down through the generations. In one of the first such stories, found in the Bible's Book of Genesis, one of the first things that Noah did after the waters of the great flood receded was to disembark from the Ark and plant grapevines. Even today, grapes are prevalent in the area where Noah's Ark is purported to have landed. After reaping the fruit from his vines, Noah made the juice into wine. Later in the story Noah became drunk, disgracing his son Ham, who "saw the nakedness of his father" upon walking into Noah's tent. The story illustrates that even God's chosen people can overindulge with alcohol if they are not careful, and that the whole family can be affected.

Figure 1.3 A *Quaichs* is a cup made from silver that was used in Great Britain. [Dorling Kindersley Images]

Historically, societies raised and cultivated vines anywhere that they would grow. An example of this is Georgia, a former kingdom and former province of the former Soviet Union, located to the northeast of Turkey, where Noah's Ark landed on Mount Ararat. This and other areas located around the Black Sea may have been where the first grapes were grown. As societies moved around, they took the vines with them to grow in different areas all over the world. There are records in Egypt of vineyards dating back to 2900 B.C. Now vines can now be found on every continent except Antarctica. Some of the vines grew naturally, such as the vines found in the Americas, whereas others, such as the vines in Australia, had to be transplanted.

In the early years, the countries that had the vines were the countries that had the wine. This early trade was documented in the form of written law as early as 1792 B.C., when the Babylonian King Hammurabi included several punishments for dishonest wine traders, including the death penalty. This set of laws was known as the Code of Hammurabi. The fact that laws were made to govern the early wine trade industry attests to the social and cultural importance it had as a commodity in society.

Wine in Ancient Egypt

Wine was the drink of prestige and privilege in ancient Egypt. Its consumption probably was limited to the rich and the clergy. It is clear from hieroglyphics and archaeological evidence that wine was used in religious ceremonies and was buried with the dead. When tombs of the Pharaohs were opened, clay jars used for holding wine were discovered. The jars were marked similar to the way bottles are marked today, indicating where the grapes were grown, the year the grapes were harvested, and who made the wine. Apparently, this wine was part of the dead pharaoh's provisions for the afterlife. Many pharaohs also had their own private vineyards; hieroglyphics showing the harvesting of grapes and the production of wine also have been found. The Egyptians also had begun to master the art of glassmaking, and they used this skill to make bottles for storing wine.

The drinking of wine also had social implications in ancient Egypt. If a young man allowed a woman to take a sip of his wine or beer, the couple immediately became engaged.

Because Egypt is located in the desert, its people had to figure out how to irrigate their vineyards. The guaranteed growth that the water provided was very important because of the trade route that the Egyptians set up with the Greeks first and later the Romans.

Greek and Roman Winemaking

To say that winemaking and drinking played an important part in ancient Greek and Roman life is an understatement. The importance of wine can be illustrated by looking at the ancient meaning of the term *symposium.* Today a symposium

Figure 1.4 A Graeco-Roman ivory carving of a female offering wine to a youth. [Dorling Kindersley Images]

refers to a meeting of learned individuals gathered to talk about many aspects of a single subject. Its Greek derivative, however, means "to drink together."

Wine was so strongly embedded in Greek culture that the Greeks specifically had a god for wine: Dionysus. The importance of wine in Greek life was celebrated each year by a festival to honor Dionysus. The people participating would sacrifice live animals, drink wine, watch plays, drink wine, and then drink more wine. According to Hugh Johnson's book *Vintage: The Story of Wine*, their wine also may have included pinesap, hallucinogenic mushrooms, and a natural form of the hallucinogenic drug we know as LSD. The Greeks believed that when they consumed wine, they consumed the god and that this was why they felt good when they drank. As they started to feel bad from the wine's aftereffects, they credited this feeling to the god leaving their bodies.

Wine had a role in Greek literature and science as well. Homer included wine in his stories about the Battle of Troy and Odysseus. In addition, Hippocrates, one of ancient Greece's scientists, made many notes concerning wine's effects on different parts of the human body.

The Romans also had a god of wine whom they called Bacchus. Roman leaders, however, did not always appreciate this god or his followers. In 186 B.C., the Roman Senate banned the worship of Bacchus, or Bacchanalia, because his worshippers were accused of many sorts of crimes and vices ranging from promiscuous sex to murder. A witch-hunt followed this ban, during which over 7,000 people were accused of treason. Many years later, Julius Caesar lifted the ban in response to public pressure. By this time, however, Bacchus's role had changed into to that of a savior figure; he became the god of the underworld with power to grant his followers an afterlife.

Figure 1.5   The Roman god Bacchus.
[Dorling Kindersley Images]

Christian authorities, believing in only one God, discouraged the worship of Bacchus, and by A.D. 692, a ruling from Constantinople, a stronghold of the early Christian church, forbade anyone from worshipping the wine god. Winegrowers could not even utter his name during winemaking; women could not dance in public; and plays were banned. Anyone caught violating any of these new church laws could be excommunicated, according to Hugh Johnson.

France

For centuries, French wine has served as the epitome of wine. Even today, when wineries in other countries claim that their wine is made in the "old-world" style, they are referring to French-style winemaking. For example, if a winery near Santa Barbara, California, says that it makes wine in the old-world style of Burgundy, the winemakers mean that they are using the same grapes and the same methods that winemakers use in the Burgundy region of France.

The winemakers of France, in turn, have been influenced by the styles and techniques of other countries. Because France played a role in many wars, including World War I, World War II, and the Hundred Years War, France has had access to the ideas and methods of all the other countries with which it has had contact.

Wine Regions of France   For many centuries, France and Germany fought over the province of Alsace. After World War I, the small strip of land bordering France and Germany came into French control again. This province produces grapes that are considered German grapes and that produce classic German wines such as Riesling and Gewürztraminer. Alsace growers also grow Tokay,

Pinot Gris, and Pinot Blanc. The major distinction between German and Alsatian wines is that Alsatian wine is dry like French wines rather than sweet like German wines.

Other areas in France, such as the Bordeaux, Loire, and Rhône regions, also are important regions in France's wine history. In the Bordeaux region, Château Haut-Brion is noted as the first great wine; its unique taste comes from an innovation used in the wine's storage. Long before the advent of scientific techniques in wine production, these wine producers used new barrels to store wine, which they kept filled to the bunghole at the top. Even though the wine producers did not understand why this type of storage made a difference, it did make a very big difference in the flavor of the wine, making Château Haut-Brion an extraordinary wine.

The Loire, another famous wine region of France, is known for the extraordinary white wine produced there. Some of the biggest names in wine, including Pouilly-Fumé, Sancerre, and Vouvray, are produced here. White grapes flourish among the many castles built for the nobility in this valley along the banks of the Loire River. The grape-growing region in the Rhône, just north of Avignon, France, known as Châteauneuf-du-Pape, takes its name from a Roman Catholic pope. Pope Clement V resided at the Châteauneuf-du-Pape, or "New Castle of the Pope," during the fourteenth century. The Rhône region is also home to the

Figure 1.6 This wine press was used many years ago to squeeze the juice out of the grapes. [Dorling Kindersley Images]

Hermitage, named after Henri Gaspard de Sterimberg, a knight who fought in Pope Innocent III's crusade. When he returned from the crusade, he became a hermit and spent the next thirty years dedicated to viticulture. The wines of the Hermitage are made from the Syrah grape and are some of the fullest-bodied red wines made in Rhône.

Philippe the Bold, Duke of Burgundy was perhaps the first person to impose rules or laws regarding what could be grown in his Duchy. He dictated what farmers could and could not use to fertilize their ground, and in 1395 he banned the Gamay grape from Burgundy because the wine it produced was "foul." Many years later, the Rhône region gained the distinction of being the first region to implement an Appellation d'Origine Contrôlée (AOC) several years before any other region. In 1923, the Baron Le Roy of the Château Fortia almost single-handedly wrote the regulations for the entire region. Many of the other regions used this document as a guide in 1936 when an AOC was created for the rest of France. These laws covered everything about the production of grapes, including which rootstocks could be used and how many grapes could be grown per hectare (approximately 2.5 acres). These early laws still control how French wines are made today.

Germany

When all wine regions are evaluated and compared, Germany breaks all the rules regarding the needs for successful winemaking, yet many experts say Germany makes some of the best wine in the world. The climate in Germany is generally considered too cold and harsh for good grape production and the land is deemed

Figure 1.7 The traditional costume of an Alsatian Wine Master. [Dorling Kindersley Images]

too hilly. According to master sommelier Kevin Zraly, about 66 percent of the land consists of steep hillsides with an angle of about 60 degrees. Fourteen percent of the land can be described as hillsides with an angle of 45 degrees, and only 20 percent can be described as flat land. This type of terrain is not ideal for growing grapes, but during the Roman occupation of present-day Germany, Romans determined which grapes did best in this hilly land, and they were able to produce their much-loved wine. Because of the terrain and climate, however, the wine produced in Germany was much sweeter than the wine the Romans had produced in the past.

Because of Germany's geographic location, there are approximately one hundred sunny days in the country. Since there is so little direct sunlight, the grapes must stay on the vine longer than is usual in other regions. The longer that the grapes are on the vine, the more sun they get, which promotes more sugar to develop and reduces the acid content of the grapes.

In addition to these natural phenomena affecting the wine's sweetness, a particular winemaking technique also plays a role in giving German wines their sweet flavor. The winemaker will reserve some of the unfermented juice, called the Süssereserve. Once the wine is made and the yeast will no longer ferment additional sugar, the Süssereserve is added back into the wine. This juice raises the sugar content and lowers the alcohol content.

Another accidental discovery gave Germany one of its most distinctive wines. In 1775, the Abbot of Fulda, who had the personal responsibility of ordering the harvesting of grapes, was attending a very important church conference. The conference took longer than expected, and the monks back at the Abbey watched anxiously as the grapes began to rot on the vine. Finally, they sent a rider to get the Abbot's permission to harvest. By the time the rider returned with the permission, the monks thought that the crop had been lost, but they harvested the grapes anyway and made them into wine. They were surprised that it became one of the best wines they had ever tasted. The wine was sweet, rich, and very complex. They called the wine Spätlese, or "Late-Picked," and the technique of hand-picking grapes with what has become known as "Noble Rot" continues to this day.

Italy

Even though grapevines have grown in Italy for well over 3,000 years, only two regions are well known for wine: Piedmont and Tuscany. Many of the grape growers in these regions have bent to public demand for wines made from Cabernet Sauvignon, Chardonnay, and Merlot grapes, but this is a recent development. Traditionally, the grape varieties of Italy are Nebbiolo, Sangiovese, and Trebbiano. Other grapes that have their origins in Italy include Pinot Blanc and Pinot Gris (which is referred to as Pinot Grisio in Italy). The Gewürztraminer grape, while sounding German, may have come from, or been named for, the village of Tramin in Italy.

In 1963, the Italians adopted laws very similar to the French AOC called Denominazione di Origine Controllata, or DOC. These laws cover the geographic limits of each region, the grapes that are used, how many grapes are produced per acre, the minimum alcohol content, and how long the wine should be aged.

Recently there has been conflict in Italian winemaking because the traditional Italian grapes are being replaced with grapes that are identified with those grown in France. Some Italian winemakers insist on making wine only from those grapes that have always been common to Italy.

California

Wine was first made in California when Spanish missionaries planted vines in the mid-1700s as they spread the Christian faith north of Mexico. Since the 1960s and 1970s, California wines have been considered some of the best wines in the world. The true beginning of the rise of California wines occurred in 1976, when a California winery competed in a blind tasting in France. Warren Winiarski's Stag's Leap 1973 Cabernet Sauvignon was named the top wine that year, beating out some of the French first growths, including Château Haut-Brion and Mouton-Rothschild.

The Mite That Almost Brought Down the Industry   The grapes now thought of as great California grapes such as Chardonnay, Merlot, and Cabernet Sauvignon did not come America; these are truly European grapes, or *vitis vinifera*. There are three main species of grapes: *vitis vinifera* (native European), *vitis labrusca* (native American), and French-American hybrids. People arriving in America were used to drinking wines made from *vitis vinifera* grapes. When they found grapes growing in America, they were overjoyed to know that they could continue to make and enjoy wine, but they were disappointed by the flavor of the wine made from *vitis lambrusca* grapes. To amend this, they sent home for cuttings of the *vitis vinifera*. When they planted the European grapes, they found that the vines did not survive in the American soil. They continued to experiment, however, sending cuttings back and forth across the ocean. Over the years both the people in America and Europe thought that the only thing they were shipping back and forth were grape vines. When all of the vines in Europe started to die, people started looking for what was causing the vines to die. They found that a little mite, ***Phylloxera vastatrix*** (phylloxera for short), very hard to see by the naked eye, was attacking the root. The mite had emigrated from America to Europe on the vines that had been shipped from America. When vines were tested in America, the mites were found, but the roots of the *vitis labrusca* were resistant to the mite. In 1869, Professor Gaston Barzille proposed that if American roots were grafted to French vines, it might solve the problem of phylloxera. He was right. This grafting created the new French hybrids that are used today. Unfortunately, the problems with phylloxera mites remain a threat to the industry, but advances are being made to solve new problems before they are as devastating as the first phylloxera mite crisis.

Other United States Wine Regions

California was not the only state known for its wine prior to 1919. New York, Missouri, Michigan, Pennsylvania, Ohio, Iowa, and North Carolina were also known for their wines in the early eighteenth century. Thomas Jefferson, one of the founding fathers of the United States, had attempted to grow vineyards and produce wine in Virginia before the Revolutionary War began in 1775.

Beer

A fermented beverage of grain, water, hops, and yeast, beer comes in many flavors and colors and is usually carbonated. Beer has been the most popular alcoholic beverage in the United States for many years, but its roots go back thousands of years.

The Early Years

How man first stumbled upon the method to make beer is a mystery, but likely it was an accident. Discoveries on archaeological digs prove that many different peoples from many different places made beer. Depictions of man drinking beer or remnants of beer-making paraphernalia have been found in the areas that were ancient Mesopotamia, Egypt, China, Rome, Greece, Assyria, and Peru.

The Middle Ages and Europe

In the Middle Ages, both men and women brewed beer; women who undertook making beer at home were known as "brewsters." During this time, the Church controlled much of the production of alcohol. Monks were responsible for brewing, as they would be for the next several centuries. Beer was such an important part of life during this period that the Catholic Church named a patron saint for brewers. In, A.D. 640, the Bishop of Metz died away from his home. He was so loved that the people of his town went to retrieve his body the next year. When the returning group stopped to rest in the village of Champigneulles only one goblet of beer was left to feed them. As in the story of the loaves and fishes, the beer was plenty for the whole group, regardless of how much they drank. The group thought that this was a miracle, and eventually the Bishop was elevated to the status of the first Patron Saint of Brewers, St. Arnulf (Arnold).

The first guild of brewers was formed in Belgium during the reign of Duke Jean (John) I (1251–1294) and was known as the "knights of the mashing fork." Beer had become so important at this point that there is a clause about ale in the Magna Carta , which was signed by King John of England in 1215.

It was the Germans, however, who enacted the first laws or regulations for the production of beer. In 1487, Duke Albert IV set forth the first set of regulations, which was the basis for William VI's famous Reinheitsgebot of 1516. These

Figure 1.8   These beer barrels were used by Mary, Queen of Scots to smuggle messages to the French around the English. [Dorling Kindersley Images]

regulations are still followed in German beer production today. They basically state that the only ingredients allowed in beer production are malted grain, hops, water, and yeast.

Early America

Beer was the preferred beverage aboard sailing ships, including the Mayflower, because water did not always make the voyage without turning bad. The alcohol and hops in beer insured it would be safe for consumption.

According to Gregg Smith, the author of the book, *Beer: A History of Suds and Civilization from Mesopotamia to Microbreweries,* an error in navigation had placed the Mayflower off course, and the crew was required to spend extra time searching for a suitable drop-off place for the Pilgrims. When the boat finally landed in what is now Massachusetts, the crew was worried they would not have any beer for the return trip to England. (Incidentally, John Alden was the cooper, or barrel maker, on the Mayflower; he had the weighty task of ensuring the beer supply. Alden's descendents include two Presidents (John Adams and John Quincy Adams), a Vice President (Dan Quayle), poet Henry Wadsworth Longfellow, actor Orson Welles, and actress Marilyn Monroe.)

Beer also played a role in the colonization of North America. In the early American colonies, beer cost about one cent per quart. Demand for the beverage was high, and by 1680, there were dozens of government-licensed taverns. Many illustrious individuals owned breweries in these years. According to Gregg Smith, John Harvard, founder of the college that is now called Harvard University, made sure that the students and faculty would be able to acquire beer; he included the construction of a brew house in the plans of his college, which opened in 1636. (Harvard had learned to brew from William Shakespeare .) When the beer supply ran low in 1639, the students at Harvard revolted and were successful in raising the supply. The first large-scale commercial brewery was opened in 1638 by William Penn (Pennsylvania's namesake) in Pennsbury, Pennsylvania.

Breweries also were owned by some famous Revolutionary-era generals, including George Washington. Other early generals who owned breweries were Charles Sumner, Ethan Allen, and Israel Putnam. Perhaps one of the most famous early brewery owners was Samuel Adams, even though he did not reach the height of his fame as a brewer until recently, when a widely marketed beer with his name on the label was released. On December 16, 1773, Samual Adams (cousin to future President John Adams and now the namesake for Sam Adams Brewery) and John Hancock, along with other members of the Sons of Liberty, dressed in Native American garb and drank pints of beer before raiding an English ship in an act of rebellion that would become known as the Boston Tea Party.

Taverns as well as breweries were owned by some of our country's founding fathers. Our second President, John Adams, owned and managed a tavern. He also enjoyed "a large tankard of cider every morning," according to grandson Charles Francis Adams.

According to the *Professional Guide to Alcoholic Beverages* by Robert and Kathleen Lipinski, the oldest tavern in America still in existence is Fraunces Tavern in lower Manhattan, in New York City. The tavern was founded in 1762 by Samuel Fraunces, who was of African descent. At the end of the Revolutionary War, General George Washington said goodbye to his officers at the Fraunces Tavern.

The Rise of the Microbreweries

In recent years, customers have become more quality-oriented, and small breweries have begun to spring up all over the country. Almost every major city in the United States has a brewpub and many have microbreweries. Customers like the idea of fresh and the finished product can be tweaked for a unique taste or to quell the taste of the locals. The names of the breweries often represent local names, landmarks or areas such as, Devil Mountain Brewery/Bay Brewing Co. in Benicia, California, near San Francisco, or Pike's Peak Brewery in Colorado Springs, Colorado. Several others include the Dallas County Brewing Co. in Adel, Iowa; Mystic Brewing Co. in Mystic, Connecticut; Bluegrass Brewing Co. in Louisville, Kentucky; and Capitol City Brewing Co. in Washington, D.C.

Spirits

A spirit is almost exactly what it sounds like. It is the vapor, or the essence, of the alcoholic liquid. Spirits refer to alcoholic beverages such as whiskey, gin, and vodka. Spirits are usually very concentrated and contain from 35 to 95 percent alcohol by volume. In order to produce spirits, alcohol is distilled or extracted at temperatures between 180° and 200°F. Anything that has sugar can be fermented into alcohol and distilled into a spirit. Different spirits will not be discussed at this point except in passing and only to show developments that took place to enhance the production of distilled alcohol.

The Early Years

One of the early uses of distillation was for perfumers to extract oils for perfumes. As early as 1000 B.C., the Chinese distilled rice wine to help make gunpowder. By 800 B.C., a distinction between the terms *distilling* and *fermenting* was made in several cultures; most notably, Chinese and Indian writings contain descriptions of the difference between that which was fermented and that which was distilled. Little evidence exists to prove that Europeans were distilling until the Middle Ages. In Greece, Aristotle pointed out in 4 B.C. that seawater could be distilled into drinkable water, and by A.D. 700, Poland and Russia knew that freezing could separate alcohol and water. Arab countries were using alcohol for medical purposes.

The Middle Ages

Sometime between 1235 and 1312, Arnold de Villanova taught distillation as part of alchemy at Avignon and Montpellier. He became recognized as the "Father of Distillation," even though the technology existed more than two millennia before he was born.

By the 1400s, the practice of distilling was widespread in Europe. The Polish began distilling the drink vodka with fermented potatoes in about 1405. They may have done it earlier, but the product probably was used for perfume or as a curative agent used in drugs. The name *vodka* is Russian and means "water of life." Whiskey and several other drinks derive their names from that meaning as well.

Brandy, which is distilled wine, was also produced during the 1400s. The areas producing it, Cognac and Armagnac, became famous for their brandies. Armagnac, though it is not as well known, is the older of the two towns. Distilling began there between 1411 and 1422. Brandy distillation did not begin in Cognac for about another hundred years.

The news of how to take a fermented alcoholic beverage and distill it in to a stronger drink quickly spread throughout Europe. In 1494, whiskey production was recorded in Scotland, and Irish whiskey was first produced in 1556. A French apple brandy called Calvados came into production in 1533. The Church spread the production of distilled spirits during the Middle Ages. Monasteries had the time, resources, money, and labor to devote to such an undertaking, and the process probably traveled from monastery to monastery.

Laws concerning distilling that were passed during this time started with Ivan the Great of Russia who limited the production and sale of vodka in 1474. In

1546, King Jan Olbracht of Poland decreed that all of Poland could distill. By the end of the Middle Ages, governments had realized that they could profit by imposing a tax on the production of alcohol. In 1644, the Scottish Parliament was the first to levy a tax on whiskey and many other governments followed suit. The distillers responded by hiding their stills and continuing to produce alcohol illegally.

Early America

The year that George Washington took office as the first President of the United States, 1789, bourbon whiskey was born in Kentucky. This whiskey may have been named after the county where it was first made—Bourbon County, Kentucky. Another theory states that the name was derived from the French royal family, the Bourbons. This theory states that most other whiskey hailed from the British Isles, which was an enemy of the United States at the time. Therefore, the makers of bourbon whiskey named their drink after an ally, the French. While there is some disagreement as to where the name came from, Bourbon County is its most likely home. A Baptist minister, Elijah Craig, was the first person to produce bourbon, and he became known, as "the Father of bourbon." By 1890, there were over 1,576 registered distilleries throughout the state of Kentucky. Kentucky still makes bourbon, but today, there are only 16 distilleries in the state. While total consumption of hard alcohol is down from thirty years ago, the trend seems to be that people are willing to spend more money for a drink. Because the consumer is substituting quality for quantity, the industry is striving to meet the need for high-quality specialized drinks.

As in brewing, in recent years distillers have been emphasizing quality. There are different recipes for quality. Some involve barrel aging for many more years than is required by law. Some increase the corn content, whereas others say the secret is making the beverage in small batches.

Prohibition

During the period in United States history known as Prohibition, the production, sale, and transportation of alcohol in the United States was illegal. Prohibition lasted from January 16, 1920, when Congress passed the Eighteenth Amendment to the Constitution, to December 5, 1933, when the Twenty-first Amendment was passed. However, the seeds of Prohibition were planted in America long before passage of the Eighteenth Amendment.

In the 1830s, the Temperance Society advocated only moderate, if any, consumption of alcoholic beverages. Later, the group took the more radical stance of total abstinence, and the group became known as "teetotalers." Their work laid the groundwork for the legislation to come. In 1851, Neal Dow of Maine wrote the country's first prohibition law. When it was passed by the Maine legislature, Neal Dow became known as the "Father of Prohibition." By 1855, similar state laws were passed in Rhode Island, Massachusetts, Vermont, Minnesota, Michigan, Connecticut, New York, New Hampshire, Nebraska, Delaware, Indiana, Kansas, and Iowa. These laws were never enforced, however, because most people were more concerned with the impending Civil War than with Prohibition.

The Temperance movement, however, had sympathizers at the highest levels of government during the Civil War. In 1862, the advisors of President Abraham Lincoln asked him to dismiss the successful General Ulysses S. Grant from his command because of Grant's excessive drinking. As Grant continued to be successful, Lincoln went against his advisors, suggesting that a barrel of General Grant's preferred whiskey should be sent to all of the Union generals. General Grant later became President Grant, but the alcohol debate continued and intensified.

The anti-alcohol movement continued in American society until 1917, when World War I began. By September of that year, President Woodrow Wilson, acting under special powers granted by the Food Control Act, was allowed to lessen the production of beer by not allowing grain to go for beer production. President Wilson also limited the alcohol content in beer to less than 2.75 percent by weight. His reasons may have reflected darker motives than just helping the war effort. Most of the owners of the big beer brewers were of German decent. It was easy at the time for people to play the ethnicity card, trying to shut down the brewers because the United States was at war with Germany.

In December 1917, Congress proposed the Eighteenth Amendment to the Constitution. The Amendment was known as the Volstead Act, and it outlawed the "manufacture, sale or transport of intoxicating liquor" (but not consumption). Within thirteen months, two-thirds of the states had ratified this new amendment. It became a law on January 16, 1919, and took effect the following year. All of the states ratified the amendment with the exception of two: Connecticut and Rhode Island. (Interestingly, these two states had earlier prohibition laws that already had been abolished. However, they still were required to uphold the new Constitutional amendment.) The votes in the state legislature had not even been close: 85 percent of the senators and 79 percent of the members of the House of Representatives voted for the measure. Prohibition's long-term effect on the country was devastating. An entire industry had been abolished. In the opinion of the late Max Allen, 1997 International Bartender of the Year and Bartender Emeritus at the Seelbach Hilton Hotel in Louisville, Kentucky, Prohibition was at least partially responsible for the Great Depression. People who had jobs in the liquor industry were suddenly without work and there were no new jobs to replace them. Allen also noted that Kentucky was especially hard hit because one in every three jobs was somehow tied to the industry of making and distributing alcoholic beverages.

Prohibition was repealed fourteen years later by the Twenty-first Amendment, but until then crime and corruption related to Prohibition were widespread. Bootlegging, which originally refered to the concealment of a pint-size flask in a boot for a trip, began in earnest between the United States and Canada. Canada also had imposed prohibition in 1918, but it only lasted one year. Once

Canadian prohibition was repealed and the United States' prohibition was imposed, the door opened for illegal smuggling from Canada to the United States.

The careers of many American gangsters took off during this period. Al Capone and other gangsters smuggled a variety of alcoholic beverages over the Canadian border with Elliot Ness and other U.S. Treasury officers in pursuit. In the end, Capone did go to jail, but the charges were related to tax evasion rather than any infractions related to the Eighteenth Amendment. The alcohol that was successfully brought across the border was usually sold at a "speakeasy," an illegal bar. To enter a speakeasy, the customer had to pass a guard at the door. The customer would knock on the door and the guard would open a little slat in the door to look out. The customer would say the password; if the password was correct, the customer would be allowed to enter. The speakeasies of the Prohibition era first came into existence in 1899 in New York City when the sale of regulated alcohol was legal. During the first years of the speakeasy, the owners sold unregulated alcohol . Many famous people visited speakeasies. The Prince of Wales, who would later become King Edward VIII, (and later the Duke of Windsor) was drinking at a speakeasy when the police raided the establishment. The future king was lucky to have a quick-thinking host who moved Prince Edward into the kitchen, put a chef's toque on his head, gave him a pan and told him to cook eggs until the raid was over. The police never knew the Prince was there.

Another common practice during Prohibition was the making of homemade gin. The person would acquire a basic neutral alcohol. After placing the neutral spirit in the bathtub, the person would add extracts or oils of juniper berries to the spirit, giving the mixture the flavor and kick of gin. After the mixture was finished, it would be bottled. This became known as "bathtub gin."

One of the more covert ways people were encouraged to break the law involved California wineries. The wineries continued to grow and many switched from making wine to making unfermented grape juice concentrate. The makers of this concentrate made sure that anyone who could read would still be able to enjoy wine. Producers often put the following warning label on packages of grape juice concentrate: "WARNING: IF SUGAR AND YEAST ARE ADDED FERMENTATION WILL OCCUR."

The alcoholic beverage industry did whatever it could to survive during Prohibition. Many of the major distilleries and breweries switched to making industrial alcohol, or "near beer." Some of the breweries made other products, such as candy, malted products, soda, or cheese.

In 1928, Democrat Alfred E. Smith ran for President against Republican Herbert Hoover. Hoover used the campaign slogan "Rum, Romanism, and Rebellion," because one of Smith's issues was the repeal of Prohibition. Smith did not win, but he did get the county talking, and by the next presidential election, the country was ready for a drink. Democrat Franklin D. Roosevelt beat Hoover, and within the first nine days of his administration, he asked Congress to amend the Volstead Act. Congress proposed the Twenty-first Amendment on February 20, 1933, and the states went to work. Two-thirds of all states are needed to adopt a new amendment to the Constitution. On December 5, 1933, with nineteen shopping days left until Christmas, the Eighteenth Amendment was history, and by the end of 1933, people were legally drinking alcohol again. When someone asked Elliot Ness, the U.S. Treasury agent who worked to stop Al Capone and other bootleggers, what he would do now that Prohibition was over, he answered, "I think that I am going to have a drink."

Post-Prohibition

When Prohibition was repealed on December 5, 1933, Congress, for the very first time in history, directly created business opportunities for the citizens of the United States. While several California wineries had been able to hold on through the fourteen years of Prohibition by selling grape juice or industrial alcohol, most of them failed. In fact, most of the wineries all over the United States failed. When Prohibition was repealed, very few had the capital to resume production. In addition, most states continued to enforce prohibition locally, and World War II delayed the full return of the business of alcohol production. The wine industry in the United States would not recover for over thirty years. According to Harold Grossman, author of *Grossman's Guide to Wines, Beers, and Spirits*, 7th edition, grape production did not return to pre-Prohibition levels until 1975, and American wine did not take its true place in the world market until some fifty years after Prohibition. According to the Wine Institute, U.S. consumption of wine rose from 0.25 gallons per capita, or 33 million gallons, in 1934 to 2.01 gallons of wine per capita, or 565 million gallons, in 2000.

The beer industry was as damaged as the wine industry by Prohibition. Many of the breweries that existed before Prohibition were not able to reopen their doors, mainly because of a lack of funds. However, new breweries opened, and it has taken much less time for the beer industry to bounce back from Prohibition. As of 1998, two of the top five beverage companies in the United States are Anheuser-Busch, with over $11 billion in revenue, and Adolph Coors, with almost $2 billion. In 2000, beer sales in the United States exceeded 196,847,000, 31-gallon barrels.

Key Terms

Code of Hammurabi
Dionysus
Bacchus
Bacchanalia
Dom Pierre Perignon
The Christian Brothers Order
Appellation d'Origine Contrôlée (AOC)
Old-World style
Denominazione di Origine Controllata (DOC)

Phylloxera vastatrix
Vitis vinefera
Vitis lambrusca
French-American hybrids
Prohibition
Eighteenth Amendment
Volstead Act
Twenty-first Amendment
Microbreweries

Study Questions

1. How was alcohol discovered?
2. Who were Dionysus and Bacchus?
3. Why was legislation, such as the Code of Hammurabi, the AOC, and the DOC, necessary?
4. Why were religious orders involved in the industry, and what are the uses of wine in religion?
5. What was the effect of the *Phylloxera* mite on the wine world?
6. What effect did Prohibition have on the alcohol industry?

Chapter

2   *Alcohol Safety*

After reading this chapter, you will be able to:

- ❑ Identify the major areas of legal concern for foodservice operations.
- ❑ Discuss legal liability related to alcohol sales for foodservice operations.
- ❑ Explain what Dram Shop laws are.
- ❑ Detect the signs of intoxication in a person.
- ❑ Discuss Blood Alcohol Content.
- ❑ Identify the BAC line in your state.
- ❑ Conduct alcohol training and industry certification.

It provokes the desire, but takes away the performance.

—William Shakespeare

Alcoholic Beverages and the Hospitality Industry

Society has been trying to protect itself from abuses brought on by overindulgence in alcoholic beverages since there have been alcoholic beverages to consume. As long ago as in ancient Babylon, laws such as the Code of Hammurabi were designed to restrict possible violence and damage caused by alcohol abuse. The restaurant operator who combines the sale of food with that of alcoholic beverages, or who sells alcoholic beverages exclusively, faces many challenges.

In general, there are two primary classifications of establishments that serve alcoholic beverages. The first includes full-service restaurants, in which beer, wine, and spirits are served primarily as an accompaniment to food. The second includes establishments in which beverages are sold as the primary offering. Generally, bars, taverns, and nightclubs fall into this category.

While alcoholic beverage control boards in each city and county generally have specific powers and responsibilities, the final control over alcohol sales usually rests with the state liquor authority or the state alcohol beverage control board. Matters regulated by some or all states include licensing, illegal sales, hours of operation, dram shop liability, and alcohol service training.

Figure 2.1 A waiter serves a customer a beer in an outdoor café. [Dorling Kindersley Images]

Alcohol Regulations

Licensing

Under the Twenty-first Amendment to the U.S. Constitution, ratified on December 5, 1933, each state has the right to control the sale of alcoholic beverages within that state. A liquor license, once granted, may be revoked or suspended by the state if the licensee (the person who holds the license) violates prescribed laws.

Illegal Sales

Two areas of major concern for foodservice operators who plan to sell alcoholic beverages are the minimum legal age for drinking and drivers who operate motor vehicles while under the influence of alcohol. When Congress threatened to shut off federal highway funds to states that did not raise their legal minimum age requirements to twenty-one, every state that had not already done so promptly adjusted its laws.

Restaurants and bars must carefully check identification cards, such as drivers' licenses, in order to verify that every patron is of legal drinking age. In most states, the following types of sales are considered illegal:

1. Sales to minors (under age twenty-one).
2. Sales to visibly intoxicated persons.
3. Sales to habitual drunkards.

Sales to anyone on this prohibited list may result in the suspension or revocation of a liquor license. Illegal sales can also lead to civil liability for resulting injuries and, particularly in the case of serving a minor, criminal liability for which penalties could include jail and a fine. The prudent foodservice operator will take care to avoid illegal sales.

Hours of Operation

The hours during which a restaurant or a bar can serve alcoholic beverages are strictly regulated by the state, the city, and or the county in which the establishment is located. The days on which alcoholic beverages can be sold—both in foodservice establishments as well as in retail and package outlets—also are strictly regulated. Some areas prohibit Sunday sales altogether, while other areas allow by-the-drink sales only after 12:00 P.M., and then only in establishments which also serve food. Some areas allow only the sale of beer on Sundays, while other areas allow the sale of all alcoholic beverages. In many jurisdictions, alcohol cannot be sold until after 6:00 P.M. on local and national political election days. Clearly, the prudent operator must rely on state and local authorities when determining on what days and at what times it is legal to sell alcoholic beverages.

Figure 2.2 A well-stocked bar. [Dorling Kindersley Images]

Dramshop and Common Law Liability

Every state has strict laws forbidding people to drive motor vehicles if they have been drinking. Many states have now developed third-party liability legislation that holds the restaurant or tavern operator responsible, under certain conditions, for the actions of his or her patrons who consume excessive amounts of alcoholic beverages. These laws, commonly called dramshop *laws,* impose penalties on the server or on the operation that provided the alcoholic beverages.

The objectives of dramshop laws are to discourage owner/operators from selling alcohol illegally and to afford some kind of compensation to those victims whose injuries are a result of an unlawful sale of alcohol. The potential liability is very significant. Some illegal sales have resulted in verdicts that have financially ruined the bar or the restaurant that wrongfully served the alcohol. Because of these laws, operators are becoming increasingly concerned with alcohol awareness and abuse.

A person who is injured by the acts of an intoxicated individual also may have the right to bring a lawsuit based on the common law theory of negligence. In some states, such lawsuits may be filed against the operation that made the illegal sale, independent of any claim under a state's dramshop laws. Under the common law theory of negligence, operators must reasonably foresee that a sale to an obviously intoxicated customer could create a risk of harm to others. The foodservice operation must provide reasonable care to prevent such occurrences.

Dramshop Laws

Dramshop is an outdated term once used to describe establishments that sold alcoholic beverages. Dramshop laws date to the mid-1850s, and they made owners and operators of drinking establishments liable for injuries caused by intoxicated patrons. Before that time, tavern owners and bartenders were exempt from such liability—the theory being that the *consumption* of alcohol, not the *serving* of it, made customers liable. The dramshop laws changed that. More than a dozen states have dramshop acts on the books, and over three dozen states have modern legislation that closely emulates the original dramshop laws.

Because the general public is demanding responsible alcohol service, those who serve alcohol are being held to higher standards of care. Because dramshop legislation and common law liability vary from state to state, the prudent operator should seek the advice of qualified counsel.

Selling alcohol to people who are already intoxicated is illegal. It is difficult to determine someone's level of intoxication based solely on the basis of how much alcohol that person has consumed. The effects of alcohol will differ greatly from person to person. To qualify as *illegal,* the person's appearance or actions must indicate he is intoxicated. Although intoxication is sometimes difficult to detect, that difficulty may not be a defense to a charge of an illegal sale. Bartenders and servers are expected to be familiar with the indicators of intoxication. These indicators include slurred speech, bloodshot and watery eyes, flushed face, and poor coordination, which is often evidenced by difficulty in performing such acts as making change or handling money, lighting a cigarette, or walking without staggering or stumbling. Behavioral evidence of intoxication may also include being overly friendly, boisterous, loud, argumentative, crude, and or annoying to other customers.

In a lawsuit, intoxication is usually proved in one of two ways. The first, used primarily when a criminal charge of driving while intoxicated (DWI; also known as driving under the influence, DUI, in some jurisdictions) is involved, is to show an elevated blood alcohol content (BAC) in a person. BAC is the percent by weight of alcohol in the person's blood. The BAC is determined by analyzing the person's blood, breath, urine, or saliva. Alcohol affects people differently, and several factors affect the amount of alcohol absorbed in a person's blood. Among them is the amount of alcohol consumed, the time involved, the person's body weight, food in the stomach, and the person's general health, especially liver condition.

Alcohol and Its Effects

In general, for a 160-pound person drinking for an hour on an empty stomach:

Number of Drinks	Blood-Alcohol Content
Two	0.04%
Three	0.07%
Five	0.11%
Seven	0.16%

A drink is defined as 1½ ounces of 80-proof liquor, 12 ounces of beer, or 5 ounces of table wine.

ALCOHOL-INDUCED CHANGES

Blood-Alcohol Level	Effects (for Most Drivers)
0.01% to 0.05%	Mild alteration of feelings and slight intensification of mood. Bad driving habits are slightly pronounced.
00.05% to 0.10%	Feeling of relaxation. Vision, hearing and speech are impaired. Minor disturbance of balance. Longer reaction time. Fine motor skills (such as braking) are impaired. Judgment impaired.
0.10% to 0.15%	Judgment and memory seriously affected. Physical coordination impaired. Motor skills badly impaired. Driving becomes very difficult.
Over 0.15%	Difficulty in standing, walking and talking. Distortion of all perceptions and judgment. Major impairment of all physical and mental functions. Irresponsible behavior. Euphoria.
0.40% or more	Death can occur.

Source: The Courier-Journal, Louisville, KY, Saturday, June 23, 2001.

Figure 2.3   Each container holds equal amounts of alcohol. [Dorling Kindersley Images]

In general, a 170-pound man with an empty stomach would likely reach a BAC of 0.08 percent after drinking four servings of alcohol in an hour. A 137-pound female would reach the same level after drinking three servings of alcohol in an hour.

In order to reduce the alcohol-related problems on American highways, the National Highway Traffic Safety Administration (NHTSA) made it illegal to operate a motor vehicle with a BAC at or above 0.10. Each state has laws specifying the BAC level at which one can be charged with driving under the influence and the consequences.

See Table 2.1 for BAC-related data for the fifty states and the District of Columbia.

According to the U.S. Department of Labor, as of December 2001, twenty-nine states, Washington, D.C., and Puerto Rico had 0.08 as the established BAC level, whereas twenty-one states remain at the 0.10 level. In October 2000, Congress passed 0.08 BAC as the national standard for impaired driving regulations. States that do not adopt 0.08 BAC by a certain date will be denied a portion of their federal highway construction funds. Massachusetts is the only state that does not prohibit drinking and driving with a specific BAC level. Some states also have adopted a zero-tolerance standard for teenage drivers. In these states, teenage violators will have their licenses suspended for operating a motor vehicle with any detectable blood-alcohol levels.

Because states increasingly are formulating legislation that lowers the limit at which one is considered legally impaired, the prudent operator may stay abreast of these laws by consulting with qualified counsel and by joining a state chapter of the National Restaurant Association.

Table 2.1

State	BAC defined as illegal per se	State	BAC defined as illegal per se
Alabama	0.08	Montana	0.10
Alaska	0.10	Nebraska	0.08
Arizona	0.10	Nevada	0.10
Arkansas	0.10	New Hampshire	0.08
California	0.08	New Jersey	0.10
Colorado	0.10	New Mexico	0.08
Connecticut	0.10	New York	0.10
Delaware	0.10	North Carolina	0.08
District of Columbia	0.08	North Dakota	0.10
Florida	0.08	Ohio	0.10
Georgia	0.08	Oklahoma	0.08
Hawaii	0.08	Oregon	0.08
Idaho	0.08	Pennsylvania	0.10
Illinois	0.08	Rhode Island	0.08
Indiana	0.08	South Carolina	0.10
Iowa	0.10	South Dakota	0.10
Kansas	0.08	Tennessee	0.10
Kentucky	0.08	Texas	0.08
Louisiana	0.08**	Utah	0.08
Maine	0.08	Vermont	0.08
Maryland	0.08	Virginia	0.08
Massachusetts	None	Washington	0.08
Michigan	0.10	West Virginia	0.10
Minnesota	0.10	Wisconsin	0.10
Mississippi	0.10	Wyoming	0.10
Missouri	0.08		

**Effective 9/30/03.

Source: U.S. Department of Labor, September, 2002.

The second way that intoxication can be proved is by providing a witness for the behavioral indicators of intoxication mentioned earlier in this chapter. A witness can be anyone who observed the patron in an intoxicated state, such as a bartender, wait staff personnel, other customers, or the police.

Training and Industry Certification

Proper training of management and staff is essential and should include specific training for recognizing the signs of customer intoxication. Requiring management and service staff to participate in training programs such as TIPS (Training for Intervention Procedures for Servers), offered by Health Communications Incorporated; or C.A.R.E. (Controlling Alcohol Risks Effectively), sponsored by

Figure 2.4 People enjoy alcohol in an outdoor German *Bier Garten.*
[Dorling Kindersley Picture Library/Osterreich Werbung]

the American Hotel and Lodging Association, is helpful. While only a few states *require* server education, servers who have obtained this type of certification have gained information about alcohol and its effect on people, the common signs of intoxication, and how to help patrons avoid becoming intoxicated. In some cases, server certification in alcohol awareness may assist in a *reasonable care* defense should the establishment be sued under common law theory of negligence. Frequent refresher courses are an important component of alcohol service training. Employee meetings provide a good opportunity to reinforce the message that alcohol must be served responsibly. Some states, Maryland being one example, have laws that require all establishments that serve alcohol to be certified in an alcohol awareness training program. More and more states are formulating policies that show they will not tolerate people getting behind the wheel of a motor vehicle if they have been drinking.

Key Terms

Common law
Dramshop laws
Intoxicated
Reasonable care

Blood-alcohol content
TIPS
C.A.R.E.

Study Questions

1. What are three cases in which alcohol sales are illegal?
2. What are dramshop laws?
3. What are some telltale signs of intoxication?
4. What does the acronym BAC stand for?
5. What is the BAC considered illegal in the state in which you live?
6. Name two training programs related to alcohol safety.

Chapter 3

Wine Labels and Bottle Shapes

After reading this chapter, you will be able to:

❑ Explain the differences in bottle shape.
❑ Describe how to identify a wine based on the label.
❑ Distinguish the country of origin on a wine label.
❑ Identify varietal wine.
❑ Discuss different countries' systems of denoting wine quality.

Wine is bottled poetry.

—Robert Louis Stevenson

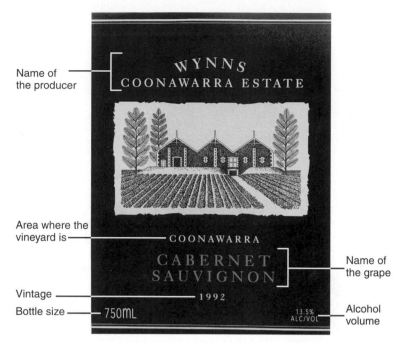

Figure 3.1   The customer needs to know that Coonawarra is in Australia when reading this label. The rest of the information is very clear. [Dorling Kindersley Images]

A good way to begin learning about wines is to become familiar with the distinctions in wine bottle shapes and the information that is included on wine labels.

Wine Bottles

The first clue to what is in a wine bottle comes from the bottle itself. Anyone who knows the basic bottle shapes can easily deduce the wine inside. Quality wine traditionally comes in five differently shaped bottles.

The first bottle type has high "shoulders." The wine within these bottles is full-bodied. If the bottle is green, the consumer can expect a red wine, usually Cabernet Sauvignon, Merlot, Zinfandel, and sometimes Shiraz. When bottles with this shape are clear, they will contain white wines such as Sauvignon Blanc, Fume Blanc, and Semillon. Darker bottles help eliminate the wines' exposure to light allowing wines to age longer. Clear bottles indicate the wine should be consumed instead of aged.

The second bottle type has gently sloping shoulders. This bottle, tinted green, is used for medium-bodied wines such as Pinot Noir, Gamay, and Syrah. Chardonnay is the main white wine found within this bottle type; these bottles may be clear.

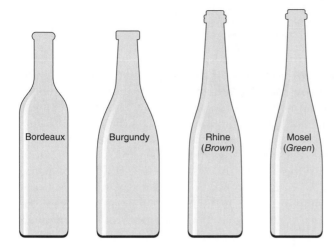

Figure 3.2 Different wine bottle sizes. [Pearson Education/Prentice Hall]

The third bottle type is thinner and taller than the second, but it looks similar to the second type. These bottles come in two shades, brown and green, which signify different grape-growing areas. The brown bottle signifies the Rhine area in Germany, while the green bottle signifies the Mosel area in Germany or the Alsace area in France. This type of bottle is used mainly for Riesling and Gewürztraminer grapes.

The fourth bottle type also is shaped like the second type, but the glass is noticeably thicker at the bottom of the bottle. This type of bottle is used for sparkling wine and is shaped to withstand the pressure of the carbonation in the wine.

The fifth bottle type is shaped more like the first bottle, but it has a longer neck. The tall high shoulders are still as pronounced, but they are a little lower. This bottle type is used for Sherry, Port, Marsala, and Madeira.

A recent trend is to move away from the classic wine bottles. This trend allows winemakers (mostly American) to distinguish their wine on the shelf so it is easy to pick out among the vast rows of classic wine bottles. These new wine bottle shapes are mainly a marketing tool and generally do not provide information pertaining to the contents of the bottle.

Being able to identify bottle types can give the consumer a basic idea about the bottle's contents, but some questions remain unanswered:

- Who made the wine?
- Where was the wine made?
- Where were the grapes grown?
- How much wine is in the bottle?
- What is the wine's level of alcohol by volume?

The wine label can answer all these questions.

Wine Labels

In general, as the amount of information included on a wine bottle's front label increases, so does the quality of the wine. For example, all wine labels must indicate the country of origin. If, the region is added, one can expect a higher-quality wine. If the label also displays the area or district, the wine will be of even higher quality. If a label identifies a wine as being from the Margeaux district of the Bordeaux region of France, for example, the consumer will know that the wine is from a particular 3,364-acre area. This knowledge allows the consumer to identify the specific area of origin, hence the quality of the wine. By including the name of the vineyard or the producer on the label, the consumer can further narrow down the wine's place of origin and quality. If the name "Château Ferriere," the producer, is added to the example label above, the place of origin is narrowed down to 12 acres.

Wine label language also often includes the words *reserve, vintage, estate, château, produced by,* and *imported by.* The word *reserve* can appear in several ways, such as Private Reserve, Special Reserve, or Vintners Reserve. Usually the term *reserve* connotes a special wine, but it has no legal definition in the United States. Therefore, theoretically, a winemaker's best "reserve" could be one of the industry's worst.

Vintage simply refers to the year that the grapes were grown. For example, if 95 percent of the grapes were grown in the 2002 growing season, the bottle is a 2002 vintage wine. The word *vintage* does not refer to quality in the United States. Some import wines, however, only declare vintages when the grapes are of exceptional quality. Champagne, for example, only declares a "vintage" year two or three times in a decade. Madeira has a vintage year even fewer times than that.

Estate refers to where the grapes are grown. If a winery wants to claim that they have an estate bottled wine, 100 percent of the grapes must have been grown in that winery's vineyard. The French use the word *château* in a similar manner. Château is the French word for castle or house.

The terms *produced by* and *imported by* are self-explanatory. A bottle of wine "produced by" a winery is made by that winery, and a bottle of wine "imported by" a company refers to the company that brings the wine into the country where it is sold.

Wine Label Regulations

United States The law mandates that alcoholic beverages must be labeled with certain information. These labels can be confusing to a person unfamiliar with reading wine labels. The required information includes (1) what is in the bottle, (2) who made the alcoholic beverage, (3) where the alcoholic beverage was made, and (4) how much alcohol by volume is in the bottle.

Other factors can add to the confusion of label reading. For instance, the requirements for label information are different for the different classes of alcohol

Figure 3.3 A California wine label. [Dorling Kindersley Images]

(wine, beer, and spirits). Further, alcohol producers can add optional information to the label.

In the United States, ten specific pieces of information are required on wine labels:

1. Name of the wine
2. Name of the producer
3. Name and address of the bottler
4. Name of the importer
5. Name of the shipper
6. Alcohol content (expressed as a percentage of the volume)
7. Volume of the bottle's content
8. Country of origin
9. Sulfite advisory (According to U.S. laws, wine producers must warn if the wine contains sulfites because some people are allergic to them. These sulfites might be added to wine as sulfur dioxide to act as an antibacterial agent for the wine.)
10. Government warning.

Sometimes the information might be duplicated. For example, the producer and the bottler might be one and the same. When this is the case, this information only has to be listed on the label once.

There are five optional pieces of information that the wine label also can include:

1. Quality of the wine
2. Vintage of the wine

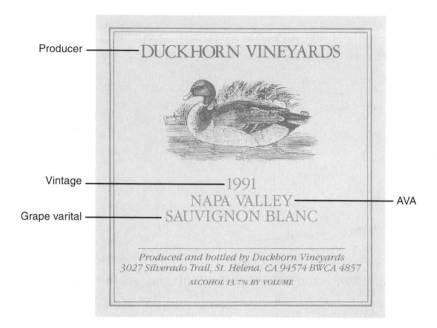

Producer ——— DUCKHORN VINEYARDS

Vintage ——— 1991

NAPA VALLEY ——— AVA

Grape varital ——— SAUVIGNON BLANC

Produced and bottled by Duckhorn Vineyards
3027 Silverado Trail, St. Helena, CA 94574 BWCA 4857

ALCOHOL 13.7% BY VOLUME

Figure 3.4   A California wine label. [Dorling Kindersley Images]

3. Type of wine
4. Growing region, or *appellation*
5. Descriptive information about the wine.

International Wine Production Laws and Regulations   Different countries have different laws regarding the production of wine. Most countries have an agency or several agencies that regulate how the grapes are grown and how the bottle is

Figure 3.5   A French wine label.
[Dorling Kindersley Images]

labeled. In the United States, wine production is regulated by the Department of the Treasury and enforced by the Bureau of Alcohol, Tobacco, and Firearms. Companies or individuals from other countries that import wine into the United States must follow all of the United States laws regarding labeling.

Many of the areas that grow grapes in the United States are broken in to what are referred to as American Viticultural Areas (A.V.A.). The areas are similar to the regions in other countries and are specific geographical locations that have been given appellation status by the bureau of Alcohol, Tobacco, and Firearms. Appellations are specific regions in which wine grapes can be grown and are determined by a country's regulatory agency.

France has a similar system—Appellation d'Origine Contrôlée (AOC)—which was founded in the 1930s. The AOC system establishes regulations for winemaking and provides quality control for French wine. A winemaker in France must follow rules concerning where grapes can be grown, which grapes can be grown in different areas, the minimum alcohol content, and how many grapes can be grown per acre. AOC also is the highest quality rank for wine in France.

There are three additional levels denoting quality in French wine:

1. Vin Délimité de Qualité Supérieure (VDQS)
2. Vin de Pays (Country Wine)
3. Vin de Table (Table Wine).

In Italy, the Denominazione di Origine Controllata (DOC) and DOCG (the "G" stands for Garantita and means guaranteed) are very similar to the AOC in

Figure 3.6 An Italian wine label.
[Dorling Kindersley Images]

Figure 3.7 A Spanish wine label. [Dorling Kindersley Images]

France and A.V.A. in America. The DOC, however, is a much newer system; it was started in 1963. The DOC regulates the size of the regions, the grapes that can be used, how many grapes can be grown per acre, and the minimum alcohol content of the finished wine. Its control also extends to the percentage of each variety of grapes used in a wine and the length of aging. The DOCG is the highest quality rating for wine in Italy. In order to protect the quality of wine within this category, the National DOC committee has adopted standards for wines admitted into the DOCG category. These standards include limits on the number of grapes grown per acre and a higher minimum alcohol level.

Spain's classification system is broken down into five quality levels:

1. Denominación de Origen Calificada (DOC)
2. Denominación de Origen (DO)
3. Vino de la Tierra (VdlT)
4. Vino Comarcal (VC)
5. Vino de Mesa (VdM).

The first two levels represent the top wines of Spain. The last three are comparable to the Vins de Pays wines of France. The DOC level, added in 1991, includes only the very best wine of Spain.

Australia has a more limited labeling program known as the Label Integrity Program (LIP). In general, the LIP regulates vintage, varietal, and geographic claims on labels.

Figure 3.8 This Austrian label is very similar to the German counterpart. [Dorling Kindersley Images]

The German system of regulation started in 1971. The system is fairly simple but extensive. German wine is first graded into one of two categories:

1. Qualitätswein (quality wine)
2. Tafelwein (table wine).

The Qualitätswein category is then divided into two types:

1. Qualitätswein mit Prädikat (QmP)
2. Qualitätswein bestimmter Anbaugebiete (QbA)

The difference between the two is that QbA wines are region-specific (from one of the thirteen regions in Germany) quality wines that meet certain alcohol content and grape variety requirements and are examined by authorities. QmP is quality wine with distinction from the thirteen regions or the top wine of Germany. Every requirement for QbA must be met but also the wine must not be chaptalized. *Chaptalization* is the process of adding sugar to the unfermented grape juice, which raises the potential alcohol content after fermentation. This means that the grapes that constitute these wines must ripen longer on the vine, thus gaining natural sugar and hence a higher alcohol content when fermented. There are six levels within this higher wine category. The six levels of QmP are listed below in descending order of quality.

1. Eiswein (ICE-vyn)—German for "Ice wine." This is a rare wine produced from grapes that are left on the vine until they freeze. Then, the grapes are picked and crushed while they are still frozen. The grapes must be at least ripe enough to make beerenauslese.
2. Trockenbeerenauslese (TRAWK-uhn-bay-ruhn-OWS-lay-zuh)—German for "dry-berries-out-picked." These grapes literally dry on the vine, resembling raisins when picked. The sugar and the juice are very concentrated and produce a very sweet wine. Many times the grapes also are infected with Noble Rot (*Botrytis cinerea*). This wine was first made in 1921 and tends to be the most expensive German wine. (A bottle simply marked *trocken* is a dry wine.)
3. Beerenauslese (BAY-ruhn-OWS-lay-zuh)—German for "berries-out-picked." These grapes are individually picked out of the grape bunches. The grapes are sometimes infected with Noble Rot.
4. Auslese (OWS-lay-zuh)—German for "out picked" or selectively picked. This wine is made from grapes that are very ripe when picked; the other clusters of grapes are left on the vine to ripen more.
5. Spätlese (SHPAYT-lay-zuh)—German for "late picking." The grapes for this wine are picked at least a week after the normal harvest. The extra time allows the grapes more sunlight, which in turn increases the sugar level in the fruit. The wine tends to be more intense and sweet than Kabinett.
6. Kabinett (kah-bin-NEHT)—German for "cabinet," this wine is the least expensive and driest of the German wines in the QmP category.

Key Terms

A.V.A.	QbA
VDQS	QmP
LIP	Alcohol by Volume

Study Questions

1. What can you tell from the different style of wine bottles?
2. What is some of the information a wine label should include?
3. If a wine label does not have very much information, what can you say about the wine?
4. What is an A.V.A., and how does it differ from an AOC?
5. What is the difference between QbA and QmP?
6. What is LIP?

Chapter 4

Getting to Know Alcohol: Tasting and Pairing

After reading this chapter, you will be able to:

❏ Explain how to taste and analyze wine.
❏ Explain how to taste and analyze beer.
❏ Explain how to taste and analyze spirits.
❏ Analyze food for proper pairing with wine, beer, and spirits.

To pontificate, to let opinions rule your appreciation of wine and to be unable to feel, as the candles gutter and the moon rises on a warm summer night, that the wine on the table, however unsung and lacking in renown, is, for that short moment, perfection itself, is to miss the whole heart of wine—and of life too.

—Oz Clarke

Tasting and Analyzing Wine, Beer, and Spirits

The only six tastes the human tongue can detect are sweet, salt, sour, bitter, umami (a savory protein flavor), and spicy. The nose provides the mouth with the details of these general flavor sensations.

If sweetness is detected in a wine, what kind of sweetness is it? Does the wine have the taste of honey or raisins? Perhaps what is being tasted is orange blossom or strawberry jam. Only the individual person can answer those questions. Two people tasting the same wine may have two completely different analyses of that wine.

The process of tasting wine, beer or spirits is done in an orderly way. The purpose is for the person who is tasting to spend time contemplating what they are seeing, smelling, and tasting. The seven "Ss" can be used by new wine tasters so they easily can remember the process of tasting. This system allows the taster to comment on the wine by seeing, swirling, smelling, sipping and spitting or alternatively, swallowing and savoring, the wine.

Wine

Seeing Some professional wine tasters have color ranges for wine. They say that white wines range in color from green-yellow to walnut brown. Red wines range from "partridge eye" (a very light pink) to coffee brown. Other professional

Figure 4.1 A tilted wine glass is the best way to see wine. [Dorling Kindersley Images]

wine tasters describe a wine's color in terms of light, medium, or dark. A wine's color comes from the grape skins, age, air, and the barrels in which wine is stored.

Just by looking at the color of the wine you can tell a lot about it. For example, the age of wine can be determined from its color. White wines grow darker as they age, whereas red wines grow lighter. Since white wines take on more color as they age, a white wine will brown if aged long enough. Red wines lose color or become less purple and more brown. Another color attribute to look for is the rim variation. The rim variation is the difference between the color in the center of the glass and the color at the edge of the glass. No or little variation in the color signifies a young wine. A big color difference signifies an older wine or a wine that has not aged well. The barrels, which sometimes are used to age wine, also add color and flavor to the wine; it can take some of its color from the burned inside of the barrel. The alcohol level, residual sugar, acid, and tannin are the elements that allow the wine to age. When wine exposed to air it begins to oxidize, which causes the wine to age. If left long enough, it will age past its prime in the glass in front of the drinker. Part of the reason for the closure at the top of a bottle is to shield the wine from the air. Real cork does "breathe," allowing the wine to oxidize a little and creating new qualities in the wine's flavor and aroma.

Swirling   Smell is an important sense to use in wine tasting. In order to smell all the nuances of a wine, the taster swirls the wine. Swirling the wine allows it to combine with air and release esters, ethers, aldehydes, ketones, and alcohol. The

Figure 4.2   Swirling wine in a glass. [Dorling Kindersley Images]

release of these elements allows the person to smell many different aromas. Without swirling the wine, wine simply smells like alcohol and possibly fruit.

The easiest way to swirl a glass is to hold the stem of the glass on the table and rotate it in a small circle. The wine will be affected by the centrifugal force of the rotation, allowing it to swirl against the glass. When a taster becomes more experienced at swirling, he or she can swirl wine without using a table to hold the glass steady.

Smelling   Once a taster swirls the glass of wine and releases its aroma, the next task is to describe the scent. The best way to train oneself to describe a wine's aroma is to ask a broad question first: What do I smell? Is that wood, flowers, spice, nuts, caramel, vegetables, or chemicals? What is the broad category of aromas being smelled? Once it is established that the scent derives from fruit, for example, the taster can narrow it down by asking the next questions: What kind of fruit is it? Is it citrus, berry, tropical, dried, or tree fruit? Once that question is answered, the next question is: Specifically, what fruit am I smelling? If, for example, the taster is smelling a berry, is it strawberry, blackberry, or raspberry?

Sometimes people are not able to pinpoint the aroma because they are not used to smelling things without the visual cue. Don't be too surprised if more than one specific aroma can be detected in a single wine. It is also probable that two or more tasters will have different descriptions for what they are smelling. Dr. Ann Noble at the University of California at Davis has devised an Aroma Wheel to help wine tasters articulate what they are smelling in a wine.

Sipping   As mentioned previously, there are a maximum of six sensations that a tongue will taste: (1) sweet, (2) sour, (3) salt, (4) bitter, (5) umami, and (6) hot (spicy). Without the nose, humans only can perceive these general tastes. Salt rarely plays a part in wine tasting, but the other five tastes play a major role in how wine is perceived.

The first flavor a taster might perceive is sweetness, or lack thereof. The sweet flavor can be a clue to how much residual sugar is in the wine. Fruit flavors can trick people into believing that they are tasting something sweet when they are not. Sometimes the only way a taster might distinguish between sugar and fruit is by closing or pinching the nose when he or she tastes. When the taster does this, the sweetness from the sugar will remain, but the sweetness from fruit will disappear.

Wine has a sour taste when acid is present. The acids most commonly found in wine are malic acid, citric acid, lactic acid, and tartaric acid. Malic acid is the same acid that is found in apples; this accounts for the apple flavor people taste in some wines. Citric acid is the same acid found in citrus fruits such as lemons, grapefruit, and oranges. Lactic acid is the same acid found in milk, and tartaric acid also is found in most fruits and vegetables. An acid can cause a vinegar flavor in wine; in most cases, this flavor signals that the wine has turned bad. Usually the bitter flavor people pick up in wine is caused by tannin, which is a substance found naturally on grapes but which can also come from oak barrels.

Finally a hot, but not necessarily spicy, flavor can be picked up from wines high in alcohol. The combination of the alcohol, tannin, and acid make up the body of the wine. Alcohol makes up a very large part of the body of wine because alcohol is a flavor enhancer. As a general rule, the more alcohol a wine has, the more body the wine will have. Light-bodied wines will have less alcohol, and full-bodied wines will have more alcohol.

When tasting wine, a taster will take small amounts of the liquid into his or her mouth from the glass. Holding the wine at the bottom of the mouth, the taster draws air in through a small hole between the lips across the wine allowing the wine to bubble. This allows some of the flavors to better show themselves too.

Spitting or Swallowing and Savoring

If only a few wines are being tasted, wine professionals may swallow the wine; however, many wine professionals spit. Wine judges may taste hundreds of wines in a day, so swallowing each one would be unwise. The best time to taste wine is late in the morning at about 10:30 or 11:00 A.M. The palate is awake and fresh because the mouth has had an eight-hour break. Breakfast wakes the palate. Later in the day, the palate has had to endure eight hours of flavor bombardment, which makes it more difficult for the palate distinguish between tastes.

Describing the Taste   Once someone has tasted a wine, the next step is to describe it. How do wine tasters depict the wine to others? The terms used to describe wines can be broken into three categories: general terms, positive terms, and negative terms. Most of the words used by wine professionals are self-explanatory. For example, a Cabernet Sauvignon might be described as firm and beefy. This description communicates to a wine professional that the wine has good tannin and/or acid level and that the wine is full-bodied. Alternatively, the wine might be described as thin and flabby. This would mean that the wine lacks flavor, body, and acid. Some of the more common words to describe wine are listed bellow.

General Terms

Aroma—A single smell found in wine, such as honey, lemon, raspberry, or grass.
Assertive—A character in the wine that stands out in the smelling and tasting.
Body—The texture or taste of the wine in the mouth. The body of a light-bodied wine can be compared with skim milk, a medium-bodied wine with 2 percent milk, and a full-bodied wine with cream.
Bouquet—The mixture of the many aromas found in a single wine.
Finish—The flavor a wine leaves in the mouth after the wine is swallowed.
Legs—The tears of wine that run down the inside of the glass after swirling.
Light—A wine low in alcohol, or light-bodied.
Long—A wine with an aftertaste that lasts.

Mature—A wine that is ready to drink.
Nose—The aroma or bouquet of a wine.
Spritz—A wine with a little effervescence.
Underdeveloped—A wine that needs to age before drinking.
Well Developed—A wine that is ready to drink.
Young—A wine that has not fully matured.

Positive Words

Aftertaste—Also known as the finish, aftertaste is found in complex wines and is the flavor left in the mouth after the taster has swallowed the wine.
Aromatic—The aromas and/or flavors of the wine have a spicy or herb quality.
Balanced—A wine that is balanced has the perfect combination of flavors, acid, alcohol, fruit, tannin, and sugar; none overpowers the others.
Beefy—A full-bodied wine.
Big–Full–Heavy—A full-bodied wine that is high in alcohol and has good balance.
Bright—A young wine with fresh and fruity aromas and flavors.
Character—A wine with specific qualities related to its style or variety.
Chewy—A very rich and intense full-bodied wine.
Crisp—A noticeably acidic wine, but the acid does not overpower the wine.
Delicate—A quality wine that is light and well-balanced.
Dense—A full-flavored wine or wine with a deep color.
Earthy—A dirt aroma in the wine.
Elegant—A high-quality wine.
Fat—A full-bodied sweet wine.
Finesse—A high-quality, well-balanced wine.
Firm—A well-balanced, high-tannic or acidic wine.
Fleshy—A full-bodied, high-alcohol, smooth wine.
Forward—An early maturing wine.
Fragrant—A wine with a floral aroma or bouquet.
Fresh—A simple, well-balanced, fruity wine.
Grapey—A wine with the flavors and aromas of grapes.
Grassy—A wine with the aroma of freshly cut grass.
Green—A young, underdeveloped wine.
Heavy—A full-bodied, highly alcoholic wine.
Herbaceous—A wine with the aroma of herbs.
Jammy—A wine with a concentrated fruit flavor.
Meaty—A full-bodied wine with rich flavors.
Mouth-filling—A wine with a rich, full-bodied flavor.
Nutty—A wine with a flavor or aroma of nuts.
Penetrating—A wine with an intense nose, usually with high alcohol.
Peppery—A wine with a spicy, black-pepper flavor.
Perfumed—A wine with a fragrant aroma.

Rich—A wine with a balanced, full flavor.
Robust—A wine with a full flavor.
Round—A wine with a well-balanced, mellow, and full-bodied flavor.
Scented—A wine with a fragrant aroma.
Silky—A wine with a smooth texture and flavor.
Simple—A wine that is not complex.
Smoky—A wine that has a smoky flavor.
Smooth—A wine that has a smooth texture and finish.
Soft—A wine that is mellow and well balanced.
Solid—A wine that is full-bodied from high levels of acidity, alcohol, fruit, and tannin.
Stalky or Stemmy—A wine with a green flavor.
Steely—A white wine high in acidity and well balanced but otherwise lean.
Supple—A wine that is soft but well structured.
Vanilla—An aroma in wine caused by aging in new oak barrels.
Vegetal—An aroma in wine of a vegetable character in the nose.
Yeasty—A wine with a yeast aroma.
Zesty—A white wine with a fresh, crisp flavor and aroma.

Negative Words

Acetic—A wine with an excess of acetic acid or vinegar flavors.
Aggressive—A wine with slightly high tannin or acid.
Astringent—A wine with very high tannin or acid levels.
Austere—A young wine with a high level of tannin and/or acid that might soften with aging.
Baked or Burned—A burned caramel flavor caused by overexposure to heat.
Barnyard—A wine that has an aroma similar to animal fecal matter.
Bitter—A wine with a high tannin level or another element that makes the wine bitter.
Coarse—A poor-quality wine with body.
Corky or Corked—A spoiled wine.
Dried out—A wine that has lost its fruitiness.
Flabby—A wine without enough acidity.
Flat—A wine that lacks flavor because of its lack of acidity.
Grip—A young wine with high tannin or acid levels and with a firm texture that needs more time to develop.
Hard—A wine with too much tannin or acid.
Hollow—A wine with very little flavor or a disappointing flavor.
Hot—A wine out of balance with a high alcohol content.
Lean—A wine with very little flavor.
Metallic—A wine with a tin-like flavor.
Moldy—A wine with a mold-like aroma or flavor.
Neutral—A wine with very little flavor or aroma.

Off—A wine that is flawed or spoiled.

Oily—A wine with an oily character in the flavor or in the aroma.

Overdeveloped—A wine that has aged past its prime.

Oxidized—A wine that has been exposed to air. This exposure has changed the quality of the wine from good to bad.

Raw—A wine with a young and underdeveloped flavor.

Rough—A wine that is overly tannic or acidic.

Sharp—A wine with too much acid.

Short—A wine with very little flavor in the finish.

Sour—A wine with a lot of acidity.

Stewed—A wine that has been exposed to heat and tastes cooked.

Tart—A wine that is high in acid and leaves a sharp, sour note in the mouth.

Tired—A wine that has been overaged.

Tough—A full-bodied wine with lots of tannin.

Watery—A wine with a watered-down flavor.

Woody—A wine that has been aged too long in oak barrels.

Beer

Beer is the most popular alcoholic drink in the United States. While most of the beer consumed in the United States is light in body with no heavy flavors or aromas, this is only a small fraction of the types of beer available. The qualities beer tasters look for include appearance, aroma or bouquet, flavors (such as hops and malt), a balance of flavors, aftertaste, and mouthfeel. Thus the "Ss" can again be used to evaluate beer. The only "S" that is not used is swirling, because the carbonation would be lost.

Seeing　When evaluating the quality of beer, the first impression can come from the beer's head retention. No head or too much head on a beer can signify poor quality. Other factors may affect a beer's ability to retain a head as well. Check the glasses to see if they are greasy, as this may cause the beer to go flat. Too much head on a beer may mean that it was poured improperly from the bottle or that the pressure in the keg line is too high.

Color and clarity are other variables to look at when evaluating beer. Generally, the color of a beer reveals information about the body of the beer. Lighter-colored beer has a lighter body, and darker-colored beer has a heavier body. Clarity has little to do with the body or flavor of the beer, but a cloudy beer might have a bacterial contamination. Cloudy beer may also mean that the beer was frozen or that the keg lines through which it was drawn are dirty. However, clarity is not the only determinant of quality, because some beers are supposed to be a little cloudy.

Smelling　As with wine, much of the flavor of beer comes from its aroma. Some beers have caramel notes or fruit aromas (such as apples, pears, raspberries, or other fruit). One thing that a taster should be able to smell is the malt or the toasted grain used to make the beer. Caramel notes come from the malt in the beer. These notes also can produce toffee, roasted nut, and toasted-bread aromas. The fragrance of hops—bitter herbs that are added to beer to counter the sugar and to preserve the beer—should also be prominent in most beer; hops give beer a range of scents, from floral to spicy to an almost antiseptic aroma.

Sipping   A beer taster should focus on the flavors and quantity of the malt and the hops used in making the beer. Most of the sweetness in beer comes from both the malt and the hops. The malt can give beer unfermented or residual sugars. Hops add floral and fruity flavors that can be perceived as sweetness, but they do not add sugar. Most beer also has a degree of bitterness. This bitterness comes from the malt and the hops as well. The malt displays a higher degree of bitterness the longer it is roasted; the hops are bitter by nature, so the amount of hops the beer maker adds to the beer directly affects how bitter the beer is. The more hops the beer maker adds, the more bitter the beer will be.

Swallowing   While wine tasters spit during wine tasting, beer tasters generally do not. They are looking for aftertastes that are only present if the beer stays on the palate. These aftertastes are affected by the amount of carbonation the beer contains. The carbonation is a flavor carrier; therefore, if the carbonation is low, the beer will taste flat. If the carbonation is too high, the beer will taste acidic.

Spirits

The "S" process is used for tasting distilled spirits as well as wine. To reiterate, this system involves seeing, swirling, smelling, and sipping and spitting or swallowing and savoring the beverage being tasted.

Seeing   All distilled alcohol is clear when it comes from the still. Depending on the spirit, there should be only one of two colors that are seen in the bottle: clear and golden. If the spirit is clear, the taster knows that the spirit was not aged, but distilled and placed in the bottle for sale. If the spirit has some golden coloration, the spirit was aged in a charred wooden barrel. The burned wood imparts the golden color to the alcohol.

Swirling   Swirling allows air to interact with the hidden aromas of the alcoholic drink and lets some of these aromas come to the nose more easily. A wine glass can be used to taste spirits; swirling is achieved in the same manner as for wine tasting.

Smelling   When tasting spirits, alcohol is the first aroma that comes into contact with the nose. Once the taster gets beyond that, the aromas found in some alcohol spirits, especially those aged in wood, can range from vanilla, caramel and oak to herbal aromas.

Sipping   To taste a distilled spirit, place a small amount of the liquid on the tongue. The liquid should be allowed to flow across the tongue so that most of the taste buds can be activated. This should be done a second time; the taster evaluates the spirit based on the second taste that runs across the palate. If the spirit is to hot on the palate, the taster should breath in through his or her mouth. The alcohol will cool the mouth with exposure to air.

Spitting or Swallowing and Savoring   When tasting spirits, unless the tasting is limited to a very few selections, the taster should always spit so that the alcohol does not overcome the taster.

Pairing Alcohol and Food

A meal without wine is like a day without sunshine.

—Louis Pasteur

Like boys and girls locked away in same-sex prep schools, most wines yearn for a bit of flesh.

—Jay McInerney, in *Bacchus and Me*

Take a moment and imagine a nice summer day, a back porch, barbecue chicken and ribs, and all of the side dishes one can eat. The potato salad is creamy, smooth, and refreshing; the pasta salad screams "vinaigrette!" The children are playing football and the adults are sitting on the porch having a drink. What are the adults drinking? The beverage of choice could be beer, or it could be Chardonnay, Merlot, or a mixed drink, such as a Mint Julep. Only the drinkers can answer the question; the person consuming the beverage determines which drink will accompany the food he or she is eating. Interestingly, in this situation, people do not agonize over a drink choice; the drinker just chooses something. The choice might be based on habit, or it might be that the individual just "knew" what would go well with the food. When people go out to eat, however, people become more intent on pairing the proper drink with a meal.

There used to be a saying: "White wine with white meat, red wine with red meat." In today's dining climate, however, this saying does not hold true. Properly matching food and wine is a little more complicated now, partially because winemakers are better at making wine today than they were even twenty years ago. Today they try to impart specific qualities in the wine. Now, when pairing any beverage with food, the diner needs to think about the body of the beverage and the body of the food. For instance, food with an intense flavor requires a wine with an equally intense flavor. This is especially true in the case of wine; beer and spirits are a little easier to match with food.

Wine

One of the most confusing things about pairing food and wine is that there is no "wrong" answer. What food goes with what wine is based totally on opinion and personal experience (i.e., what one person tastes is different from what another person tastes). If the pairing tastes good to the person doing the tasting, it is a good combination.

There are some general principles of tastes that do affect how well wine and food complement each other, however. For instance, a Beaujolais-Village and Beaujolais-Nouveau (both red wines made from the Gamay grape) are better paired with chicken than with sirloin steak. Because wines made from the Gamay grape do not have much body, these often go well with more delicately flavored foods. Pinot Noir grapes can be made into wines that have a large range. Pinot Noir wines, therefore, can pair as well with chicken or salmon as veal or pork. Veal or pork would overpower wines made from Gamay grapes, however, causing the wine to taste weak.

In his book, *Windows on the World: Complete Wine Course, 2003 Edition,* Kevin Zraly states that he likes to pair Chardonnay (a white wine) with steak. The reason he gives is that "Chardonnay is a red wine masquerading as a white wine." In other words, the body and the complexity of the steak is more complementary to Chardonnay than one might think. This is not to say that a full-bodied Cabernet Sauvignon would not be wonderful with same steak as well.

The main thing to remember when pairing wine with food is to balance the flavor of the food and the flavor of the beverage. The flavors of the wine need to either complement or contrast with the flavors of the food. Consider the qualities of the food and consider the qualities of the wine. Qualities in wine can be broken into four basic categories: sweet, fruit, acid, and tannin . Food tastes can be broken into six categories or qualities: sweet, salt, sour, bitter, umami, and spicy or hot. When pairing food and wine, the qualities of the wine and the qualities of the food are important to consider to achieve a good match.

In wine, sweet can range from very sweet to mildly sweet, but in all cases the term "sweet" refers to sugar. Sweet wines can be paired with food with a savory quality or a sweet quality. Keep in mind that a sweet flavor in food will intensify the flavor of the wine, so make sure the wine is sweeter than the food choice. Hot and spicy food should be paired with wines that will cool the effect of the spice; sweet wines tend to do this. Spicy Asian food is matched well with a German Gewürztraminer because the food is spicy and the wine is sweet.

Fruit flavors and aromas in wine are sometimes confused with sweet. This becomes critical when pairing wine with food. Fruit flavors and aromas can be sweet like the raspberry in a White Zinfandel, or they also can be sour like the lemon or lime flavor in a Sauvignon Blanc or the cherry flavor in a Pinot Noir. (There is no sugar in Sauvignon Blanc and Pinot Noir wines.) The fruit flavors and aroma come from the acid in the wine. Before pairing a fruity wine with food, determine if the fruit is sweet or acid. White Zinfandel compliments cheese and fruit, whereas Sauvignon Blanc goes well with chicken. For beef or game, Pinot Noir is strongly recommended.

Acid flavors in wine should be paired with savory foods and proteins such as chicken or fish. In turn, the protein in the food intensifies the acidic flavors and overall strength of the wine.

The tannin (the drying element) in wine is best paired with a food that is acidic. The acid refreshes the palate from the drying effects of the tannin and helps to make the wine milder. Salt in food also makes wine milder and helps tame some of the bitterness and drying effects of the tannin. An example of this type of pairing is Italian food with tomatoes, such as pasta with meat-and-tomato sauce, which pairs well with medium- to full-bodied red wine high in tannin. The acid in the tomatoes and the salt in the meat with both tame the tannin in the wine.

Light-Bodied Whites   Light-bodied white wines seem to be made specifically for delicate-tasting fish and seafood and, therefore, go well with Japanese cuisine. Light-bodied white wines include Pinot Grigio, Pinot Blanc, and some Rieslings. These wines are excellent choice for people who have never had wine or who have had bad experiences with wine.

Medium-Bodied Whites   Wines such as Sauvignon Blanc, Gewürztraminer and some Chardonnays go well with firm white fish and crustaceans. These wines also can go with pork and veal. If the wine is high in fruit (and sometimes sugar), a wine in this category may go well with Mexican, German, or Chinese cuisine.

Full-Bodied Whites   Chardonnay and Viognier are examples of full-bodied white wines. These wines are great with roasted poultry and richer tasting oily fish. If someone is trying to avoid red wines but has a rich-tasting dish such as steak, this category of wine would be an excellent choice.

Light-Bodied Reds   Light-bodied red wines match many of the same aspects in food that full-bodied white wines do. Roasted poultry and rich oily fish go very well with these reds, which include Gamay, some Sangiovese, Barbera, and some Pinot Noir wines. Many white wine drinkers enjoy these light-bodied red wines also. (A great time to make the switch from white to red is on the third Thursday in November, when Beaujolais Nouveau becomes available. Beaujolais Nouveau (made from Gamay) is similar to a white wine because it is best served chilled and goes well with chicken. These wines also pair well with southern Italian cuisine such as pasta and pizza.

Medium-Bodied Reds   Pinot Noir is joined by Merlot, Syrah, Sangiovese, Zinfandel, Malbec and, in some cases, Cabernet Sauvignon in this category. Medium-bodied red wines go well with veal, pork, venison, rabbit, and game birds.

Full-Bodied Reds The reigning king of this category is Cabernet Sauvignon. Wines made from Merlot, Zinfandel, Syrah (Shiraz), and Nebbiolo also fit in this category. These wines go well with lamb, beef, and game meat. These tend to be the more intense and tannic wines on the scale.

Sparkling Wines When you are in doubt as to what to serve, a safe bet is sparkling wine. Sparkling wine seems to go with everything. From the appetizer to the dessert, sparkling wine can compliment almost any food. However, the sweetness in sparkling wine will affect its overall compatibility with food.

Fortified and Dessert Wines Fortified wines, for the most part, are served after dinner or with the dessert course, with the notable exception of sherry. Sherry can be served with the soup course if the right soup is being served. Sherry pairs very well with shellfish bisques but can also pair well with other soups, depending on the intensity of the soup and the sherry. Many sweet wines go wonderfully with fruit as well. Sometimes a sweet wine can go with savory flavors. Two perfect examples of this type of pairing are sweet Sauterne with savory foie gras and Porto with Stilton cheese.

Beer

Almost anything will pair well with beer. Beer's bubbly constitution makes it food friendly. Even hot and spicy foods go well with this beverage (the same cannot be said of many wines). When pairing beer with food, however, one should think about the weight, or heaviness, and flavor of the beer. For example, it is better to pair a heavy beer with a rich taste, such as a stout ale (a dark, full-bodied beer) with steak than it is to pair it with a lighter food such as chicken. A light lager (a light-bodied beer) will also go with the steak, but the stout will overpower the chicken, making the dining experience less than perfect.

Sometimes surprises are found when pairing beer with specific dishes, such as beer and dessert. Most people do not order beer with dessert, but sometimes it can go well with sweets such as a chocolate nut torte. Beer with a nutty quality or a strong aroma or flavor of nuts or cinnamon will generally work well with desserts.

Distilled Liquor

Liquor drinkers usually like a specific drink, and they have a certain way they like to drink it. The benefit to most distilled alcoholic drinks is that they are wonderful before- and after-dinner drinks. Most liquors stimulate the appetite and aid digestion; this may be one reason people often have a brandy after dinner. On the other hand, distilled spirits can dull the palate. This will prevent the diner from fully enjoying the flavors of the food and the alcoholic drink.

Key Terms

The seven "Ss"   Sour
Light-Bodied   Bitter
Medium-Bodied   Fruit
Full-Bodied   Umami
Tannin   Spicy
Sweet

Study Questions

1. What food pairs well with sweet wine?
2. What food pairs well with wine with high levels of tannin?
3. What food pairs well with acidic wines?
4. What are the seven "Ss"?
5. How can a wine have a fruity taste but not be sweet?

Chapter
5
The Vineyard

After reading this chapter, you will be able to:

❐ Explain the elements needed to grow grapes.
❐ Differentiate regions for grape growing.
❐ Discuss the enemies of grapes.
❐ Explain how producers tell when the grapes are ready for picking and wine production.
❐ Describe the materials winemakers use to store and age wine.
❐ Describe what barrels are made from and how barrels are made.
❐ Explain what happens to the bottles of wine after they are bottled.
❐ Discuss how corks are made and the material used to make them.

Every glass of wine we drink represents a whole year of vineyard culti-
vation and perhaps several years of effort in the winery. . . . Yet most of
us throw it away, straight down our throats, without even trying to
"read" it.

—Jancis Robinson

Figure 5.1 A vineyard. [Dorling Kindersley Images]

A vineyard is a plot of land that has been devoted to growing grapes. Vineyards produce grapes with the help of what the French call *terroir. Terroir* refers to how the soil, the weather, the climate, other environmental factors, and the skill of the vintner affect the grapes. Grape growing, or farming, literally and figuratively merges science and art. The same grape can produce very different products depending on where it is grown and how the vintner handles the grapes.

The Grape

Not all grapes are the same, even though they all belong to the *Ampelidaceae* family. To the vintner, grapes that belong to the genus *Vitis* are the most important members of the family. The most important *Vitis* grape is the *Vitis vinifera,* which yields most of the world's wines. *Vitis vinifera* wines include all of the major varieties such as Merlot, Cabernet Sauvignon, Syrah, Pinot Noir, and Chardonnay. Other species of grapes native to the Americas are used to make wine; these include *Vitis labrusca, Vitis riparia,* and *Vitis rotundifolia.* Grapes also are classified by the color of the grape as well as by their species. Green grapes are called white grapes, and purple grapes are referred to as red grapes.

The Enemies of the Vine

The most feared enemy of grapevines is a small plant louse *Phylloxera vastatrix.* This parasite burrows down to the root of a plant and lives by destroying the vine.

Phylloxera vastatrix is native to America, but it was exported accidentally to Europe in the 1860s, where it effectively destroyed the grape farming industry over the next forty years because *Vitis vinifera* grape roots are not resistant to phylloxera. By the mid-1870s, all of France was affected. The only solution was to graft American rootstock (which was much more resistant to phylloxera) to the European vines. Grafting, a method developed to increase the resistance of a plant, is now practiced worldwide, except in Chile, Cyprus, and some parts of Portugal.

Recently there has been another outbreak of phylloxera in California. This outbreak was caused by a mutated strain that is less inhibited by the American rootstock. This phylloxera is called "Type B."

The phylloxera louse is not the lone enemy of the vine. Molds and fungus can also be a problem in areas with high humidity. Some of the more common fungi are *Botrytis cinerea* (Noble Rot) and *Guignardia bidwellii* (Black Rot). Even though Noble Rot can be a condition some grape farmers encourage (see Chapter 1), it can be a bad situation for other farmers. Generally, farmers of white grapes are more likely to welcome Noble Rot. Even if they are not trying to make a sweet wine (see Chapter 13), Noble Rot will add to the complexity of white wines. In the same way, red grape farmers fear Noble Rot because it will destroy what they are trying to produce in the wine. Most red grape farmers are tying to make dry wine.

Black Rot is unwelcome by everyone. This fungus grows on the leaves of the vine and on the grapes. Grapevines are at risk when the environment is hot and humid. Another enemy is Pierce's Disease, which is caused by a bacterium that is carried by insects called sharpshooters. The insects spread the bacteria, which can cause the entire vine to die. At the minimum, the leaves will turn yellow and the fruit will wilt. There is no known solution to Pierce's Disease. Other molds, bugs, and bacteria exist that affect the growth of healthy grapes, but these vectors—organisms that transmit pathogens—occur on a more limited basis.

The Soil, Weather, Environment, and Climate

The soil in which that the grapes grow influences how they taste. For example, grapes grown in mineral-rich soil take on some of the minerals as nutrients, helping influence the final product. A chalky soil will produce a chalky flavor in wine.

Figure 5.2 A vineyard. [Dorling Kindersley Images]

Another factor determining the wine's final taste is the water in the soil. Soil receives water one of three ways: (1) rainfall, (2) irrigation, or (3) an underwater aquifer.

Water can affect a vineyard dramatically because the vineyard needs water for the vines to grow. If a vineyard receives its water from rainfall, too little rain can mean the grapes will not grow properly; they will lack the flavor and mass they should have. Too much rain and the flavor will literally be washed away, and the bloated grape will produce a weak-flavored wine. The ideal is to achieve big grapes with full flavor. A vintage can be, in all respects, perfect—only to be ruined by a last-minute rain.

The idea of irrigation is not new; the concept is to get water to where it is not. The Romans built huge irrigation systems to ensure crop success, including grape crop success. Currently, irrigation is used in locations that are perfect for growing grapes except that the annual rainfall falls short of what the vines and grapes need for making good wine. Irrigation allows the grape farmer more control over the product, but the crop can still vary from a huge success to a miserable failure.

Sometimes the farmer is fortunate because the vineyard is located next to a river or an underwater aquifer that is able to feed the vines and the grapes no matter what the annual rainfall turns out to be. Most of the time rainfall is not a problem in these regions, but every so often the extra water that the river or the underground aquifer provides to the vines is a real boon to the grape farmer, increasing the yield and the quality of the grapes.

Climate has almost everything to do with what type of grapes a vineyard will be able to grow successfully. Many studies have been done to match the grape with the land and the climate. In France, laws require different grapes to be grown in different places. The French invented this system by trial and error, and, in the end, the French ended up with a codified system for grape growing. For example, Chardonnay and Pinot Noir grapes are grown in Burgundy, whereas the Cabernet Sauvignon, Merlot, and Sauvignon Blanc grapes are grown in Bordeaux. This system has been in place for many years, even before scientific studies were able to verify the proper growing locale for specific types of grapes.

Dr. Albert Winkler, a professor at the University of California at Davis, has developed a similar system for other areas of the world. The Winkler system divides the areas of the world into five regions based on the overall heat received during the growing season, using a baseline temperature of 50° F. (This temperature is used as a baseline because grapevines do not grow well under 50° F.) During the growing season, from April 1 to October 1, the mean temperature is taken each day. The mean minus 50 equals the summation for the day. These summations are added together for the span of the growing season to come up with the heat index for the regions. Regions are numbered from 1 to 5, with higher numbers representing hotter regions.

Region 1

Region 1 includes the lowest temperature areas that have a heat index of less than 2,500 degrees. These regions include Germany; areas in northern France such as Burgundy, Chablis, and Champagne; and areas in California including Santa Barbara, Santa Cruz, and Monterey. The suggested grapes for this type of area are Riesling and Gewürztraminer, which grow well in Germany, and Chardonnay and Pinot Noir, which grow well in Burgundy, France.

Region 2

Region 2 includes areas with heat indexes of 2,501 to 3,000 degrees. These areas include northern Italy; Bordeaux, France; and areas in California, including northern Sonoma, the southern Napa Valley, and some areas spanning between Los Angles and San Diego Counties. Grape varieties that grow well in this region are Merlot, Cabernet Sauvignon, and Sauvignon Blanc.

Region 3

Region 3 refers to places such as The Rhône Valley of France, the middle of Italy, and areas in California such as north Sonoma County, middle Napa County and southern Monterey County. The heat index ranges from 3,001 to 3,500 degrees.

Grapes suitable for growing these areas include Zinfandel, Gamay, and Syrah (Shiraz).

Region 4

Region 4 includes areas with a heat index of 3,501 to 4,000 degrees. This designation refers to places such as southern Italy and Spain or areas in California such as the northern Napa Valley, Los Angles, and Orange and San Diego Counties. The recommended grapes for these areas are limited to varieties such as the Thompson seedless grape. Many of these areas can successfully produce grapes that are listed in the first three regions, but the growing season is shorter.

Region 5

Region 5 is the hottest of the five regions, having a heat index of 4,001 degrees or more. The areas that fall within this region are northern Africa, southern Spain, and a very large portion of the middle of California, spanning from Shasta County in the north to Kern County in the south. These areas are recommended for the Thompson seedless grapes and other sweet grapes.

Training, Wire Training, and Pruning

The grape farmer is distinct from the vineyard owner because the grape farmer is growing grapes; the farmer does not plan to produce wine from them, but he or she might sell the grapes to a vintner to make wine. Most grape farmers focus on quality, not quantity; the farmer produces grapes knowing that the grapes must have certain qualities before a winery will accept them. Usually they trim the number of bunches on a vine so that the vines only have to parent a fraction of

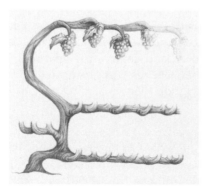

Figure 5.3 The vine is "trained" to follow the wires so that the rows of grapes that are created are easy to care for and harvest. [Dorling Kindersley Images]

the grapes that would have otherwise grown. This practice results in better, healthier grapes. In turn, the increased quality in grapes raises the quality of the wine made from those grapes.

The grape farmers also train the vines to grow in a certain way so that the vine and the grapes will receive more sunlight than they would have under the canopy of regular vine growth. Many times the tops of the vines are tied to expose the grapes to the sunlight. Sometimes this is done by tying the vines in a circle or in a heart shape, and sometimes the vines are tied so that the row of vines looks like a single, thin line stretching across the vineyard. If those same vines had not been tended, the row of vines would have grown much thicker, almost like the canopy of a tree, shading some of the grapes.

Pruning refers to cutting the vine or bunches of grapes. This practice helps increase sunlight to the grapes and also reduces the amount of the grapes that the vine makes, increasing the quality of the remaining grapes.

Testing the Grapes

Throughout the growing season, farmers check the grapes to make sure that they are developing properly. The grower mainly checks for sugar levels, or *brix*. The brix level is perhaps the single most important quality in grapes being grown for wine production because a certain amount of sugar needs to be present in order the yeast to produce alcohol during fermentation.

The grape farmer knows the sugar level that the grapes require to produce specific wines. Most countries forbid the addition of sugar to boost alcohol levels during fermentation, so the winemaker must make the most of the natural brix level. The sugar level in the grapes will depend on where the grape is being grown, what the weather has been like that year, and how much rainfall the vineyard has had.

Harvesting

When the sugar and acid levels of the grape reach the right levels, the grapes are picked. This usually must happen quickly for several reasons. For example, rain can ruin the grapes because the root will quickly transfer water from the ground to the grapes. This will water down the concentrated flavors that the grape farmer has been working toward all season. The grapes also will continue to ripen, destroying the perfect levels of sugar and acid that the grape farmer has worked to achieve all season. A freeze also could destroy the crop, so when the word is given to harvest, the grapes need to be picked quickly.

Figure 5.4 When gathering grapes by hand, the workers use a "hod," or basket, to be more efficient. [Dorling Kindersley Images]

Figure 5.5 Mechanical harvesting of grapes in a vineyard. [Dorling Kindersley Images]

Labor versus Machines

At one time everything that needed to be done to grapes to insure a great harvest was done by hand. Now, considering the size of some vineyards, this is impractical. However, in countries such as Germany, France, Portugal, and Chile, most of the vineyard work is still done by hand. This reliance on nonmechanized labor is related to the size of the vineyards and, in Germany's case, the terrain.

In France, a large vineyard may be split between several members of a family; machines do not make financial sense when the owner only has to care for the single row he or she owns. Germany poses a much different problem for grape growers. Most of the land is so hilly that machines are useless; therefore, most of the work is done by hand.

Machines are used in other locations at every stage of the winemaking process to decrease the cost of labor and to speed the process. Machines are used to cultivate and pick grapes almost everywhere else in the world at large vineyards. The machines that are used include a mechanical pruner, a mechanical harvester, a mechanical crusher-stemmer, a bottle filler, and an automated corker. The pruner trims the vines to exact a quality yield from the grapes. The harvester pulls bunches of grapes off of the vine; a mechanical harvester is able to complete an acre of land in less than an hour. Once the grapes are harvested, a crusher-stemmer removes the stems and extracts the juice. After fermentation, a mechanical filler fills the bottles, and finally, a mechanical corker places the cork in the bottle.

Yield

Vines are pruned to produce high-quality grapes. Some vineyards produce a yield of 2 tons of grapes per acre or less, while others produce an excess of 12 and 14 tons per acre. The yield of the acre has a great deal to do with the quality of the grape. As the yield of a vineyard climbs, the quality tends to fall off. Therefore, the grape farmer limits the production so the quality will be higher.

Juice Extraction

Once the grapes are gathered, they are placed on a press and crushed. One of the first methods of crushing the grapes involved the winemakers crushing the grapes with their feet. Even though this method is effective, it is rarely used today. There are several types of presses in use today: (1) a mechanical crusher-stemmer, (2) a crank-operated press, and (3) a balloon press. While these methods vary, the results are roughly the same.

Once the juice has been squeezed out of the grape, the mixture of juice, skins, seeds, and stems can be left together to allow the skins to color the juice.

Figure 5.6 and 5.7   Grapes are crushed with many different presses from the hand driven to the mechanical. [Dorling Kindersley Images]

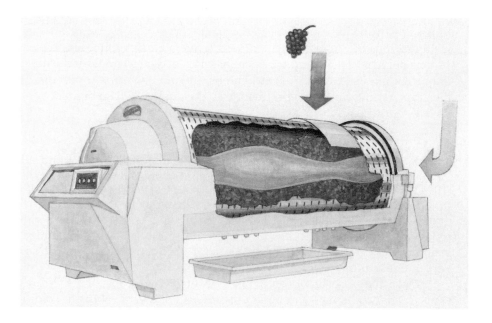

The red color is only found in the skins of grapes. These skins dye the otherwise clear juices. This method is used almost exclusively for red grapes when the winemaker is trying to make red wine. Alternatively, once the juice is collected, the skins, seeds, and stems can be skimmed off, allowing the juice to remain its natural color. This method is used for both red and white grapes when the winemaker is trying to make a white wine. Sometimes a winemaker wants to make a white wine from red grape. An example of this is "white" Zinfandel. White Zinfandel is made by crushing the grapes and then skimming the skins off; this quick skimming does not allow the grape skins any time to dye the wine. Sometimes the skins of grapes also add tannin to the juice, which allows the wine to age. For a visual explanation of how the two wines are processed refer to color insert Figure 2.

Fermentation and Storage

Once the winemaker obtains the desired color, the juice enters the fermentation process. Fermentation might happen in an oak barrel (this method will also add tannin from the wood), a glass container, or a stainless steel container.

Historically, fermentation occurred because of the natural yeast in the grapes. Today it is common practice for the winemaker to add yeast. (For more information about fermentation, read Chapter 6.) The yeast eats the sugar in the grape juice, turning it to wine. The fermentation process takes less than a month; the yeast will naturally stop producing alcohol when the sugar is exhausted or when the juice reaches about 15 percent alcohol by volume (some yeast strains can produce a little more alcohol).

Once the wine is fermented, it needs to mature, or age. Aging can take place in a bottle, a stainless steel tank, or in an oak barrel. The winemaker picks the storage container very carefully because different qualities can be imparted to the wine as a result of the storage container used. The most common storage containers are an oak barrels or bottles. Barrels are used for wines that will age for a long period, whereas bottles are used for wines that will be ready for consumption quickly.

The Cooper and the Barrel

The cooper, or barrel maker, cuts the staves (slats) of the barrel and allows the staves to dry before putting them together. Machines almost always are used to cut the staves now, but a little over 100 years ago, the whole process was done by hand. There are three methods used to dry the wood for barrels: time, air, and kilns. The wood can be laid out to air-dry for up to three or four years, but most wood is kiln-dried to save time and money.

After the staves are dried, they are held in place on the barrels by large iron hoops. Finally, each end of the barrel has a head which, is made from several pieces of flat wood that are hinged together. After the barrel is assembled, it is "toasted" or charred on the inside to the winemaker's specifications. Alcohol pro-

Figure 5.8 A cooper begins to build a barrel.
[Dorling Kindersley Images]

ducers do this to add color to wine stored in barrels. Generally there are three levels of toast: low, medium, and high.

Depending on its intended use, the barrel can be made with a choice of wood. The most common wood used for barrel making is white oak. There are two major types of white oak used: French and American. French oak comes from

Figure 5.9 A cooper continues to build a barrel. [Dorling Kindersley Images]

forests in France, and the trees usually range in age between 150 and 250 years old. (French oak grows slowly because of low levels of rainfall in its environment.) Only the upper part of the trunk is used for barrels, so each tree can yield about two barrels. The rest of the tree is used for firewood, planks, beams, and veneer wood. Some of the most sought-after French oak is Limousin Oak from the Limousin Forest near Limoges, France. Limousin oak is used for Cognac, White Burgundy wines, and California Chardonnay. French oak is said to give a subtle oak quality to the wine.

American oak, on the other hand, is much younger and cheaper than its French counterpart. The demand for American oak is lower because this oak gives a very forward oak quality to wine aged in it.

Barrels come in different sizes; the smallest size is 5 gallons. Some of the Italian barrels are large enough for thousands of gallons of wine, however. Winemakers usually use a barrel that holds about 55 gallons. The size of the barrel influences the flavor of the liquid in the barrel. The smaller the barrel, the more flavor the barrel imparts because the wine has more direct contact with the wood of the barrel. The number of times a barrel has been used also influences how the liquid tastes. If the barrel is made from *new oak,* or wood that has never been used before, the wood will affect the taste more. If the barrel is made from *old oak,* or a barrel that has been used before, the liquid's taste will be less influenced by the wood.

Many American winemakers use new oak barrels to make their wine, whereas the French usually use old oak. This difference dramatically affects the

Figure 5.10   A cooper finishes a barrel. [Dorling Kindersley Images]

Figure 5.11   A barrel is being charred.
[Dorling Kindersley Images]

wine and makes the wine's nationality easy to pick out by the trained wine professional.

Aging

After a wine is made, the winemaker has a choice to bottle the wine and sell it or to age it in oak barrels. The aging can last as little as 3 to 6 months to as long as 20 years (in the case of vintage Madeira). Not all wine is aged in oak barrels. While Chardonnay and Cabernet Sauvignon wines are known for their oak aging, Riesling and Gamay grapes have a much more delicate body and are not aged in oak barrels. Many of these wines are bottled directly after they are made.

Racking, Filtering, and Fining

Racking, filtering, and fining are all ways to clarify wine. Racking is exclusive to champagne. The bottles of champagne are placed in a rack at an ever-increasing angle, allowing gravity to pull the sediment towards the bottle's neck. The bottle is turned a quarter-turn each day until the sediment eventually works itself to the neck of the bottle, where it is frozen and removed.

Filtering is done with a machine. The wine flows through a series of tubes and filters, which takes most, if not all, of the sediment out. The wine is then bottled and sold. Most winemakers today use this method of clarification.

Fining is a more natural way to filter. Agents are used to "filter" the sediment out of the wine. Egg whites have been employed as a fining agent, but isinglass, which is a gelatin-like substance, is more commonly used today. Bentonite and charcoal are used for fining as well.

Blending

Sometimes a wine made from a single grape is not exactly what the winemaker wants. The tannin level may be too high or the acid may not be well balanced. The winemaker can blend wine made from another grape or from another vintage to sweeten or soften the original wine.

Winemakers are limited in how they can blend by their country's laws, however, which may dictate how much or how little of the second wine they can add. For example, if a winemaker in the United States wants to make and label his or her wine "Chardonnay," 75 percent of the wine that is bottled in the bottles marked Chardonnay must be made from the Chardonnay grape. The other 25 percent can be any other grape the winemaker wants to use. In Australia, the winemaker can blend different grapes at will and list both of the varieties on the label.

Bottling

Once the wine is ready to age or to sell, the winemaker bottles it. Bottles vary in size; the most common size is 750 milliliters (25.4 fluid ounces). Generally, a bottle of wine contains between 4 and 6 glasses of wine. Bottles of other sizes range from 187 milliliters (6.3 ounces) to 15 liters (507 ounces). Each size of bottle is identified by a particular name. These bottle names and sizes are listed in Table 5.1.

Table 5.1 Wine Bottle Names and Corresponding Sizes

Name of the Bottle	Size of the Bottle	Glasses of Wine	Bottles
Split	187 milliliter	1	N/A
Half-bottle	375 milliliter	2–3	½
Bottle	750 milliliter	4–6	1
Magnum	1.5 liters	8–12	2
Jeroboam (Double Magnum)	3 liters	16–24	4
Methuselah (Imperial)	6 liters	32–48	8
Salmanazar	9 liters	48–72	12
Balthazar	12 liters	64–96	16
Nebuchadnezzar	15 liters	80–120	20

Source: Lipmski and Lipmski, Oxford companion to wine

Most of the terms in Table 5.1 are reserved for champagne bottles, but Bordeaux wines use similar terms. For instance, a Double Magnum equals four 750-milliliter bottles (16–24 glasses of wine). A bottle that equals six 750-milliliter bottles (24–36 glasses of wine) is a Jeroboam, and an Imperial is a bottle that holds 8 regular bottles (32–48 glasses of wine).

Corks and Corking

Once the wine is bottled, the winemaker needs to shield it from the air, which can oxidize the wine prematurely. Even though a screw-top closure would do, most winemakers or bottlers prefer real corks. A real cork is made from the bark of an evergreen oak tree. This spongy material has been used as a stopper for wine and beer bottles since the late 1600s or early 1700s. Most corks average about 1¾ inches in length, but the size can vary from 1½ inches to 2½ inches.

Longer corks are reserved for wines that will age well. For example, the wines of Bordeaux (which are all known for longevity) all use a 2¼-inch cork, allowing them to age longer. The idea is that there is more of a barrier between the air and the wine. Red wines tend to be bottled with the longer corks, while white wines have the shorter corks because most white wines should be consumed when they are young.

Lately there has been a shortage of good cork, so winemakers have turned to three alternative solutions. The first is the screw top. Unfortunately, in the past the screw top was a sign of poor-quality wine. Nevertheless, some winemakers

Figure 5.12 Cork in several different forms.
[Dorling Kindersley Images]

have decided to fly in the face of this old notion, topping their wine bottles with screw tops. The second alternative is to take the extra cork material that is not formed into real corks and to compress it into composite corks.

The third option, which is becoming increasingly popular, is to use a rubber or plastic cork. This synthetic cork is becoming more desirable as cork tree bark is become increasingly rare. The winemaker is able to conserve the bark of the trees and still give customers a shape with which they are familiar. Even though there are some benefits to the synthetic cork, such as being able to store the bottle right-side up, it has not been proven that wine stores properly in bottles stopped with synthetic corks.

Key Terms

Terroir	Nebuchadnezzar
Vitis vinifera	Corks
Vitis labrusca	Brix
Trained vine	Hod
Phylloxera vastatrix	Vectors
Noble Rot	Pierce's Disease
Black Rot	French oak
Magnum	Cooper
Jeroboam	Racking
Methuselah	Filtering
Salmanazar	Fining
Balthazar	Winkler heat-index system

Study Questions

1. What is important about the region system set up by the University of California–Winkler?
2. Why does University of California–Winkler suggest that Chardonnay grapes be grown in Region 1 and not Region 4?
3. Why are machines used in the cultivation and harvesting of grapes?
4. What are some enemies of vines and grapes?
5. How do grape growers and winemakers test grapes to tell if the grapes are ready to make wine?
6. What is a cooper?
7. What is the name of the largest bottle used to store wine and how much does it hold?
8. What is the name of the smallest bottle and how much does it hold?
9. What is the name of the standard bottle and how much does it hold?

Chapter

6 *Fermentation*

After reading this chapter, you will be able to:

- ❏ Explain the process of fermentation.
- ❏ Discuss the ingredients necessary for fermentation to occur.
- ❏ Apply the science of fermentation.
- ❏ Discuss how different types of alcohol are fermented.
- ❏ Describe how winemakers determine alcohol content using brix, specific gravity, and a hydrometer.

Any successful fermentation proceeds along a predictable course. . . . The only significant influences upon the fermentation that can be manipulated by the brewer are those of the yeast . . . and the temperature and duration of the ferment. Changes in any one of these can affect the residual sugar, mouthfeel, clarity. . . .

—Gregory Noonan, in Brewing Lager Beer

Different types of alcohol are simple to distinguish from each other. Beer traditionally has a foamy head, a color ranging from pale gold to chocolate brown, and distinctive yeasty smell. Wine, when swirled in the glass, can create golden- to burgundy-hued "legs" that run down the sides of the glass. There may be some bubbles in the wine, but a foamy head will only last seconds. In addition, wine usually has at least twice as much alcohol (by volume) as beer. Hard alcohol has a somewhat sharper smell than either beer or wine and a much higher alcohol content. It's hard to believe that all of these types of alcohol begin with the same basic process. Despite these obvious differences, however, all alcohol is produced using one initial method: fermentation.

Fermentation

Fermentation is a biochemical process that produces alcohol as a byproduct, or waste product, of an organic exchange. Fermentation requires three basic ingredients: water, yeast and sugar. As simple as this seems, however, the endless variations in which these ingredients can combine can change the final product in as many. Other ingredients also may be added to achieve different products and results.

Water

Generally, only fresh water is used for creating alcohol, but even among fresh water sources, the composition of the water varies greatly. For example, the Great Salt Lake is saltier than any ocean, and water from the Cuyahoga River in Ohio once contained so many pollutants that it actually caught on fire. As these examples illustrate, diverse water sources bring different levels of purity and different minerals to the fermentation process. The water's source will affect the final product's taste as well. Mineral levels that are present in water from one part of the country are different in water from other parts of the country. Water from a mountain spring has different characteristics than water out of the tap, and fresh water formed in a limestone basin possesses different characteristics than fresh spring water. Brewers, distillers, and vintners are particular about the water they use because they know it will affect the final product; some distillers prefer water with a high lime content, and some brewers look for specific minerals or a higher salt content.

Yeast

Yeast is a one-celled, chlorophyll-free plant that lives on simple sugar. There are endless varieties of yeast, and different areas of the world have different strains of yeast. Many strains exist naturally in the air or on the grapes themselves, but some yeast is commercially grown and marketed and can be purchased by brewers and vintners to impart specific qualities. Any strain of yeast used for fermentation must be alive. Fortunately for alcohol producers, yeast is very hard to kill. Heating it above approximately 137° F. is deadly to yeast, but it can be frozen or freeze-dried and revived for later use by thawing or reconstituting.

Sugar

The type of sugar the alcohol producer chooses alters the taste and alcohol content of the end product. There is surprising flexibility in this ingredient; some sugars are sweeter than others, and many have other subtle or obvious taste differences. Fructose, maltose, and glucose are the main sugars used in fermentation. Each has a different chemical structure and source. Sugar comes in forms such as granulated or powdered sugar and honey. Some forms feel more complex on the palate than others.

The sugar used to make wine is derived from the juice of the grape. Fruit and fruit juices, also known chemically as fructose, are very often used to make wine: grapes plums, raisins, and berries all produce nice wines. Any starchy food also can be used, because starch easily breaks down to sugar.

Potatoes, a glucose sugar, are a good source of sugars for alcohol production, and they constitute the chief ingredient in some vodkas. Whiskey producers ferment with corn, and rum's sugar source for fermentation is the sugar cane plant. Tequila is made from the blue agave, a member of the desert lily family, which is similar in appearance to cactus. Beer brewers use barley that has germinated (malted barley), which breaks down into a sugar called maltose. Almost any food that contains sugar can be fermented into alcohol. Like water, all of these sugars have components other than their sugar content that modify the fermentation process and create different flavors and colors.

The Science of Fermentation

Food is used by living organisms for nutrition to survive and reproduce. Yeast, a living organism, operates on this same principle, and, like any other living organism, it also produces waste: alcohol and carbon dioxide. This organic process is *fermentation.*

Yeast consumes simple sugars. These simple sugars, such as glucose and fructose, are made up of carbon (C), hydrogen (H), and oxygen (O) molecules. All simple sugars are made from these three types of molecules; the way the molecules are arranged determines the form of the sugar. Think of these molecules as being ingredients in a recipe. Scientists write their recipes in a string of letters and numbers. The numbers serve two purposes: to show how many of the molecules are present or to show how much of the ingredient is present in total in the recipe. A small number behind a letter, such as the 2 in H_2O (one water molecule) tells how many parts of hydrogen are present. In this case there are two molecules.

When there is no number following a letter, like the O in H_2O, it means that there is only one part. In water, therefore, there are two hydrogen molecules and one oxygen. A large number in front of the chain of numbers signifies that there is more than one chain of this particular configuration. So, in scientific shorthand, $2H_2O$ represents two water molecules.

Scientifically, glucose is written like this: $C_6H_{12}O_6$. This means that glucose is composed of six carbon atoms, twelve hydrogen atoms and six oxygen atoms linked together like a group of people holding hands. When yeast is added to the simple sugar, it consumes the sugar. When the living organism is finished consuming the simple sugar, it expels the digested sugar in a different form. After the sugar is digested, the individual molecules stop "holding hands" and grab onto a new set. This change allows the yeast to expel two different forms of waste: alcohol (C_2H_5OH), and carbon dioxide (CO_2).

To summarize, when yeast is added to a glucose molecule, it eats the sugar and changes the way the molecules are connected. The yeast's waste is reorganized into molecules of carbon dioxide and alcohol. In scientific shorthand, scientists write this process down so it looks like a mathematical equation:

$$\text{Yeast} + C_6H_{12}O_6 = 2C_2H_5OH + 2CO_2 + \text{Energy}$$
$$\text{or}$$
$$\text{Yeast} + \text{Sugar} = \text{Alcohol, Carbon Dioxide, and Energy}$$

Notice that the chemical reaction does not change how many molecules of carbon, hydrogen, or oxygen are involved; the process cannot add or subtract new molecules. There are still six carbon, twelve hydrogen, and six oxygen molecules, but they are arranged differently on each side of the equation. When this exchange takes place, energy is expelled, as shown in the equation.

The amount of alcohol from fermentation depends on the amount of sugar available for the yeast to consume. If there is not much sugar, there won't be much alcohol expelled by the yeast. If the yeast is mixed with a liquid that has a very high sugar content, however, the yeast will continue to eat the sugar and produce alcohol until the alcohol level reaches about 15 percent of the total volume. The yeast stops functioning at this point because the alcohol creates a toxic environment for the yeast; the alcohol reaches an incapacitating level, the yeast is overwhelmed, and alcohol production ceases.

Brewers can predict the anticipated alcohol level because the sugar content of malted barley, which is the most common ingredient in beer, is easily controlled. Alcohol content in wine can fluctuate wildly due to variations in the weather from season to season and because of the difference in grape varieties. However, a winemaker can still predict how much alcohol will end up in the final product, depending on how much sugar is the initial product. The alcohol content is measured by determining the *specific gravity* (SG) of the liquid, which is the density of a given volume of liquid as compared to the weight or density of an equal volume of water at the same temperature. Water is understood to have the SG of 1.000. Alcohol is lighter than water, so it will always have a number less than 1.000. Any liquid with any amount of sugar has a SG greater than 1.000 so it has a density greater than water. As the yeast changes the sugar to alcohol, the specific gravity lowers as the carbon dioxide floats into the atmosphere.

Winemakers and brewers test their sugar infused liquid before, during, and after fermentation with an instrument called a *hydrometer.* The hydrometer is a vertical scale inside a waterproof glass tube that is weighted at one end. It is used to test the density, or specific gravity, of a liquid by comparing it with the density of pure water. The hydrometer floats upright in the liquid like a buoy. The higher the top of the hydrometer floats, the denser the liquid; the more it sinks, the less dense the liquid. Alcohol is less dense than water. The more alcohol by volume, the lower the hydrometer will sink.

Winemakers also have another tool called a *refractometer,* which helps determine the potential alcohol level of grapes on the vine based on the sugar level, or brix. The refractometer tells the winemaker how much sugar is in the grapes. This is important because sugar is food for the yeast, and the more sugar available for the yeast's consumption, the higher amount of alcohol the yeast can expel. A winemaker can figure out the potential alcohol level by multiplying the brix by .55. Table 6.1 shows what potential alcohol level a winemaker might expect based on the specific gravity and the brix.

Fermentation of Beer

Most beer production starts with barley that has been malted and roasted. A grain is malted by adding water to it so that it begins to grow. During the malting stage, enzymes begin converting the carbohydrates to a sugar that yeast can consume. Roasting the barley stops it from growing and adds a darker color to the grain. The malted roasted barley then is crushed and water is added; this combination is called a *wort* and is not unlike a grain soup or stock. The wort is brought to a boil to destroy enzymes, stabilize salts, and to sterilize the wort. The wort is then cooled and yeast is added, or *pitched.* Sometimes, however, the wort is exposed to air, allowing natural yeast, which are present in the air everywhere, to ferment the sugars into alcohol and carbon dioxide. In an open tank, the carbon dioxide byproduct is allowed to dissipate into the atmosphere. Sometimes this carbon dioxide is captured and sold to other companies for other uses such as carbonating water or soda.

Table 6.1 Potential Alcohol Content Derived from Brix and Specific Gravity

Brix of the Grape	Specific Gravity of the Juice	Potential Alcohol (% by Volume)
17	1.070	8.8
23.7	1.100	12.5
28	1.120	15.0

Figure 6.1   Beer is being fermented with the carbon dioxide escaping into the brewery. [Dorling Kindersley Images]

Most of the time yeast is picked out very carefully; the brewer chooses the yeast for specific properties that will influence the final product. Again, there are literally thousands of different strains of yeast, each able to do something a little different from the other. Once the yeast has converted the sugar to about 4 to 6 percent alcohol, the beer is almost ready to be bottled. A little more sugar is added just before bottling creating an opportunity for a secondary fermentation. This time the most important product is not the added alcohol, but the carbon dioxide. The carbon dioxide is trapped in the bottle, creating the carbonation that allows for the *head.*

Fermentation of Wine

Grapes are an excellent choice for fermenting. Up to 33 percent of the mass of a grape is sugar. Grapes are the only fruit that can claim such a high sugar content. Additionally, the grapes contain enough water to ensure fermentation. The gray "dust" that we end up wiping off of most grapes before we eat them is natural yeast, which, if we do nothing, may turn the grapes into "wine on the vine" anyway.

Given that grapes already contain the necessary ingredients for fermentation to occur, the only steps left are to crush the grapes into juice, remove the stems and seeds (and skins, unless a little color is preferred), and let the juice sit.

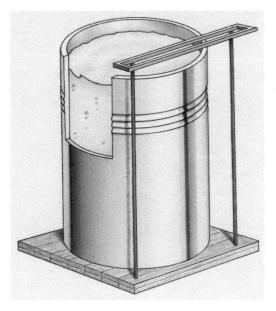

Figure 6.2 Sometimes a fermentation happens in a stainless steel vat. [Dorling Kindersley Images]

If sparkling wine is the desired product, a secondary fermentation (just like with beer) is allowed to occur in the bottle.

Fermentation of Spirits

Spirits are made by a process called distillation (see Chapter 15), but before alcohol can be distilled it must be created by fermentation. There are two different products that can be distilled: beer or brewed beverages and wine. The distilled beer is made from a grain, such as corn, rice, or barley, that is fermented. Distilled wine is made from any fruit or vegetable that is fermented. The beer or wine that is to be distilled may not be what most people think of as beer or wine. For example, to make vodka, the producer starts with potatoes. The producer makes potato water that is fermented into a potato "wine." This wine then is distilled into what is known as vodka.

Key Terms

Alcohol	C_2H_5OH
Fermentation	Enzyme
Secondary Fermentation	CO_2

Carbonation
Carbon Dioxide
Glucose
Hydrometer
Brix

Wort
Pitching Yeast
Specific Gravity
Refractometer

Study Questions

1. What three ingredients are essential to fermentation?
2. What does fermentation produce?
3. How is the alcohol content predicted in fermentation?
4. What is secondary fermentation, and what types of alcohol need it?

Chapter 7

Light-Bodied White Wines: Riesling, Gewürztraminer, Müller-Thurgau, and Pinot Blanc

After reading this chapter, you will be able to:

- ❏ Discuss white grapes that usually produce light-bodied wines.
- ❏ Explain where the grapes for these wines are grown.
- ❏ Describe the flavor and aroma profiles of wines made from these grapes.

Who after wine, talks of war's hardships or of poverty.

—Horace

Riesling, Gewürztraminer, and Pinot Blanc grapes most commonly are associated with Germany, but these grapes also grow in a small eastern region of France called Alsace. Each of these grapes has their own personality and, for the most part, they live in the same types of neighborhoods all over the world. They are known for producing wines that are sweet, but they also produce some wines that are dry. The wines made with these grapes tend to be light-bodied or a little watery in nature with very few (if any) lingering flavors.

The sweet wines made from these grapes come from late harvest grapes or are produced by adding a süssereserve, an unfermented grape juice. The sweet grape juice balances the high acid of German grapes and wine. (German grapes are high in acid because of the short growing season in the country.) Outside of Germany, the same grapes make wines that are higher in alcohol, but each of the wines made from these grapes displays different and specific characteristics which can be recognized as a signature of the grape.

Riesling

The Riesling grape is a pale, greenish-yellow grape that is very hardy and can withstand hardships ranging from weather to diseases. The vine buds late; as a result, the grapes are late to ripen. Riesling wines are white and usually sweet, but some areas produce a drier version of Riesling. A dry Riesling wine will be labeled Johannesburg Riesling, while a sweet wine will simply be called White Riesling.

The aromas in Riesling wines include green apple, passionfruit, peach, flint, kiwi, and even lime, depending on the ripeness of the grapes at the crush and where the grapes were grown. Riesling can develop other aromas and flavors including honey, lemon, apricot, spice, and even gasoline. A tart, citrus flavor can come from the grapes not getting enough sun. The taster should be able to tell where the grapes were grown by the overall flavor of the wine and the alcohol content. Many wineries mimic the Riesling style, but the areas in which these wineries are located have warmer climates and longer growing seasons. Therefore, the wines have a higher alcohol content.

Germany

When most people think about German wine, one of the first grapes that comes to mind is Riesling. This perception partially is due to the fact that Riesling makes up about 20 percent of all German wine production. German wines tend to be low in alcohol (only about 8 percent) and tannin, but high in sugar and acid. Many German wines are produced from hand-picked grapes because of Germany's hilly terrain. The landscape does not allow for mechanized harvesting. Winemakers only pick the grapes that have achieved the desired ripeness. This human factor in the production process allows for many levels in the quality of wine produced in Germany.

German Riesling wine tends to be very light and fruity with a hint of minerals and earth. Some of the fruits detected include apple, lemons, peach, and grapes. Other aromas and flavors in German Riesling might be flowers and, if the wine is older, gasoline.

France: Alsace

Even though the Riesling wines of Alsace and the Riesling wines of Germany are bottled in similar bottles and made with the same grapes, they are very different. Riesling wine from the French region of Alsace is very dry and has a high alcohol content. The winemakers in Alsace ferment all of the sugar out of the juice, allowing the alcohol content to finish with up to a hefty 12 percent.

Twenty-five percent of the grapes grown in Alsace are Riesling. Other varieties grown in the region include Gewürztraminer, Pinot Blanc, Tokay, and Pinot Gris, all of which are used to produce dry white wines.

United States: California

In California, Riesling most often is grown in cool areas, but these areas still tend to be warmer than Germany. In addition, California receives more sunshine than Germany. This results in grapes with less acid, more sugar, a higher alcohol content and more fruit flavors than a German Riesling. It is the goal of many California winemakers to produce Riesling that is more like the sweet wines of Germany and less like the dry wines of Alsace.

Figure 7.1 Unlike wines from other French regions the wines from the Alsace region list the grape varietal on the label. [Dorling Kindersley Images]

United States: New York

The quality of Riesling wines that come from New York can be compared with those from Germany and Alsace. The best New York Riesling wines come from the Finger Lakes region, which is located southeast of Rochester and southwest of Syracuse. Some very good Rieslings also come from the North Fork of Long Island. New York Riesling wine can vary in sweetness from extremely sweet to bone dry.

United States: Washington and Oregon

Even though Washington and Oregon share the same coast with California, the wines that are produced in these two states are distinctly different from California wines. Washington and Oregon are located north of California; therefore, the growing season is shorter, and the grapes do not ripen as much. This means the wines tend to be lighter and crisper than California Riesling. Oregon follows Alsace's lead when producing Riesling wine. They ferment the sugar out of the juice, which results in a dry wine.

Washington's Riesling wines range from dry to sweet. A dry Riesling wine from Washington simply might be marked as dry or it may come marked "Johannesburg Riesling"; the sweeter Riesling wines might be marked as late harvest. Washington Riesling wine also might be marked "White Riesling," which means that the wine is not dry, nor is it completely sweet. The wine would be referred to as *off-dry* or *semi-sweet*.

Figure 7.2 A bottle of Australian Riesling. [Dorling Kindersley Images]

Australia and New Zealand

Australian Rieslings tend to have a greenish-gold hue. Apple can be detected as an aftertaste in Australian Rieslings, but there is a powerful lime note both in the smell and the taste that will be very forward.

Australian Riesling also tends to be higher in alcohol and fairly intense in flavor (no other Riesling can compare with the lime overtones). Most of the Riesling grapes are grown in South Australia, which is a state in the country of Australia. The growing areas in South Australia that do very well with the Riesling grape are the Clare Valley, the Barossa Valley, and the Eden Valley.

New Zealand is comprised of two islands: the North Island and the South Island. The majority of New Zealand Rieslings come from the South Island from areas called Nelson, Marlborough, Canterbury, and Central Otago. Two areas on the North Island also are growing Riesling with success: Gisborne/Poverty Bay and Wairarapa/Martinborough.

New Zealand Riesling wines are a close cousin to the Riesling wines of New York and Oregon in taste and aroma, with the distinct difference being that New Zealand wines have some tropical fruit to them, including hard-to-miss grapefruit and citrus notes.

Gewürztraminer

Even though Gewürztraminer grapes are known for producing white wine, the Gewürztraminer is a pink-skinned grape. These grapes are low in acidity. The resulting wine is perceived as sweeter than other wines, having nothing to balance the sugar in the flavor. The name of this grape tells the taster what to expect. The German word *Gewürz* means spicy. This signature spiciness can be detected in almost any wine made with Gewürztraminer grapes. The Gewürztraminer grape is not native to Germany; this grape was most likely a transplant from Italy, where it is still grown. Today Gewürztraminer is grown all over the world, with some of the variations producing medium-bodied wines.

Gewürztraminer wines are distinctive because of the aromas of spice they contain. The wine also can have notes of honey, rose, cinnamon, and some tropical fruit, depending on the ripeness of the grapes at the crush and where the grapes were grown. The taster is able to tell the type of grapes that were used to make this wine by the overall aroma and flavor.

Germany

Of all of the German wines, Gewürztraminer is the most forward in its flavor. Gewürztraminer is not one of the major grapes of Germany; this spicy grape makes up only a small percentage of what the Germans produce every year. The Gewürztraminer grape is grown in only three of the thirteen winemaking regions of Germany: the Rheinhessen, Palatinate, and Baden. The wines produced in these areas with the Gewürztraminer grape are, not surprisingly, spicy and sweet.

France: Alsace

While the Gewürztraminer grape most likely was born in Italy and has a German name, the wine came to fame in the Alsace region of France. Alsatian Gewürztraminers are fermented dry, like all wines in the region. (The wine also will have the name of the grape varietal on the label; this which is different from the way the rest of France labels wines.) The wine is fairly high in alcohol and low in acid, allowing the spiciness and fruit of the wine to come out. Some of the best wines in Alsace are late harvest, which are called *Vendange Tardive*. Because of the late harvest, the grapes are very ripe and they allow the alcohol and the sugar to preserve the wine, aging them very well for white wines.

United States: California

California Gewürztraminer has not always had a good reputation. The wine rarely tasted as good as its Alsatian and German counterparts because this grape did not do well in the warmer climates of California. In recent years, however, the flavor of the California Gewürztraminer has improved because wine producers are growing the grapes in the cooler regions of northern California such as the Anderson Valley in Mendocino County and the Russian River Valley in Sonoma County.

United States: New York

Gewürztraminer grapes can be found in the same places in New York as the Riesling grape: the Finger Lakes region and the North Fork of Long Island. The Gewürztraminer wines of these areas, however, pale in comparison to the wines of Alsace.

United States: Washington

Even though the first commercial wine released in Washington in 1967 was Gewürztraminer, the grape has been losing ground in the state ever since. Many growers are planting other grapes, and the use of the Gewürztraminer grape is declining.

New Zealand

New Zealand is the perfect place to grow white wine grapes; the climate almost seems to cater to these grapes, including Gewürztraminer. The areas in which Gewürztraminer grapes are grown include the regions of Gisborne/Poverty Bay and Wairarapa/Martinborough on the North Island and Nelson and Central Otago on the South Island.

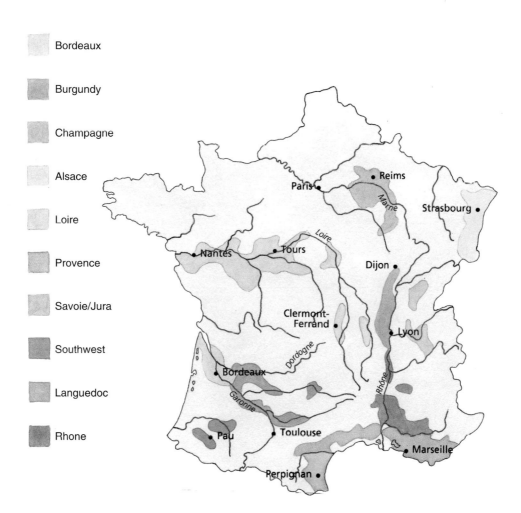

France's wine regions. [Dorling Kindersley Images]

Bordeaux

Burgundy

Champagne

Alsace

Loire

Provence

Savoie/Jura

Southwest

Languedoc

Rhone

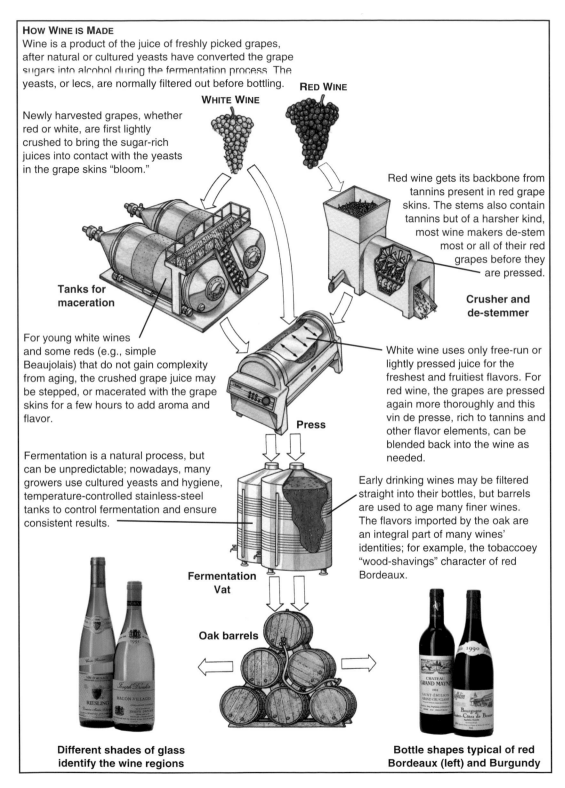

HOW WINE IS MADE

Wine is a product of the juice of freshly picked grapes, after natural or cultured yeasts have converted the grape sugars into alcohol during the fermentation process. The yeasts, or lecs, are normally filtered out before bottling.

WHITE WINE

RED WINE

Newly harvested grapes, whether red or white, are first lightly crushed to bring the sugar-rich juices into contact with the yeasts in the grape skins "bloom."

Red wine gets its backbone from tannins present in red grape skins. The stems also contain tannins but of a harsher kind, most wine makers de-stem most or all of their red grapes before they are pressed.

Tanks for maceration

Crusher and de-stemmer

For young white wines and some reds (e.g., simple Beaujolais) that do not gain complexity from aging, the crushed grape juice may be stepped, or macerated with the grape skins for a few hours to add aroma and flavor.

White wine uses only free-run or lightly pressed juice for the freshest and fruitiest flavors. For red wine, the grapes are pressed again more thoroughly and this vin de presse, rich to tannins and other flavor elements, can be blended back into the wine as needed.

Press

Fermentation is a natural process, but can be unpredictable; nowadays, many growers use cultured yeasts and hygiene, temperature-controlled stainless-steel tanks to control fermentation and ensure consistent results.

Early drinking wines may be filtered straight into their bottles, but barrels are used to age many finer wines. The flavors imported by the oak are an integral part of many wines' identities; for example, the tobaccoey "wood-shavings" character of red Bordeaux.

Fermentation Vat

Oak barrels

Different shades of glass identify the wine regions

Bottle shapes typical of red Bordeaux (left) and Burgundy

All grapes follow a similar path when wine is being made. [Dorling Kindersley Images]

Stainless steel fermenting tanks. [Dorling Kindersley Images]

Men working on a barrel of Madeira wine in the Adegas de Sao Francisco in Madeira. [Dorling Kindersley Media Library]

White Wines

Chardonnay, Pinot Gris (Grisgio), Sauvingnon Blanc, and Reisling are four different white wines with varying shades of white.

Rosé and White Zinfandel

With Rosé and White Zinfandel, both the lighter-shaded red and the white wines are made from red grapes.

[Original photography by Jim Smith]

Red Wines

Cabernet Sauvignon, Syrah (Shiraz), Beaujolais (Gamay), and Burgundy (Pinot Noir). These wines distinguish themselves by their colors and their aromas.

California Cabernet Sauvingnon, California Syrah, French Beaujolais Village, and California Burgundy (some California producers borrow this famous French name).

California Merlot, Italian Chianti (Sangiovesc), Red Zinfandel, and California Pinot Noir. The depth in the color of the wine can allude to the depth in flavor.

[Original photography by Jim Smith]

Porto

This fortified wine has different quality levels, and different colors. The California Tawny Port is lighter in color than the Special Ruby Porto or the Late Bottled Vintage Porto. The price of the porto increases with higher quality.

Sherries

This fortified wine has different quality levels, each with a distinct flavor and color.

Aperitifs

These alcoholic beverages are used before the meal to stimulate the appetite.

Sparkling Wines

These California sparkling wines are clearly marked to indicate their sweetness, or how much residual sugar is in the bottle. Brut is the driest, while Extra Dry is semi-sweet.

[Original photography by Jim Smith]

Distilled Spirits

Distilled spirits can be made from almost anything with sugar. The difference in color shows if the spirits were aged in wood. The tequila, vodka, gin, and first rum were not aged in wood, whereas the last two rums were.

The four whiskies (whisky) are distilled from grain, while the brandy is distilled from wine. Each has a different quality that makes it distinct.

Cordials

Each has a high sugar content and the distinct flavor of coffee, fruit, or mint. Cordials can vary in flavor and are usually used as mixers.

[Original photography by Jim Smith]

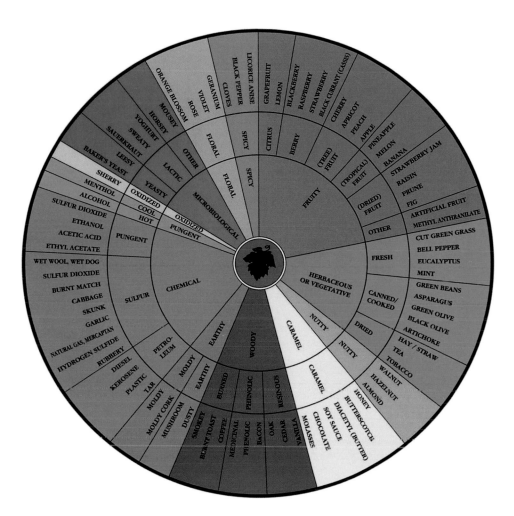

This wine aroma wheel can be used to better identify and describe the aromas and flavors of wines during tastings. [The Aroma Wheel copyright © ACNOBLE 1990. Colored, laminated copies of the Wine Aroma may be obtained from AC Noble at the Department of Viticulture and Enology, University of California, Davis CA 95616 USA. acnoble@ucdavis.edu   www.winearomawheel.com.]

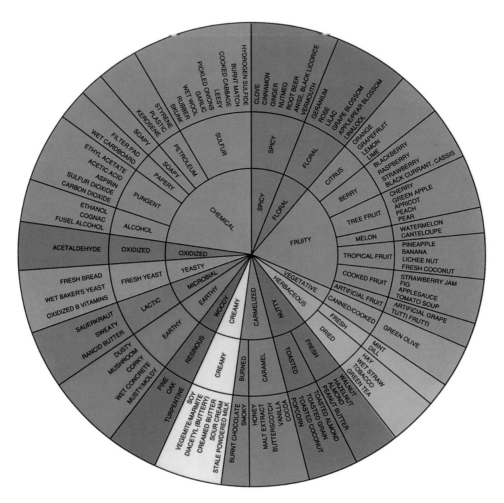

Use this wine wheel to better identify the aromas and flavors of sparkling wines and Champagnes during tastings. [The Sparkling Wine Aroma Wheel may be obtained from Ann Noble at the Dept. of Viticulture and Enology, University of California; Davis, CA 95616 USA.   acnoble@ucdavis.edu   www.winearomawheel.com.]

Müller-Thurgau

The Müller-Thurgau grape is a relatively new grape. It is a hybrid created in 1882 by crossing Riesling and Silvaner grapes. Some botanists claim that two clones of Riesling actually parented the grape; others claim that the Müller-Thurgau grape is a result of crossing the Riesling and Chasselas grapes. Müller-Thurgau grapes are easy to grow and ripen early, so this variety has quickly replaced other varieties in the vineyard. In Germany, it is second only to Riesling. Müller-Thurgau grapes produce a wine that is relatively low in alcohol and low in acidity with nice subtle fruit flavors.

Germany

The wines made from Germany's Müller-Thurgau, such as Liebfraumilch, are less expensive than other German wines. These wines are simple and very straightforward. Müller-Thurgau's popularity with German grape growers has translated into a passport to all destinations that have a cooler climate and a short growing season.

Other Regions

Some of the other places in the world that Müller-Thurgau grapes are grown are considered cooler or colder grape-growing areas, including England, Austria, New Zealand, Oregon, and Canada. The areas in which Müller-Thurgau grows successfully gives this grape the distinction of being grown in some of the most remote vineyards, including those closest to the North and South Poles.

Pinot Blanc

Pinot Blanc is a white grape that makes light-bodied, almost neutral-tasting, wines that can reflect flavors and characters found in Chardonnay in many ways. However, the buttery apple, pear, tangerine, and citrus found in Pinot Blanc wines seems to be a shadow of the mighty Chardonnay. The ripeness of the grape tends to lead to higher alcohol content than Chardonnay, and Pinot Blanc can have a high acid level. While the two grapes have similarities, they are not related. Pinot Blanc is more closely related to the Pinot Gris and even to the Pinot Noir (a red grape) than to Chardonnay.

The characteristics of the Pinot Blanc grape do lend some support to the perception that there is a connection between Pinot Blanc and Chardonnay grapes, however. Many times Pinot Blanc vines are planted in the same vineyards as Chardonnay (for example, in the Côte d'Or); sometimes Pinot Blanc is even produced the same way Chardonnay wines are. This results in a more intense, fuller-bodied Pinot Blanc wine.

France: Alsace and Burgundy

The best Pinot Blanc wines come from the Alsace and Burgundy regions of France. The wines made from Pinot Blanc in Alsace and Burgundy have more body than Pinot Blanc from other areas, yet they are still light-bodied wines. (Due to the laws in Alsace, the name of the grape is always on the label.) Pinot Blanc from Alsace is best served before meals as an aperitif because its high acid level and light body will stimulate the appetite.

In Burgundy, Pinot Blanc is the underdog grape. Most wine production in the area is Chardonnay. Only a small percent of total production is Pinot Blanc, and even then Pinot Blanc is handled much like the neighboring Chardonnay. This results in a more intense wine, which is out of character with the normal Pinot Blanc, and many times it is taken for a weak Chardonnay. No hint on the label is given to the customer, so many make the wrong assumption about the lineage of the wine.

Italy

In Italy, Pinot Blanc is known as *Pinot Bianco.* The Pinot Blanc (Bianco) grown in Italy makes some flavorful wine and can rival wine made from Alsace. The majority of Pinot Blanc from Italy is grown in the northernmost regions such as Collio and Alto-Adige.

United States: California

Most of what is called Pinot Blanc in California is really is a grape called Muscadet. The two grapes are easy to confuse when looking at and tasting them. Several botanists called *ampelographers* (botanists that specialize in grapes) only recently found the mistake that the grape growers were making. Many of the wineries continue with the misnomer because Pinot Blanc is a more popular grape and they are in business to sell their wine. Some of the wineries in California do make real Pinot Blanc, however.

Key Terms

Süssereserve	Riesling
Off-Dry	Gewürztraminer
Semi-Sweet	Müller-Thurgau
Ampelographer	Pinot Blanc
Light-Bodied	

Study Questions

1. What are the flavor and aroma profiles of Riesling wines?
2. What are the flavor and aroma profiles of Gewürztraminer wines?
3. What are the flavor and aroma profiles of Müller-Thurgau wines?
4. What are the flavor and aroma profiles of Pinot Blanc wines?

Chapter 8

Medium-Bodied White Wines: Sauvignon Blanc, Sémillon, Trebbiano, Pinot Gris, and Chenin Blanc

After reading this chapter, you will be able to:

❏ Discuss the major grapes that make medium- to full-bodied white wines.
❏ Describe the flavor and aroma profile of Sauvignon Blanc wines.
❏ Describe the flavor and aroma profile of Pinot Gris.
❏ Describe the flavor and aroma profile of wines made with other white grapes.

Place a substantial meal before a tired man, and he will eat with effort and be little better for it at first. Give him a glass of wine or brandy, and immediately he feels better: you see him come to life again before you.
—Brillat-Savarin

Many wonderful wines can be made from white grapes; laws, weather, climate, and many other factors contribute to the huge ranges of aromas and flavors these wines produce. While there are large variations in taste and aroma, all of these wines tend to have an alcohol level of about 12 to 13 percent, and the flavors of these wines tend to linger for a short period in the mouth of the drinker.

The grapes that produce medium-bodied wines grow all over the world in many different climates with greatly varying results. Many of these are grown in areas that are not well suited to the grape, but they produce good wines nonetheless.

The Sauvignon Blanc and Sémillon grapes are the main two types of white grapes used to produce medium-bodied white wines. Traditionally, these grapes are grown in the Bordeaux region. This category of wine also includes the grapes of the Loire Valley, such as Chenin Blanc, and minor grapes from Alsace, such as Pinot Gris and Muscat. Another grape that makes medium-bodied white wines is not as well known. Trebbiano grapes also can produce blockbuster white wines.

Sauvignon Blanc

The Sauvignon Blanc grape is responsible for the production of a well-known wine. However, depending on where the grape is grown and where the wine is produced, the resulting product has many different names. Wine made with Sauvignon Blanc grapes is known as White Bordeaux or Bordeaux Blanc, and wines from the Loire Valley carry names such as Sancerre, Pouilly-Fumé and, in California, Fumé Blanc. These wines range from medium-bodied to full-bodied and can have hints of oak, lemon, lime, green grass, melon, pineapple, pear, apple, green pepper, asparagus, vanilla, flint, almond, and even cream, depending on where the grapes are grown and how the wine is made. Oddly, Sauvignon Blanc also can produce the scent of cat urine or cat box. Based on this quality alone, many people can pick out a Sauvignon Blanc in a blind tasting.

The most famous of the Sauvignon Blanc wines are named for the areas in which they are grown. Bordeaux Blanc is made in the Bordeaux region of France. Sancerre and Pouilly-Fumé are produced in areas by the same name in the Loire Valley of France. In the United States and most other countries, Sauvignon Blanc is named for the grape variety. There is one exception to this rule, however. In California, thanks to Robert Mondavi, Sauvignon Blanc also can be called Fumé Blanc. Mondavi dubbed his wine made from the Sauvignon Blanc grape Fumé Blanc in honor of the wine produced from the same grape in the Pouilly-Fumé area of the Loire Valley. Mondavi did this for marketing purposes; he theorized that a name like Fumé Blanc was much easier for a customer to pronounce and, thus, ask for. The name caught on and other wineries began to use the blend of terms as well.

France: Bordeaux

White Bordeaux is made from a blend of grapes including Sauvignon Blanc and Sémillon. There is no one recipe for the perfect White Bordeaux, as the grapes are added in varying amounts depending on the vineyard in which the wine is produced. The blend varies from 100 percent of one of the grapes to a 50/50 blend of two grapes. The AOC does not require the winemaker to note this blend on the label. The white wine produced in Bordeaux can have hints of grass and pineapple, but most will find that peach and oak, with touches of cream and vanilla, are the more forward flavors.

The blend of Sauvignon Blanc and Sémillon grapes is a perfect example of the "odd couple." This contrast may account for the reason the resulting wine is so good. The Sauvignon Blanc grape tends to be high in acid, herb, and grass flavors. Wine made from this grape is usually enjoyed early in its life. The Sémillon grape is lower in acid and higher in fruit qualities. Aged Sémillon wine has more sophistication than a young wine from this grape. Therefore, the combination of the two grapes seems to be the perfect blend; each grape counteracts and enhances the qualities of the other. The blend also enhances the aging of the wine. Bordeaux Blanc (White Bordeaux) can sometimes age up to ten years with very good results. This is a very rare quality for a white wine.

France: Loire Valley

Many people feel that the Sauvignon Blanc wine produced in the Loire Valley is the model for all other Sauvignon Blanc wines. Located to the north of the Bordeaux region, the Loire Valley has two areas that are known for growing Sauvignon Blanc grapes: Sancerre and Pouilly-Fumé.

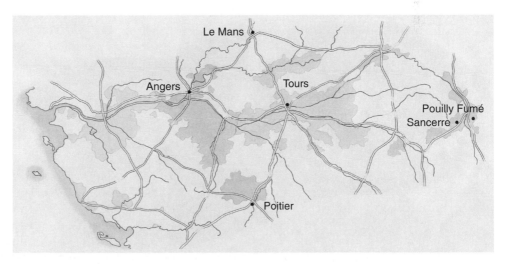

Figure 8.1 The Loire Valley. [Dorling Kindersley Images]

The wines from Sancerre tend to be fairly simple and straightforward. Very little oak is used in this area for aging or storing wine, and the wine has very sharp, but clean, high-acid quality. Assertive and forward flavors such as lemon, flint, green grass, grapefruit, and gooseberry can be found in this wine. These are the qualities that set the Sancerre apart from other Sauvignon Blanc.

Pouilly-Fumé, on the other hand, is higher in alcohol, which gives it more body than Sancerre. Many of the flavors found in a Sancerre wine can be found in a Pouilly-Fumé wine, but Pouilly-Fumé tends to be creamier; this is a quality it shares with Bordeaux Blanc wines. The Pouilly-Fumé will have a distinct flint aroma that cannot be found in Bordeaux Blanc, however. Generally, white wines from the Loire Valley tend to have a life of less than five years.

United States: California

Sauvignon Blanc ranks fourth in California white grape production. California Sauvignon Blanc tends to be the least assertive style of Sauvignon Blanc. Most of the wines produced from this grape are light- to medium-bodied, and tend to have flavors of apple, pear, lemon, almond, fig, melon, green grass, and oak. The apple and pear flavors are not the fresh-picked flavors one might expect; they are the cooked flavors of stewed apples and pears. The fruitier, cooked flavors are a result of California's longer growing season and the grapes' exposure to more sun.

Some California Sauvignon Blanc wines are a blend similar to that of a Bordeaux Blanc. The winemakers use the Sémillon grape to help the Sauvignon Blanc grape produce a wine that is more complex. However, the wine producers are limited by law to blending no more than 25 percent Sémillon grapes into wine that will be sold with Sauvignon Blanc on the label. Like Sauvignon Blanc from

Figure 8.2   A bottle of Sauvignon Blanc. [Dorling Kindersley Images]

Figure 8.3 A California Sauvignon Blanc label. [Dorling Kindersley Images]

the Loire Valley, California Sauvignon Blanc should be consumed young, within the first three to five years of bottling.

New Zealand

The Sauvignon Blanc grape ranks third in grape production in New Zealand. The Sauvignon Blanc grape of New Zealand produces some amazing wine that is unlike any other Sauvignon Blanc produced anywhere in the world. All of the good qualities of Sauvignon Blanc come together in New Zealand. The flavors of lemon, lime, green grass, melon, pineapple, pear, peach, apple, green pepper, asparagus, vanilla, almond, and cream can be found in New Zealand Sauvignon Blanc. The flavor of oak is not in this list because New Zealand wine producers age the wine in stainless steel rather than oak containers. This allows the fruit flavors to come through in a way that they do not in other Sauvignon Blanc wines. The growing season and regional characteristics of New Zealand allow for higher alcohol and acid levels, but this wine balances very well due to the mix of flavors.

New Zealand wines should be consumed during the first eighteen months to two years following production. A rare wine from this area will do well beyond about five years.

South Africa, Italy, and Other Producers

Sauvignon Blanc grapes are also grown in South Africa, Italy, Chile, and Washington state. South African Sauvignon Blanc wine is favorably compared to its New Zealand counterpart, but, at its best, the South African version is still an up-and-coming understudy to the New Zealand performer.

Sauvignon Blanc production is limited in Italy and Chile, which are mostly red grape countries. In Italy, the production of Sauvignon Blanc can be found in the Trentino-Alto Adige region, but it is overshadowed by the production of Pinot Grigio and Chardonnay. In Chile, the Sauvignon Blanc grape is the king of white grapes, with Chardonnay close behind. White grapes make up about a third of all wine production in Chile. In Washington state, Sauvignon Blanc takes a back seat to Sémillon and is often used as a blending grape for Sémillon wines.

Sémillon

The Sémillon grape always has been an important blending grape in Bordeaux, but this grape only recently found a new market for blending in Australia, New Zealand, and California. The Sémillon grape blends well with the Sauvignon Blanc grape as well as with the Chardonnay grape.

Sometimes the Sémillon grape stands alone, however. Sémillon has a low acidity level, but it usually has a higher alcohol level than other white wines, which allows the wine to age gracefully. Some of the aromas and flavors that can be found in Sémillon wines are pineapple, honey, fig, mustard, and, with age, nuts. Mustard is the most common aroma link among all Sémillon wines.

France: Bordeaux

Sémillon in Bordeaux is used mainly as a blending grape; it helps round off the rough edges of Sauvignon Blanc. Nonetheless, Sémillon is the shining star of Bordeaux in the production of Sauternes and Barsacs. In many cases, it is the only grape used because it commonly contracts Noble Rot, which helps boost the sweetness of these famous wines.

United States: California

In California, the Sémillon grape enjoys limited production and is often blended with other grapes such as Sauvignon Blanc and Chardonnay. The blend can show up at either end of the spectrum, with Sémillon or one of the other two grapes being the most prominent. Usually one of the grapes will account for about 75 percent of the blend so that the name of the grape can be included on the label. The blending grapes, or the other 25 percent of the bottle, is not mentioned on the label by name. Many times Sémillon plays the second chair to Chardonnay and Sauvignon Blanc in California.

United States: Washington State

Washington state is one of the few places in the world where Sémillon grapes are used to make wine with no other grape involved. If any blending does happen, the other grape is Sauvignon Blanc or Chardonnay, allowing the Sémillon grape to take the lead role.

Australia and South Africa

Australia and South Africa winemakers use the Sémillon grape to blend with the Chardonnay grape. However, one or two winemakers do use Sémillon as the primary grape. Some of the best Sémillon wines come from New South Wales in Australia, but the majority of wines with Sémillon grapes from Australia are Sémillon-Chardonnay blends.

Trebbiano

The Trebbiano grape (also known as Ugni Blanc, Thalia, and St. Émilion) is from Italy. The production of this grape is very limited for actual wine production, even in its home country. As a matter of fact, the French often claim the Trebbiano grape as their own because the French use it to produce distilled spirits as well as wine. The Trebbiano grape produces more wine than any other variety in the world, but the wine is used almost exclusively for blending and distilling.

One of the truly great attributes of this grape is its high yield, which is about 10 tons of grapes, or 1,600 gallons of wine, per acre. Most of this is distilled into brandy. The wine has a very high acid level with some aromas and flavors of lemon; otherwise, the wine tends to have no odor and is flavorless.

Italy

The Trebbiano grape grows in almost every region as a blending grape, but takes the lead in the Abruzzio region of central Italy and the Emilia-Romagna region of northern Italy. There are wines there that are made from 100 percent Trebbiano grapes. These wines are rather neutral in flavor, but they do have a high acid content.

Four other very popular grape varieties overshadow the production of the Trebbiano grape in Italy, however: Pinto Gris (Pinot Grigio), Pinot Blanc (Pinto Bianco), Chardonnay, and Sauvignon Blanc.

Cognac Production

The Trebbiano grape is one of three grapes used to produce the distilled spirit known as *Cognac*. Cognac, a type of brandy, is made in a small area just north of the Bordeaux region of France. In France, the Trebbiano grape is known as the

St. Émilion grape. This grape is used in conjunction with two minor grapes, the Folle Blanche grape and the Colombard grape, to produce cognac. By law, these three grapes are the only grapes allowed in the production of cognac. The grapes are picked early in the season so that they have a low sugar level and a high acid level. They are crushed, fermented, and then distilled.

The St. Émilion (Trebbiano) grape is also used to make *armagnac,* which is another brandy. There are several differences between armagnac and cognac, including the wood used to age the drinks, the area in which the grapes are grown, and the fact that armagnac production allows for the use of several grapes that cannot be used to produce cognac. The Armagnac region is located to the south of Bordeaux near the Garonne River. The Cognac region is located to the north of Bordeaux on the Gironde River.

Pinot Gris

One bottle of Pinot Gris (or Pinot Grigio in Italy) wine can differ from another Pinot Gris greatly. *Gris* means "gray," and the name probably comes from the grape's pinkish-gray hue. The wine can range in color from almost crystal clear to pink, and on the palate, the wine can range from light and crisp to fat and rich.

Italy

Pinot Grigio (Pinot Gris), is one of the most popular white grapes grown in Italy. Its popularity among grape growers is a reflection of the wine's popularity in the market. Pinot Grigio is always light and somewhat bland. It is a good choice for those just learning to appreciate wine because it is so easy to drink. Even though most Pinot Grigio wines are dry, some might have a little sweetness to them.

France: Alsace

In France's Alsace region, the Pinot Gris grape is known as Tokay or Tokay d'Alsace after the region in which the Tokay grape is grown. In other regions, the grape is known by other names. In Burgundy, it is called Pinot Beurot, and in the Champagne region, it is known as the Fromenteau grape. In Germany, the Pinot Gris grape is known as Ruländer.

As with other wines in the Alsace region, Tokay is fermented until dry. The flavors of the Tokay d'Alsace are the richest, spiciest, most full-flavored Pinot Gris in the world. For this reason they have become increasingly popular over the last twenty years. Many of these wines can age for up to ten years; most wines made from the Pinot Gris grape are long-lived if they age over two years.

United States: California and Oregon

In the United States, the Pinot Gris grape is known as both Pinot Gris and Pinot Grigio. The last twenty years have been telling for the Pinot Gris grape in Oregon. Production has taken off partially because of the early turnaround these grapes afford the winemakers. Most of the wines are ready to drink within six months of being bottled, but they also can age a few years. The production and success of this grape and the wine produced from it have made the Pinot Gris a major grape in the wine industry in Oregon.

In California, Pinot Gris wine is more like the wine that is made in Italy. It tends to be lighter in body and very easy to drink.

Chenin Blanc

Chenin Blanc grapes result in a wide range of products. The Chenin Blanc grape is produced all over the world, but the best known and most revered are from France's Loire Valley. The wines that come from this region are the best examples of what this grape can produce. The Chenin Blanc grape helps make wines that are easy to drink with flavors ranging from apples and citrus to peaches. Most of the wines produced from this grape are high in acid.

France: Loire Valley

The Chenin Blanc grapes grown in and around the city of Vouvray, France, in the Loire Valley make the best-known wine of this varietal. Other cities in the Loire Valley also grow Chenin Blanc grapes. The labels of these wines bear their names: Anjou, Saumur, and Savennieres.

These wines can range from dry to very sweet, but the acid level always remains very high and the flavor and aromas are floral and full of apples with hints of honey. Areas in the Loire Valley also produce sparkling wine from the Chenin Blanc grape.

United States: California

Chenin Blanc grapes grown in California are not as acidic as their French counterpart, nor do they have the same reputation. California brings out the peach and melon flavors in Chenin Blanc wines. The much-ignored wines from these grapes are good as starter wines because they are straightforward and not completely dry.

South Africa, Australia, New Zealand, and Other Producers

While few Chenin Blanc vines are grown in the Southern Hemisphere, South Africa, Australia, and New Zealand all have Chenin Blanc vines in their vineyards for wine production. The wines produced from this grape are not the blockbusters from France, but they are improving every year. These wines have the reputation of being very simple and straightforward with nice fruit flavors.

Vineyards in Texas, Oregon, and Idaho are among the other areas that have begun growing the Chenin Blanc grape. The production of this grape is limited in all three of these areas mainly because Chenin Blanc has to compete with other grapes for limited space in the vineyards.

Key Terms

Fumé Blanc
Sancerre
Pouilly-Fumé
Bordeaux Blanc
Tokay d'Alsace
Ruländer

Sémillon
Pinot Gris
Chenin Blanc
Cognac
Armagnac
Sauvignon Blanc

Study Questions

1. What are the flavor and aroma profiles of Sauvignon Blanc?
2. What are the flavor and aroma profiles of Pinot Gris?
3. What are the flavor and aroma profiles of the other grapes in this chapter?
4. Who coined the term Fumé Blanc?
5. What can the Trebbiano grape be used for other than wine?

Chapter 9

Full-Bodied White Wines: Chardonnay and Viognier

After reading this chapter, you will be able to:

❐ Discuss the places that the Chardonnay grape is grown.

❐ Describe Chardonnay wine.

❐ Talk about other names for wine made from Chardonnay grapes.

❐ Explain the subtle differences between wine made from grapes that are grown in different places.

❐ Discuss the flavors and aromas that a new wine drinker might encounter when tasting wine made from Chardonnay grapes.

One of the famous expressions about Chardonnay juice is that it is the perfect "blank canvas" that winemakers can fashion into just the type of wine they want to make.

—Ed McCarthy and Mary Ewing-Mulligan,
in *White Wine for Dummies*

Full-bodied wines have the fullest flavor of any white wine. The flavor comes from several areas: a high alcohol level , oak aging, and the grapes themselves. The most popular white wine, Chardonnay, falls into and makes up most of this class.

Chardonnay

Chardonnay, one if the most popular wines available today, could be described as a cool, crystal, golden glass of sun and oak. The Chardonnay grape's flexibility means that it can produce an almost endless spectrum of aromas, flavors, and, ultimately, wines.

The aroma of Chardonnay wine can range from green apple or ripe pineapple to gravel or flint, depending on where the grapes were grown and their ripeness at harvest. Chardonnay can develop other aromas and flavors, including pear, lemon, lime, grapefruit, peach, mango, and papaya. If the wine tastes of tart citrus fruit, the grapes are getting less sun and the natural acid of the grapes has not converted to sugar. Overripe grapes produce tropical fruit because of the conversion.

Nonfruity flavors can occur in Chardonnay, such as vanilla, wet wool, butterscotch, toffee, toast, nuts, and butter. Most of these flavors and aromas come from aging the wine in wood; however, if the taster is able to perceive butter, the acid in the wine may have transformed from malic acid (the acid in apples) to lactic acid (the acid in milk). The winemaker may want this process to occur because lactic acid is milder than malic acid and the wine becomes softer, smoother, and easier to drink. This process, called *malolactic fermentation,* is found mainly in Chardonnay wines and red wines. Even though the process is called malolactic fermentation, it is not truly fermentation; it is a biochemical reaction that is caused by a certain bacteria (*Lactobacillus*). Winemakers that want malolactic fermentation to occur encourage the growth of this bacteria.

France: Burgundy, Chablis, and Champagne

Many people think that Burgundy is another word for red. Most of the time it refers to a red wine, but Burgundy also can mean Chardonnay. A white Burgundy is Chardonnay.

In the United States, the terms Burgundy and Chablis refer to inexpensive California red and white wines. French Chablis, however, refers to white wine produced from Chardonnay grapes in a small area of land in the northernmost region of Burgundy. This small area of land is closer to the Champagne region and the Loire Valley than it is to the rest of Burgundy. Only three other areas in Burgundy produce white wine. Two of the three are world famous for their white wines: Mâconnaise and Côte de Beaune. Another less famous area that produces

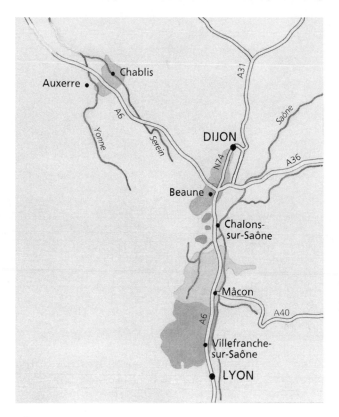

Figure 9.1 Burgundy, France, and Chablis. [Dorling Kindersley Images]

white wine is the Côte de Châlonnaise. All of the areas (with the exception of Chablis) fall between the cities of Dijon to the north and Mâcon to the south.

The labels of the finest-quality white Burgundy wines are marked with ratings. White Burgundy wine is rated at three levels:

1. Grand Cru: This is considered the best wine from the region. Grand Cru wines are the most likely to age well, keeping up to five years.
2. Premier Cru: This level is still very good wine, but the soil the grapes come from is less ideal for growing. The vineyard produces more wine than those that were Grand Cru.
3. Village Wine: Wine that comes from a certain village. This can be a real bargain if the village in question had a good vintage. This wine does not have as much staying power as the two other levels. Village wine should be consumed and not cellared.

Even though white Burgundy is aged in oak, the wine is better known for the flavor and aroma of green apples than it is for the little oak flavor that exists

Figure 9.2 A vineyard in the Mâcon area in the Burgundy Region of France. [Dorling Kindersley Images]

in it. If oak flavors and aromas are present in the wine, they should be very subtle because the wine is aged in old oak that has been used several times. The French philosophy is to allow nature to do what it will with the flavor of the grapes and not to mask it with other flavors. The old oak is seen as the salt or pepper that allows the true flavors of the grapes to be enhanced.

Chardonnay grapes also are used in the production of *champagne,* a sparkling wine. Champagnes known as *blanc de blanc* are made from 100 percent Chardonnay grapes. Of the three grapes that produce classic champagne, the Chardonnay grape is the only white grape used.

United States: California

Chardonnay is the king of California's white wines. It is widely planted, but, more importantly, it is asked for and served more than any other white wine from California. California Chardonnay is higher in alcohol than French Chardonnay and has oak and fruit flavors. Some of the flavors of California Chardonnay include tropical fruits such as pineapple, papaya, and mango.

Chardonnay grapes are grown in areas that span from the Sonoma and Napa Valleys in the north to Santa Barbara in the south. More acres of Chardonnay grapes are grown in California than of any other grape, making up about

Figure 9.3 Mâcon-Village wine from the Burgundy region of France. [Dorling Kindersley Images]

21.5 percent of all the grapes grown there. There are four distinct regions: (1) the North Coast, (2) the San Joaquin Valley, (3) the North Central Coast, and (4) the South Central Coast. Each of the regions has areas that are known for growing the Chardonnay grape.

The North Coast region includes some of the most notable areas of wine-making, including the famous Napa and Sonoma Valleys. Joining these two famous areas are all of Napa, Sonoma, Lake, Mendocino, Marin, and Solano Counties. An area that has gained a great deal of attention in the past few years is Carneros. Carneros is really part of both the Sonoma and Napa Valleys, and it spans from the Sonoma Mountains across the Sonoma Valley and continues east to the Napa Valley. The San Joaquin Valley, also known as the Central Valley, is the largest Chardonnay-producing region in California, occupying 55 percent of California's total vineyard acreage. While this region is the largest, it is the least important for the purposes of quality wine grape growing. Fewer wines of note are made in this region, even though 75 percent of all California wine is produced in the area.

The North Central Coast region begins slightly south and east of San Francisco in the Livermore Valley in Alameda County and includes all of Santa Clara, Santa Cruz, San Mateo, San Benito, and Monterey Counties. The South Central Coast includes all of San Luis Obispo and Santa Barbara Counties. This region

Figure 9.4 A California Chardonnay. [Dorling Kindersley Images]

may be the most important California region for growing Chardonnay grapes. Winemakers on the South Central Coast grow their grapes and make their wine much in the same way and with the same results as the great white Burgundy winemakers. The South Central Coast benefits from a breeze that blows off the Pacific Ocean, allowing the temperature to mimic that of Burgundy.

United States: Oregon and Washington

Oregon and Washington each claim that they are among the best places to grow Chardonnay grapes. They both have one thing in common with France, especially Burgundy: the 45th parallel. Chardonnay wine from this area is medium in body with higher acid levels than its California counterpart. Fruit flavors can vary, but the most common flavors are apples and pears. Oregon is divided into five wine-producing regions, or American Viticultural Areas (AVAs). Two of these regions are along the Columbia River: the Walla-Walla Valley in the far northeast part of the state and the Columbia Valley to its west. The other three regions are almost in a straight line from Portland to California on the west side of the state. The Willamette Valley is located along the Willamette River, which extends from Portland to south of Eugene, Oregon. The Umpqua Valley is south of the Williamette Valley, and the Rogue River Valley is located adjacent to the California border.

United States: New York

Like Washington and Oregon, New York makes a Chardonnay wine that is high in acid; however, New York Chardonnay can also be full-bodied. The wines produced in New York are reminiscent of Burgundy. The four major AVAs in New York are Long Island, the Hudson Valley, the Finger Lakes region, and Lake Erie. Some of the oldest wineries in the United States are in New York.

Emerging Areas: Idaho, Kentucky, Colorado, Arizona, and Texas

Some of the most unlikely areas are now growing Chardonnay grapes. Many of these areas are too far north or too hot to grow any grapes, much less Chardonnay grapes. An example of one such area is Idaho; Chardonnay grapes are being grown with some success near the Snake River Valley. These wines have a citrus flavor that would be expected from a wine made from grapes grown so far north. The acid in the wine is balanced by wood from barrel fermentation.

Chardonnay grapes also are being grown in western Colorado and northern Kentucky. Both of these areas have fairly temperate climates similar to the climate in Burgundy.

Figure 9.5 In Australia winemakers are allowed to blend wines to achieve the flavors and other qualities that they want. [Dorling Kindersley Images]

Australia and New Zealand

Chardonnay wine from Australia is known for two things: tropical fruit flavors and stainless steel aging. These factors produce a very different wine than those found in most other areas that grow Chardonnay grapes. The Chardonnay wines from this area tend to be full-bodied without the flavor of oak; however, theses grapes also produce more acidic wines. Sometimes the winemakers in Australia blend Chardonnay grapes with Sémillon grapes for a unique wine.

New Zealand's Chardonnays are coming of age. The Chardonnay grape is the second most-planted grape in the country. The wines these grapes produce is very similar to the Chardonnay wines of Burgundy. Unlike Australia to the north-west, New Zealand produces the perfect cross between the Oregon and the Burgundy Chardonnay wine. New Zealand Chardonnay wines are high in acid and alcohol and are aged in oak. The oak aging and the high acid add flavors and aromas that cannot be found in Australian wines.

Chile and South Africa

Both Chile and South Africa are up and coming with Chardonnay grape production. Each tends to over-oak their medium-bodied Chardonnay, but they both have shown promise in recent vintages. Chile's Chardonnay wines tend to be medium in body, but they are not comparable to Burgundy or Oregon Chardonnay. Both Chilean and South African wines are not as complex as Chardonnay from California or Burgundy, but they have good fruit flavors.

Figure 9.6 A Chardonnay wine label from Australia. [Dorling Kindersley Images]

Viognier

The Viognier grape produces a very spicy and fruity wine, not unlike wines made from the Gewürztraminer grape. However, Viognier is considered a full-bodied grape. Recently these grapes have become highly sought after because of their flavor and ease in drinking. The wine has flavors and aromas reminiscent of peach, apricot, pear, and honey. The wines that come from the Viognier grape are low in acidity and do not last very long in the bottle; they should be consumed within the first two or three years.

Viognier grapes are grown in two areas: the Rhône Valley in France and California. Viognier grapes are hard to grow outside of the Rhône Region in France because the vines are very susceptible to diseases; therefore, few California vineyards are producing Viognier grapes.

France: Rhône Valley

In the Rhône Region of France, the Viognier grape is used to make high-quality white wines, including Château-Grillet and Condrieu. Both of these wines are 100 percent Viognier.

Oddly enough, the Viognier grape also is used to make some high-quality red wines in the Côte Rôtie region. While many red grapes can be used to make white wine easily, Viognier is perhaps one of the only white grapes that plays an important part in making a red wine. (Another full-bodied white wine made in the Rhône region is Hermitage Blanc. This dry wine is made from two grapes that rarely grow outside of the Rhône: Marsanne and Roussanne.)

Key Terms

Malolactic Fermentation
Chablis
Mâconnaise
Côte de Beaune
Grand Cru
Premier Cru

White Burgundy
Champagne
American Viticultural Areas (AVAs)
Chardonnay
Viognier

Study Questions

1. What three major areas grow the Chardonnay grape?
2. What are the differences in the wines produced in these areas?

3. What are some of the flavors that can be found in Chardonnay wine?
4. What are the differences between Grand Cru and Premier Cru?
5. Which area is more likely to use new oak in the production of a Chardonnay wine, California or France?

Chapter 10

Light-Bodied Red Wines: Pinot Noir and Gamay

After reading this chapter, you will be able to:

❐ Describe the medium- to light-bodied red wines produced by the Pinot Noir and Gamay grapes.
❐ Discuss red wines made in Burgundy, France.
❐ Identify other places Pinot Noir grapes are grown.
❐ Describe the red wines made in Beaujolais, France.
❐ Describe the flavor and aroma profile of Pinot Noir wines.
❐ Describe the flavor and aroma profile of Gamay wines.

Ferment the Gamay from my Lands in a large vat. Add the laughter of a girl, the spring scents of a garden and a good dose of the spirit of Montmartre.
— Traditional Recipe from the Saint-Amour Area

Pinot Noir and Gamay are the two red grapes associated with the Burgundy region of France. The wines made from these grapes garner much attention, both positive and negative. Pinot Noir grows in northern Burgundy and is responsible for some of the best and the worst wines made, depending on the year's rainfall and growing conditions. Gamay, a grape that was once exiled from Burgundy, now has a strong foothold in southern Burgundy. Gamay grapes make the light, refreshing first red wines of the year known as Beaujolais. Both of these grapes make light-bodied wines. Pinot Noir wines range from light- to medium-bodied, whereas wines from the Gamay grape tend to be light-bodied. Some of these wines are so light that they are chilled and served as white wine (and paired with food that goes well with white wine).

Pinot Noir

The Pinot Noir grape makes some of the most famous and infamous wines in the world. Wines made with the Pinot Noir grape were celebrated by Pope Urban V. He did not want to leave France for Rome, Italy, because "There is no Beaune wine in Italy, and without Beaune wine how unhappy we would be." The former pontiff was referring to the wines made in the Côte de Beaune area in the Burgundy region. On the other hand, these wines recently have been described by writer Jay McInerney (author of *Bright Lights, Big City*) in his book *Bacchus and Me* as follows: "If it's red, French, costs too much, and tastes like the water that's left in the vase after the flowers have died and rotted, it's probably Burgundy." Some of the most famous wines are made from this grape and can be found in France in both the Burgundy and Champagne regions.

The Pinot Noir grape produces a wine with raspberry, strawberry, and cherry flavors and aromas. Plum, truffle, and oak also are sometimes found as well. The delicate nature of this grape allows for some truly amazing wine during good years, but if the elements are not synonymous with the grape, the wine will be a marginally good wine at best.

France: Burgundy

In Burgundy, there are three main areas of production for Pinot Noir: (1) Côte de Nuits, (2) Côte de Beaune, and (3) Côte Châlonnaise. The Côte de Nuits and Côte de Beaune form a region known as Côte d'Or, or "the Golden Slope." The color refers to the fertility of the land and the riches that it brings it owners as well as the golden color displayed in the fall.

The Côte d'Or has four quality levels of wine:

1. Grand Cru: This is least common of the levels and the most expensive. The wine represents the product of a single vineyard. Most red Burgundy wine at this level is made in the Côte de Nuits area of Burgundy.

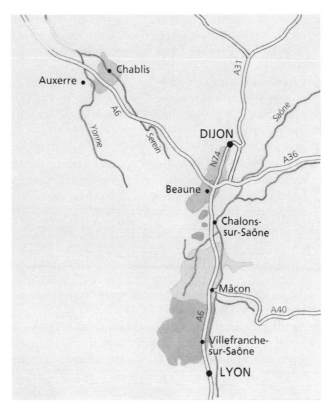

Figure 10.1 A map of Burgundy. [Dorling Kindersley Images]

2. Premier Cru: This level represents very good wine. The grapes come from a single vineyard. All of the red Burgundy at this level is made in either the Côte de Beaune or the Côte de Nuits areas in Burgundy.
3. Village: This wine is less common and more expensive than the generic wine and it usually is higher in quality. The grapes must come from the village marked on the label.
4. Generic: The generic wines are the most common, but the quality is lower and they have a lower price than the other wines. This wine can be a blend of Pinot Noir grapes from all over the Côte d'Or.

The Côte de Nuits is located in the northernmost part of Burgundy near the city of Dijon. Some of the more important towns in this region are:

1. Gevrey-Chambertin: No other name identifies more with high-quality red Burgundy than Gevrey-Chambertin. This town is home to nine Grand Cru wines and twenty-five Premier Crus. It has more acres devoted to viticulture than any other single town in this area. The wines from this town are known to be medium-bodied with very complex flavors.

2. Morey St. Denis: The wines from this town are known as sophisticated, long-lived and medium-bodied. Home to several Grand Cru wines and twenty-five Premier Crus, this town is almost as important as its neighbor to the north, Gevrey-Chambertin.
3. Chambolle-Musigny: The wines from this town are the most approachable of the wines from the Côte de Nuit region because of their light body. Some of these wines are classified at both the Grand Cru and Premier Cru level.
4. Vosne-Romanée: Some say the Pinot Noir that comes from this area is the best in the world. It is definitely some of the most expensive. This town includes some of the smallest commercial vineyards in France; many of these vineyards have no more than two acres. The wines from this town range from light- to medium-bodied.

The Côte de Beaune, which is in the northern part of Burgundy but the southern half of the Côte d'Or, has two towns of note:

1. Aloxe-Corton: This is the only town in the area to claim Grand Cru vineyards for red Burgundy.
2. Beaune: Even though there are no Grand Cru Vineyards here, this town is the center of the wine trade. Beaune also boasts forty-two Premier Crus and more acres—13,000—than any other vineyard in the area.

Just south of the Côte d'Or is a small group of four towns—Rully, Mercurey, Givry, and Montagny—that make up the area known as the Côte Châlonnaise. The wines produced here include some of the best values for Pinot Noir. The price reflects both the wine's popularity and how identifiable the wine is. Nonetheless, there are some great wines that come from this area, especially from the town of Mercurey.

France: Champagne

Even though the Pinot Noir grape is red, most white Champagne comes from this grape. Even blended sparkling wines can be least 50 percent Pinot Noir. The process of making a red grape into white wine is fairly simple. This process is outlined in Chapter 5. The special process that makes champagne is also outlined in Chapter 13.

Italy, Germany, and Alsace, France

In Italy, the Pinot Noir grape is known as Pinot Nero. Its production is limited even though there has been a large increase in the production of other "French" red grapes in Italy.

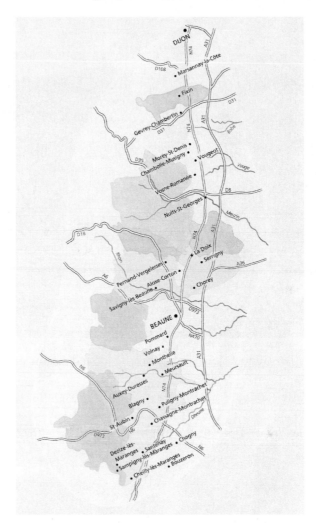

Figure 10.2 Cote d'Or. [Dorling Kindersley Images]

This same grape has yet another name, Spätburgunder, in Germany. Production of this grape is limited in Germany as well. It can be found almost entirely in the southern part of Germany.

The production of Pinot Noir is quite limited in Alsace, France, an area of France known for white wine made from grapes that are identified with Germany. In Alsace, the wine is identifiable because the grape's name, Pinot Noir, is on the label.

Figure 10.3 Pinot Noir grapes are harvested in Burgundy. [Dorling Kindersley Images]

Figure 10.4 A bottle of California Pinot Noire. [Dorling Kindersley Images]

United States: California

Pinot Noir chiefly grows in Santa Barbara, San Luis Obispo, Monterey, San Benito, Monterey, Santa Clara, San Mateo, Sonoma, and Mendocino Counties. The flavors of wines these areas produce vary as much as the ground on which the grapes are grown. Pinot Noir wines from California are known for raspberry and cherry flavors. They contain more oak and vanilla flavors than their Burgundy counterparts.

Santa Barbara and San Luis Obispo Counties are in southern California, north of Los Angeles. This area, known as the South Central Coast, specializes in Burgundian-style wines. Even though this area is in the southern part of California, the weather is cooler than some of the areas that lie to the south.

The North Central Coast region includes Monterey, San Benito, Monterey, Santa Clara, and San Mateo Counties. This region runs from the San Francisco Bay area in the north to the southern part of Monterey County, which borders the South Central Coast and San Luis Obispo County. The Pinot Noir grape is not the main grape planted in these areas, but the wine that results is well respected. The wine is less expensive than Pinot Noir produced in other places, however, because it does not have the reputation that it deserves.

The North Coast area includes Sonoma and Mendocino Counties, which are located to the north of San Francisco. Both of these counties use the Pinot Noir grapes in conjunction with Chardonnay grapes for the production of sparkling wine. They also make still wines from the grapes that grow in this area. The Russian River Valley is the biggest producer of Pinot Noir grapes in Sonoma County.

United States: Oregon

The Umpqua Valley and the Willamette Valley are the chief growing areas for Pinot Noir in Oregon. The wine made from these grapes does not have a long shelf life and should be consumed within the first five years, with a few exceptions. The wine's flavor is often compared with that of Burgundy's Pinot Noir wines, but it also has some of the qualities found in California Pinot Noirs.

Modern-day winemaking in Oregon started in the Umpqua Valley in 1962 when the Hillcrest Vineyards opened their doors. Some of the wines that come from this area are the best examples of Pinot Noir in the United States, if not the world.

The Willamette Valley, perhaps known best as the destination for travelers of the Oregon Trail, also has long been known for its fertile ground. It is the largest area in Oregon devoted to growing grapes. The Pinot Noir grape, first planted in 1966 in the Willamette Valley, is the most widely planted red grape in this area. Since this time, many of the Pinot Noir–based wines have won awards.

Oregon has the added benefit of being located on the 40th parallel, as does France, so its climate is very similar to that of France. This has long drawn attention to the area. Many French winemakers now own land in Oregon for this reason.

Gamay

The Gamay grape is the Rodney Dangerfield of grapes. It gets no respect, but most people love to drink this light-bodied and fruity wine. Most wine experts would have a hard time agreeing that the Gamay grape should be considered a major grape. The wine that comes from the Gamay grape is low in alcohol, high in acid, and high in fruit. Some growers add sugar to the juice to produce more alcohol in the final product. Many of the aromas and flavors found in wine made from the Gamay grape are found in red fruits such as raspberries, strawberries, and blackberries. However, sometimes banana and boiled fruit flavors also can be found.

Many would question that the wine made from the Gamay grapes could be great wine, but the first wine released every year is made from the Gamay grape. This wine is called Beaujolais Nouveau. Usually, Beaujolais is the only wine that is released the same year it is produced.

Many races are held each fall between the wineries of France with airplanes racing to deliver Beaujolais Nouveau to various destinations all over the world. Why do so many winemakers go to so much trouble for this wine? Beaujolais gives the first true glimpse of what all the wine made in France will be like that season. Since it is produced in a very short period of time, it also allows the people that grew the grapes and made the wine (as well as the rest of the people of the world) a chance to take time out and celebrate.

France: Beaujolais

When most Americans go to the wine shop to pick a red Burgundy, they tend to pick Beaujolais. This may be due to name recognition from the November celebration, or it may have to do with the palatability of the wine; Beaujolais wine is very easy to drink.

The Beaujolais area of France is a small area at the southern tip of Burgundy close to the city of Lyon. In this area, the Gamay grape rules supreme, occupying 100 percent of the area devoted to viticulture.

The wine in this area is not aged in oak, which allows the fruit flavors to dominate this wine. Beaujolais is not aged for two reasons. First, the flavors of the wine are very delicate and would be overpowered by any oak aging. Second, the makers of this wine do not have much time to bring the wine to market. The wine must be released on the third Thursday in November; therefore, there is no time to age the wine in oak. Unlike most other red wines, red wines from this area are better served chilled.

There are four quality levels of wine from this area:

1. Cru: This is the highest designation for this area. There are ten towns or villages that produce Cru wines. The label of the wine will have the name of the town, but it usually will downplay the overall area. Wine at this level can age up to ten years, but usually it should be consumed earlier. This is also the only level that includes wines that can be consumed at a little less than room temperature rather than chilled. The ten villages to look for are:
    Brouilly
    Chénas
    Chiroubles
    Côte de Brouilly
    Fleurie
    Juliénas
    Morgon
    Moulin-à-Vent
    Régnié
    Saint-Amour
2. Beaujolais-Village: This middle designation is for wines that come from one of thirty-five villages in Beaujolais. The wine from these villages can be blended for the best results. The name of the village is usually not added to the label. The wine can age successfully for two or three years.
3. Beaujolais: This is one of the lowest and the most common designations. This category accounts for the majority of the wine made in this area. Wines from this level should not age more than twelve to eighteen months.
4. Beaujolais Nouveau: Even though this is the lowest-quality wine, it is the most celebrated. Beaujolais Nouveau, the lightest of all of the styles in body and character, should be consumed quickly (within the first three to six months).

France: Loire Valley

The only other place in the world to grow Gamay grapes in significant amounts is the Loire Valley in France. The Loire Valley spans the longest river in France—the Loire River. This area is known for white wines.

The Gamay grapes that are grown in the Loire Valley are usually not as full-flavored as those of the Burgundy region because of the climate. The Loire Valley is north of Burgundy. This geographic placement does not allow a long growing season; therefore, the wines that come from grapes grown here are not as full-flavored as the wines made in areas with a longer growing season.

Another area that has seen new growth of Gamay is the Anjou area. As markets have turned away from rosé wines, the growers in this area have been making red wine with Gamay and other red grapes such as Cabernet Franc and Cabernet Sauvignon. In the Anjou area, wines made from Gamay grapes have become known as Anjou Rouge.

The Gamay grape is also grown in the Touraine area. Touraine-area Gamay red wines are almost as good as the wines from Beaujolais. They are very fruity. Check the label on a bottle of red wine; sometimes, the producer in this area will label the bottle with the grape variety.

Other Markets

The Gamay grape is not grown in most other markets, but a grape that has become known as the Gamay Beaujolais is. The wine that is produced from the Gamay Beaujolais grape is very much like that produced from the Gamay grape. This wine, like Beaujolais, should be refrigerated and consumed fairly quickly after it is bottled.

Key Terms

Cru
Grand Cru
Premier Cru
Burgundy

Spätburgunder
Beaujolais Nouveau
Pinot Noir
Gamay

Study Questions

1. What is the flavor profile of wines made from Pinot Noir?
2. What is the flavor profile of wines made from Gamay?
3. What is the difference between Beaujolais-Village and Beaujolais Nouveau?

Chapter 11

Medium-Bodied Red Wines: Syrah (Shiraz), Zinfandel, and Other Red Grape Varieties

After reading this chapter, you will be able to:

❐ Explain the differences and similarities between Syrah and Shiraz.

❐ Discuss red wines that fall in the category of full- and medium-bodied.

❐ Describe the flavor and aroma profiles of Syrah and Shiraz wine.

❐ Describe the flavor and aroma profiles of Zinfandel wine.

❐ Describe the flavor and aroma profiles of the other red grapes discussed in this chapter.

❐ Explain where the name Hermitage comes from and the importance of that wine.

❐ Describe how winemakers are able to produce White Zinfandel from a red grape.

One of the three or four most remarkable juices of the grape, not merely that I have ever possessed, but that I ever tasted. . . . It was the manliest French wine I ever drank.
—Professor George Saintsbury, writing about Hermitage in 1846

Most, if not all, of the grapes discussed in this chapter could be described as spicy, but this flavor is only one of the things that sets them apart from the other red grapes in this text. Syrah (Shiraz), Zinfandel, Sangiovese, Nebbiolo, Barbera, Tempranillo, and Grenache (Garnacha) also are grown in hot areas. This makes these grapes unique because all other major grapes, with the notable exception of the Gamay grape, are grown in Region 1 or 2 of the University of California–Winkler temperature classification system. The only grapes that enjoy a hotter climate are table grapes.

Syrah (Shiraz)

The name of this grape changes slightly depending on where the grape is grown and processed. In the Rhône region of France, the grape is known as the Syrah grape; in Australia and South Africa, the grape is known as Shiraz. Wines produced from this grape in all these areas are considered world class.

Each glass of wine from the Syrah (Shiraz) grape is packed with aroma and flavors. Some of the aromas and flavors are as simple as red fruits, such as cherry, raspberry, blackberry, black current, strawberry, plum, and jam. Other aromas and flavors are spicy, such as smoked bacon, mixed spice, barbecue, black and white pepper, roasted green pepper, green olive, leather, and burnt rubber or tar. Chocolate can also be detected sometimes.

France: Rhône

The medium-bodied red wines produced in the Rhône Valley are known as Côte Rôtie and Hermitage. Both of these wines are made from the Syrah grape. Côte Rôtie—literally "roasted slopes"—derives its name from the hill slopes in this area that are roasted by the sun. Hermitage takes it name from a hermit, Gaspard de Sterimberg, who planted and cultivated vines when he returned to this area after participating in the Crusades as a knight.

Côte Rôtie and Hermitage are both produced in the northern part of the Rhône. Both of these wines are medium-bodied (and, in some cases, full-bodied) wines, which can age for at least two decades. Additionally, both wines are considered the best Syrah wine the world has to offer, with the possible exception of some of the Shiraz made in Australia. While these wines have a great deal in common, two things set Côte Rôtie and Hermitage apart. First, Côte Rôtie sometimes has a little white wine from the Viognier grape added to it. Second, Hermitage, the more tannic wine, lasts up to a decade longer than Côte Rôtie. Hermitage also can have white wine added to it, but it comes from Marsanne and Roussanne grapes. Côte Rôtie and Hermitage wines both must contain a minimum of 85 percent Syrah grapes.

Three other wines produced from Syrah grapes of the northern Rhône are Cornas, Crozes-Hermitage, and St. Joseph. The Corna and Crozes-Hermitage

Figure 11.1 The term *Hermitage* originated in Rhône, France but can be used in other countries to denote the style of wine. This hermitage is from Australia but is not sold outside of Australia with hermitage on the lable. [Dorling Kindersley Images]

wines are made from 100 percent Syrah grapes. St. Joseph is usually 100 percent Syrah, but by law it can have up to 10 percent of white grapes (Marsanne and Roussanne grapes) in the wine. In Rhône, almost 95 percent of all of the red wine made is Syrah.

Australia and South Africa

The rising star in the red wine world is the Shiraz and Shiraz blends from Australia. Still relatively new to the scene, these Shiraz wines have made a splash and seem to improve each year. These wines are produced in the southern half of the Australian continent in the states of Tasmania, Victoria, New South Wales, South Australia (this state is located in the south central part of the country) and Western Australia.

Australian wines, unlike wines from the rest of the world, can be blended in creative ways. In other parts of the world, the winemakers are limited in what they can do by law. "Down under," however, they have creative license in blending and labeling. Blends can contain almost any combination of wines. For example, a Shiraz/Merlot that contains 65 percent Shiraz wine and 35 percent Merlot wine could not be duplicated in the United States. If a grape's name is on the label, the wine must contain at least 75 percent of that grape. Australians, not constrained by this law, can blend for the flavor of the wine rather than for the law.

South African wineries have been making wines for hundreds of years. However, because of apartheid, many of the wines produced have not been accessible outside of South Africa. Many other countries refused to deal with South Africa under apartheid; the end of apartheid means that there are now some wonderful wines accessible from this area.

Like Australia, South Africa also allows blends of grapes. Many people like to compare the wine of South Africa to the wines of Australia. Both of the countries are in the same hemisphere, and the wines they produce are similar in quality, aromas, and flavors. One of the major differences, however, is that the Shiraz grape is a major grape in Australia and only a minor grape in South Africa .

California, Italy, Israel, and Other Regions

The California producers of Syrah are known as the "Rhône Rangers." They produced Syrah, Mourvèdre, and Grenache grapes. These are some of the same grapes that are grown in the Rhône region in France.

Even though California wines are not considered as good as those from the Rhône, they are still good wines. Most are presented in bottles that have the sloping shoulders of the Rhône bottles and are clearly marked with the French name for the grape, Syrah.

Other producers of the Syrah grape include Italy and Israel, but the market share these wines have in these countries is very small. The fact that the Syrah grape is being grown in Israel is almost a homecoming because the Syrah grape is believed to have originated in the Middle East. There is a town in Iran by the name of Shiraz that is known for its grape production.

Zinfandel

Many people are surprised to find out that the Zinfandel grape is a red grape. Many people think that the grape is white because of the wine called White Zinfandel. The blush, or rosé, wine that is known as "White Zin" is rather tasteless and has nothing of the flavor found in the red wine made from the same grapes. A red Zinfandel has a full-bodied flavor with good tannin and aromas and flavors of blackberries, spices, and black pepper.

United States: California

The Zinfandel grape is at home in California. Although not a native, the grape was imported from Europe to California by Agoston Haraszthy, known to many as the "father of California wine" in the mid 1800s. The Zinfandel grape may have come from Italy because this grape is related to the Italian Primitivo grape.

Red Zinfandel wine can range from a lighter-bodied, lower-tannin wine such as the lighter claret wines of Bordeaux, to the full-blown, full-bodied, high-tannin wine similar to the wines of Bordeaux. Generally, the price of the wine gives away the category in which the Zinfandel falls. The lighter-bodied wines tend to be cheaper in price, while the fuller-bodied wines tend to be more expensive.

Figure 11.2   A California Zinfandel label. [Dorling Kindersley Images]

Figure 11.3   A California white Zinfandel label. [Dorling Kindersley Images]

Australia and South Africa

Some winemakers are beginning to grow and experiment with the Zinfandel grape in Australia and South Africa, but no mark has been made by any other country with this grape.

Sangiovese

Many language experts believe that the name of the Sangiovese grape comes from the Latin term *sanguis Jovis* or "the blood of Jove (Jupiter)." (Jupiter was the highest-ranking god in the Roman pantheon). The Sangiovese grape's history in Italy dates back well over 2,500 years, perhaps as far as three millennia.

The Sangiovese grape produces wines that are dark in color and medium-bodied with an unusually high acid content but medium levels of tannin and alcohol. This grape is usually blended with wine from other grapes to help cut the acidic edge. Flavors and aromas that can be expected from this grape are sour cherry, herbs and spices, rose, wood, licorice, smoke, and tobacco.

Italy

The wine produced from the Sangiovese grape in Italy is Chianti. Traditionally, Chianti was made only in the Tuscan region of Italy. This area is the oldest classified wine region in the world, dating back to as early as the thirteenth century. Historically, this area has been growing grapes and producing wine since 900 or 1000 B.C. Today, Chianti enjoys three basic quality levels:

1. Chianti Classico Riserva: This is the highest quality and the most expensive wine from this area. It is aged for at least three years before being released.
2. Chianti Classico: The middle classification is for better wines from select areas.
3. Chianti: This basic classification is for Chianti-style wines.

Chianti, unfortunately, has gotten a bad reputation over the years, which has influenced the decline of this grape. Italian winemakers in Tuscany have tried to battle this trend by changing the bottle of their top Chianti wines to the shape of a Bordeaux bottle. They have all but abandoned the older style bottle, known as a fiasco or fiasque, that was bulbous at the bottom and enclosed in a basket.

The Sangiovese and Nebbiolo grapes are the two red grapes that have dominated the Italian landscape for many centuries. One of the features of wines made from these grapes is that the liquid has an orange hue at the edge of the glass.

In recent history, wines made from the Sangiovese grape lost ground in Italian vineyards to Cabernet Sauvignon and other traditionally French grapes. Growers have replaced Sangiovese grapes with Cabernet Sauvignon and Merlot,

Figure 11.4 A California white Zinfandel label. [Dorling Kindersley Images]

hoping to raise the sales of Italian-produced wine using the better-known French grapes. The wines that come from the land that once made Chianti are now known as "Super-Tuscans."

California and Argentina

With all of its microclimates, California seems to be the right place to grow almost any grape. The Sangiovese grape has adapted well to the California ground and climate, but these grapes do not have the same intensity of flavor as the Italian counterpart. Argentina also has begun to grow Sangiovese, but with limited success.

Nebbiolo

The Nebbiolo grape is responsible for three of Italy's top wines: Barolo, Barbaresco, and Nebbiolo d'Alba. The grape is small and thick-skinned, just like the Cabernet Sauvignon grape. The wine that is produced from this little Nebbiolo

Figure 11.5 A bottle of Chianti Classico. [Dorling Kindersley Images]

grape is some of the darkest wine in the world. It is one of the boldest in flavor and has very high levels of tannin and acids. The flavors and aromas found in these wines are the intense flavors of bittersweet chocolate, rose, violet, prune, licorice, mint, eucalyptus, white truffle, and tar. Other herbal and earthy aromas and flavors can be found as well.

Italy: Piedmont

Piedmont, in northwest Italy, is the home of some of the most intense wine in the world. The wines bear the names of the areas where the grapes are grown: Barolo and Barbaresco. Barolo is the "Left Bank" of Piedmont, whereas Barbaresco is the "Right Bank." The grapes grown in these areas make Italy's greatest wines, including Asti, a sparkling wine that is the Italian equivalent of champagne. The wines that come from these areas are the Italian equivalent to the wines that come from Bordeaux.

Barolo has been referred to as the "king of Piedmont" because of its forward tannin and huge flavor. The wine needs to be aged for at least four years before even the most adventurous wine lover should drink it. Every king needs a queen, and in Piedmont, her name is Barbaresco. In a side-by-side comparison, the wines are very similar, but Barbaresco is lighter in body than Barolo.

Other wines are made with the Nebbiolo grape inside the Piedmont region, but they are not grown in the Barolo and Barbaresco areas; therefore, they are not

Figure 11.6   A bottle of Barolo. [Dorling Kindersley Images]

allowed to claim the "royal" names of Barolo and Barbaresco. Many times they are given the name of the grape and the town, such as Nebbiolo d'Alba or Nebbiolo d'Asti. Many times these wines are good examples of the wine the Nebbiolo grape can produce, but they do not have the price tag that accompanies the names of Barolo and Barbaresco.

Italy: Lombardy

The Lombardy region is in one of the northernmost regions of Italy; it shares a border with Switzerland. It is home of the city of Milan and one of only two places in the world that successfully grows the Nebbiolo grape.

The wines produced in Lombardy are light-bodied when compared to the blockbuster wines of Piedmont. They also do not have the life span of their sister wines of Piedmont, so they should be consumed early. Currently, four wines that are based on Nebbiolo grapes are produced in Lomardy: Grumello, Inferno, Sassella, and Valgella.

United States: California

Winemakers in California have been experimenting and growing the Nebbiolo grape for some time, but they have not been able to achieve the level of success the winemakers in Italy have with this grape. For some reason the Nebbiolo grape does not seem to grow very well outside of northern Italy.

Figure 11.7   A bottle of Barbera D'Alb. [Dorling Kindersley Images]

Barbera

When talking about important Italian grapes and wine, there are three "Bs" to remember: Barolo, Barbaresco, and Barbera. The Barbera grape produces a wine very different from the strong flavor and tannin the Nebbiolo grape produces; the Barbera grape is to the Nebbiolo grape as the Merlot grape is to the Cabernet Sauvignon.

Barbera is known for its low tannin and high acid levels, deep color, and ease of drinking. Many times the level of tannin is so low that the producers use new oak barrels to age the wine, boosting the tannin for longer aging. This allows the wine to show oak flavors upon drinking, but the wine also will show red fruit flavors such as cherry and currant, plus a smokiness that is hidden under the fruit.

Italy

The best wines from the Barbera grape come from the cities of Alba and Asti in Piedmont, Italy. The names come from the grape and the towns: Barbera d'Alba and Barbera d'Asti. Both wines should be drunk young. Barbera d'Alba is considered the better of the two wines and is the more full-bodied wine.

Tempranillo

The Tempranillo grape is one of two grapes that Spain has made famous; the other is Garnacha. Many times these two wines are blended together. The Tempranillo grape is widely produced in Spain. This grape produces wine that is low in alcohol and low in acid and has a thick skin, which gives the wine plenty of color.

The flavors and aromas associated with the Tempranillo grape are strawberry, spices, tobacco, and toffee. Oak and vanilla also may be found, but these flavors have more to do with aging in American oak than anything else.

Spain and Portugal

The wine that comes from the Tempranillo grape can have many names, depending on where the grapes were grown and where the wine was made. The most famous of the wines made with this grape is Rioja. Rioja is the name of a small region in northeastern Spain. Many times this wine is a blend of grapes. The producers of the wine in Spain are called *bodegas*. Very few of the bodegas own the vineyards; they just produce the wine.

Portugal also grows the Tempranillo grape, but in the Douro region, the grape is known by another name: Tinta Roriz. In the Douro, Tempranillo is blended with other grapes for the production of port. In the Alentejo region of Spain, the Tempranillo grape is known as Aragonez.

Grenache

Grenache (Garnacha in Spanish) is a grape that comes in both red and white varieties. The red variety is referred to as Grenache, while the white variety is known as Grenache Blanc. The sugar levels of this grape are high, which results in a high alcohol wine. The wines have low levels of tannin and are sweet, and the flavors and aromas are pepper, raspberry, and herbs.

Spain

In Spain, the Garnacha grape is grown in almost all of the wine regions. This grape originated here and is the premiere grape grown in the region. The resulting wines are blended with other grapes, especially the Tempranillo grape.

France: Rhône Valley

Even though the Grenache grape originated in Spain, in the southern Rhône region it joins forces with twelve other grapes to make the famous Châteauneuf-du-Pape. The name, meaning "new castle of the Pope," refers to Pope Clement who lived in Avignon, France, in the 1300s. The vineyards that help produce Châteauneuf-du-Pape all surround the city where the Pope lived for a time. For this reason, the Medieval Papal Coat of Arms can be found on most of the bottles.

The wines that come from this region are big, full-bodied wines that will age for up to two decades, provided the quality of the wine is very good to begin with.

The thirteen grapes that make Châteauneuf-du-Pape are Grenache, Syrah, Mourvèdre, Picpoul, Terret, Counoise, Muscardin, Vaccarèse, Picardin, Cinsault, Clairette, Roussanne, and Bourboulenc.

Other Regions

The Grenache grape is grown in many other regions, including the United States, Australia, Israel, Morocco, and Sardinia. Another name that the Grenache grape is known by in some of these regions is Cannonau. In all of these areas, the Grenache grape is used to blend with other wines.

Key Terms

Hermitage	Barbera d'Asti
White Zinfandel	Barbera d'Alba
Red Zinfandel	Bodega
Chianti	Châteauneuf-du-Pape
Super Tuscans	Syrah (Shiraz)
Barolo	Sangiovese
Barbaresco	Tempranillo
Nebbiolo	Grenache

Study Questions

1. What is the origin of the name of the Sangiovese grape?
2. What town in Piedmont might lead one to think that a different kind of wine made this region famous? Why?
3. What is the origin of the name *Châteauneuf-du-Pape*?
4. What grapes make up the wines labeled Châteauneuf-du-Pape?

Chapter 12

Full-Bodied Red Wines: Cabernet Sauvignon and Merlot

After reading this chapter, you will be able to:

❐ Discuss the full-bodied wine made from the Cabernet Sauvignon and Merlot grapes.

❐ Discuss the Bordeaux region, including the Left and the Right Banks.

❐ Discuss the 1855 Classification system.

❐ Identify other places that the Cabernet Sauvignon and Merlot grapes grow.

❐ Identify other wines made from these two grapes.

> *. . . drank a sort of French wine, called Ho Bryan, that hath a good and most particular taste that I ever met with.*
> —Samuel Pepys, April 10, 1663, in his journal

Cabernet Sauvignon and Merlot grapes make some of the most long-lived and notable wine in the world. Some of the wine made from these grapes, once aged and bottled, seems to last for decades, improving with time. Both Cabernet Sauvignon and Merlot grapes make a dry wine because of the level of tannin and are considered full-bodied. Both grapes commonly produce wine with intense flavors of cherry, black currant, raspberry, plum, and oak.

Cabernet Sauvignon

Cabernet Sauvignon grapes are very small, closely bunched grapes. They produce an intensely flavored wine. This is the grape most people are referring to when discussing Bordeaux wines or, for that matter, any of the long-lived, full-bodied red wines.

Properly aged, Cabernet Sauvignon wines produce aromas and flavors ranging from raw green bell pepper to black currant, depending on the ripeness of the grapes at the crush. As they age, these wines can develop other aromas and flavors, including leather, tobacco, lead pencil, mint, olive, strawberry, raspberry, and dark chocolate. The amount of sunlight and the grapes' ripeness have an effect on the wine's flavor. If grapes did not get enough sun, the wine will taste of herbs; if the grapes are overripe and sweet, the resulting wine will have stewed fruit flavors.

France: Bordeaux, the Left Bank

In France, a wine's reputation is everything. Nowhere is this more true than the Left Bank of Bordeaux. This area has produced some of the most notable wines of the last two centuries. Left Bank Bordeaux wines are the standard other winemakers use when producing a top-quality Cabernet Sauvignon.

Bordeaux is a geographically small area in southwestern France that borders the Atlantic Ocean. Two large rivers, the Garonne and the Dordogne, run through to the heart of Bordeaux where they converge into the Gironde River. The Gironde River flows into the Atlantic Ocean. The majority of Bordeaux's vineyards can be found lining the banks of these three rivers and the distinction of "Left Bank" or "Right Bank" is in reference to these rivers. The banks are named for the view someone would have floating down the Gironde River toward the Atlantic Ocean.

The prestigious growing areas of Graves, Haut-Médoc, Margaux, St. Julien, Pauillac, St. Estèphe and the Médoc are located on the Left Bank. Each of these areas has a reputation for imparting specific characteristics and qualities to wine, but common qualities can be expected from these areas as well. For example, wines from the Left Bank of Bordeaux generally have a great deal of tannin and will gain character from hibernation in oak barrels.

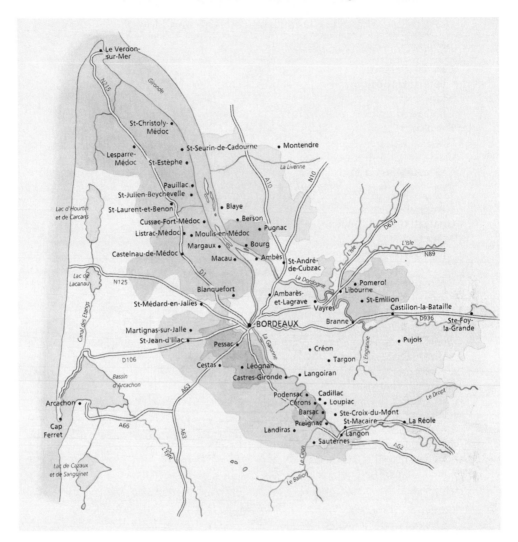

Figure 12.1 A map of Bordeaux. Bordeaux is split by a river; the land to the south of the river is the Left Bank and the land to the north is the Right Bank. [Dorling Kindersley Images]

In 1855, the French government released a list of the best wines from the Bordeaux region. This list was known as the 1855 Classification and consists of five different tiers; each one is progressively more prestigious (see Table 12.1). Classifying the wines gave the market a standard of excellence; therefore, the higher classifications of the wine command higher prices. This list has remained the same since 1855 with the exception of one change in 1973 when Château Mouton-Rothschild was elevated from a "second growth" to a "first growth." Mouton-Rothschild joined only four others' houses as a first growth or "Premier

Table 12.1 The 1855 Classification by Area and House

Premier Cru (First Growth)

Graves (Pessac)
Château Haut-Brion
Margaux
Château Margaux
Pauillac
Château Latour
Château Lafite-Rothschild
Château Mouton-Rothschild**

Deuxieme Cru (Second Growth)

Cantenac-Margaux
Château Brane-Cantenac
Margaux
Château Durfort-Vivens
Château Lascombes
Château Rausan-Ségla
Château Rausan Gassies
Pauillac
Château Pichon-Longueville-Baron
Château Pichon-Longueville-Comtesse-De-Lalande
Saint-Estèphe
Château Cos d'Estournel
Château Montrose
Saint-Julien
Château Ducru-Beaucaillou
Château Gruaud-Larose
Château Léoville-Barton
Château Léoville-Las Cases
Château Léoville-Poyferré

Troisième Cru (Third Growth)

Cantenac-Margaux
Château Boyd-Cantenac
Château Cantenac-Brown
Château d'Issan
Château Kirwan
Château Palmer
Labarde (Margaux)
Château Giscours
Ludon
Château La Lagune
Margaux
Château Desmirail
Château Ferrière
Château Malescot Saint-Exupéry
Château Marquis d'Alesme-Becker
Saint Estèphe
Château Calon-Ségur

Saint-Julien
Château Lagrange
Château Langoa-Barton
Quatrième Cru (Fourth Growth)

Cantenac-Margaux
Château Pouget
Château Prieuré-Lichine
Margaux
Château Marquis-de-Terme
Saint Estèphe
Château Lafon-Rochet
Saint-Julien
Château Beychevelle
Château Branaire-Ducru
Château Saint-Pierre
Château Talbot
Saint Laurent
Château La Tour-Carnet
Pauillac
Château Duhart-Milon-Rothschild
Cinquième Cru (Fifth Growth)

Arsac
Château du Tertre
Labarde (Margaux)
Château Dauzac
Macau
Château Cantermerle
Pauillac
Château Batailley
Château Clerc-Milon
Château Croizet-Bages
Château d'Armailhac (from 1956 to 1988 the name changed to Château Mouton-Baronne-Philippe)
Château Grand-Puy-Ducasse
Château Grand-Puy-Lacoste
Château Haut-Bages-Libéral
Château Haut-Batailley
Château Lynch-Bages
Château Lynch-Moussas
Château Pédesclaux
Château Pontet-Canet
St. Estèphe
Château Cos-Lobory
St. Laurent
Château Belgrave
Château de Camensac

**Denotes the only change ever made to the list.

Cru." The four others that have held their place on the 1855 list since its inception are Château Lafite, Latour, Haut-Brion (which is actually in the Graves area), and Margaux.

Haut-Brion was the first of the first growths added to the classification system because of the outstanding way in which the winemakers kept their grounds and cellars since well before the 1855 Classification scheme and the advent of major scientific discoveries. Even though their understanding of the science of grape production was limited, these winemakers rejected moldy grapes for the production of wine. The Haut-Brion vineyard also chose to use new barrels in which to store wine. They kept these filled to the bunghole at the top. These factors made an extraordinary wine, which was well noted at the time.

Graves, according to Hugh Johnson, is home to the "first of the first growths" and does not produce any other wine that is classified according to the 1855 Classification, but has had a reputation for producing some of the best wine in the world for almost a millennia. People, including British statesman Samuel Pepys and U.S. President Thomas Jefferson, have commented or written about wine from Graves, saying that it was the best to come from Bordeaux, and perhaps the best in the world.

Médoc and Haut-Médoc are both larger areas that are broken into the smaller regions that include Margaux, Moulis, Listrac, St. Julien, Pauillac, and St. Estèphe. The area of Margaux was able to garner the lion's share of the 1855 Classification, with more than a third of the area's total number of wines named to the list. A total of twenty-one Margaux wines grace the list, including a first growth, five second growths, ten third growths (of only fourteen), three fourth growths and two fifth growths. This should not be surprising, however, since Margaux is also the largest growing area in the Médoc. Even though Margaux has the largest number of top-growth classifications, the area does not carry a reputation as one of the great areas of Bordeaux. When the wine is good in this area, it's great; and it can be better than the rest of Bordeaux, but this is rare. In recent history, the quality of wine from the area has been, to say the least, questionable, including the first growth Château Margaux. Château Margaux's reputation as a great wine came into question in the later half of the twentieth century. While many wine experts felt as if this once great wine did not deserve first growth status, the wine has never lost the classification awarded in 1855. In the 1980s and 1990s the reputation of Château Margaux returned to a first-growth reputation.

St. Julien is one of the secret jewels in Bordeaux's crown. Even though the area does not claim a first growth, St. Julien does claim five second-growths. This is more than a third of the total named as such in the 1855 Classification. This may have to do with the forward vanilla scent in the aroma profile, which comes from the oak. Many of the wines from this area, even the unclassified ones, are high-quality wines.

While Pauillac may be second to Margaux in total number of growth classifications, Pauillac is the only area to claim more than one of the first growths. Pauillac boasts three "Premier Crus." Pauillac may be Bordeaux's most famous area; it houses 60 percent of the first growths and fifteen other lower classified wines. Château Lafite-Rothschild and Château LaTour were the two original first growths that debuted on the list in 1855.

Even though Château Mouton-Rothschild did not make the first draft, the winery was "promoted" after many years (in more ways than one) to the level of first growth from second growth. Baron Philippe de Rothschild assumed control of the family vineyard in 1920. From the moment that he took the reins, he set his sights on changing history, or at least changing the 1855 Classification. Baron Rothschild knew his wines were commanding prices similar to those of first growth wines, and he felt the quality of his wines was also at the first-growth standard. During this time he coined a motto: "First, I cannot be. Second, I do not deign to be. Mouton, I am."

In addition to lobbying the French government to change the growth status of his wine, he distinguished the winery by commissioning famous artists to design the labels for the vintages. The list of artists that agreed to design labels reads like a Who's Who of twentieth-century artists: Salvador Dali, André Masson, Andy Warhol, Robert Motherwell, Arman, and John Huston. None of these artists were paid in cash; instead, the Baron paid the artists with ten cases of Château Mouton-Rothschild in two installments. First, when the artist finished and delivered the label the Baron would give them five cases of Mouton from other vintages. Second, when the vintage that the artist created a label for was ready to market the Baron would give them five cases of the vintage with their label on it. The pinnacle for the Baron and the Château, however, came in 1973, when the Baron was finally able to add "Premier Cru Classe" to the label designed by Pablo Picasso. At this time the Baron changed his motto: "First, I am. Second, I was. But Mouton does not change."

St. Estèphe is the final area of note when traveling downriver toward the Atlantic Ocean. St. Estèphe wines are known for extremely high levels of tannin, which may be the reason that only five of its wineries are classified.

The Other Red Grapes of Bordeaux

Almost all of the wines of Bordeaux are blends of several grapes. Some of the other grapes that are used in Bordeaux to soften the big, bold tannic Cabernet Sauvignon are Cabernet Franc, Petit Verdot, and Malbec. For example, Château La Tour, one of the famous first growths of the Left Bank, is 80 percent Cabernet Sauvignon. The famous wine also has to credit Merlot and Cabernet Franc, which make up of the rest of the blend in equal parts. The ratios of grapes change from vineyard to vineyard (each Château has their own recipe for success), but the primary grape in Bordeaux's Left Bank remains the Cabernet Sauvignon.

Figure 12.2 A bottle of California Cabernet Sauvignon. [Dorling Kindersley Images]

United States: California

One of the most popular red wines to come from California is Cabernet Sauvignon. Because of its size, California can grow more grapes and produce more wines than many other areas. The Napa Valley is known for award-winning Cabernet Sauvignon, but most of Napa Valley is too hot to grow that grape in the traditional way. Therefore, the Cabernet Sauvignon from the Napa Valley is different from a traditional Cabernet Sauvignon; it is a little higher in alcohol and more balanced from what would be expected from traditional Cabernet Sauvignon. The winemakers are careful to stay in the same flavor profile, however.

The real turning point for American wine was in the late 1960s and early 1970s. Several wineries started producing world-class wine. Winemaker Warren Winiarski sealed California's place in 1976 at a wine tasting in Paris, France. The Winiarski winery's Stag's Leap 1973 Cabernet Sauvignon won top honors, beating some of the first growths from Bordeaux, including Château Mouton-Rothschild (remember, Baron Rothschild had just succeeded in having the 1855 Classification changed to reflect Mouton-Rothschild as a first growth instead of a second growth). Winiarski's wine had competed against the best wine in the world and top honors went to California instead of Bordeaux.

California's potential for great wine was more fully realized by the Baron Rothschild when he joined forces with California winemaker Robert Mondavi to make what they dubbed Opus One. Opus One is made in Napa Valley, but the wine is made very much like a Bordeaux and fetches the same price as some of the top growths. The wine is a blend of grapes and is called Meritage. Meritage can be a blend of the same grapes used in Bordeaux, although no one grape comprises 75 percent of the blend. Grapes used in the blend can include Cabernet Sauvignon, Merlot, Cabernet Franc, Petit Verdot, and Melbec. This freedom allows the winemaker to blend grapes to make the best possible wine. Baron Rothschild and Mondavi are not the only winery to produce such a wine, but they are the best known.

Labeling and blending rules change in winemaking from country to country. France and the United States winemakers can blend juice from more than one grape to achieve a desired outcome as long as at least 75 percent of the grape on the label is in the bottle. California winemakers can blend other grapes with Cabernet Sauvignon to soften this tannic wine. A wine labeled Cabernet Sauvignon must contain at least 75 percent Cabernet Sauvignon grapes.

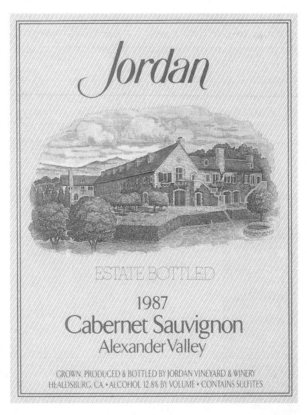

Figure 12.3 A California Cabernet Sauvignon label. [Dorling Kindersley Images]

United States: Washington, Long Island, and Other Areas

Washington state and Long Island, New York, seem to be too far north to success-fully grow Cabernet Sauvignon grapes, but some vineyards are having success. The Cabernet Sauvignon wines from these areas are a little more acidic than what is grown in California because the grapes do not get as much sun, but they are still quite good.

While the Cabernet Sauvignon grape is mainly grown in California, there are some new areas of the United States in which this grape has begun to make an appearance. Vineyards in Grand Valley, Colorado; Rogue Valley, Oregon; Bryan, Texas; and even southwest Arizona are growing this noble grape with great suc-cess.

Italy

In Italy the popular Cabernet Sauvignon grape is replacing many of the grapes that are traditional to Italy, such as the Sangiovese, Nebbiolo, Barbera, and Dol-cetto grapes. Some vineyards have seen this as a problem, but the growth of the traditionally French grapes, such as Cabernet Sauvignon, on Italian soil is a well-planned answer to the demand for wine made with this popular grape; Italian vintners are trying to capture part of the market.

Australia

Australia is not known as much for Cabernet Sauvignon as it is for the Shiraz grape. The vintners down under can blend their wines in a way that most other countries cannot because Australian laws make it easy for winemakers to do so.

Figure 12.4 A bottle of Australian Cabernet Sauvignon. [Dorling Kindersley Images]

Australia has had great success with a Cabernet Sauvignon/Shiraz blend. The Shiraz grape is very prominent all over Australia, and the mellow taste of this grape helps smooth out the harsh tannin of the Cabernet Sauvignon grapes for a full-bodied wine that is easy to drink.

Chile and Argentina

In the 1990s, the growth of the South American wine business was staggering. Even though Chile has been making wine, especially red wine, for over 450 years, and Argentina has been making wine for over 400 years, the quality of their wines has been questionable until recently. Chile's Cabernet Sauvignon crop accounts for almost 50 percent of premium grapes grown there. The vast majority of vineyards in South America can be found on a 500-mile ribbon of land spanning from Santiago, Chile, to Buenos Aires, Argentina. Other South American vineyards that grow Cabernet Sauvignon can be found in northern Chile, northern Argentina, southern Peru, northwestern Bolivia, southwestern Uruguay, and southern Brazil.

All wines are not created equal, nor are they priced equal. The wines from Chile and Argentina often are much cheaper in price than other wines, but they may still be outstanding wines.

Merlot

Merlot grapes produce full-bodied wines that are, for the most part, somewhat lighter than Cabernet Sauvignon. Merlot grapes produce a softer, easier-to-drink red wine. This fundamental difference can be traced to the size of the grape. The size of the grape and the amount of skin on the grape impacts the wine's flavor; physically, the Merlot grape is much larger than the Cabernet Sauvignon grape, so Merlot grapes have a much lower skin-to-flesh ratio. The skin influences the flavor of the wine by giving the wine more tannin.

Properly aged Merlot wine produces aromas ranging from raw green bell pepper to plums and roses, depending on the ripeness of the grapes at the crush. As the wine ages, it can develop other aromas and flavors, including black currants, tobacco, lead pencil, mint, fruitcake, olives, and dark chocolate. The amount of sunlight and the grapes' ripeness have an effect on the wine's flavor as well. If grapes do not get enough sun, the wine will taste of herbs; if the grapes are overripe and sweet, the resulting wine will have stewed fruit flavors.

France: Bordeaux, the Right Bank

Even though the Left Bank of Bordeaux is able to claim the top-ranked wines in the 1855 Classification, the Right Bank of Bordeaux can claim Bordeaux's most expensive wine: Château Pétrus. The small vineyard of Château Pétrus is the

Figure 12.5 Vines growing on the Right Bank of Bordeaux are usually Merlot. [Dorling Kindersley Images]

Cinderella of Bordeaux because the wine is not produced on the prestigious Left Bank and Château Pétrus remains unclassified. With little more than 28 acres, almost all of which is planted with Merlot grapes, Château Pétrus only produces about 4,000 cases of wine a year. Some of the vintages end up being made of 100 percent Merlot grapes; up to 5 percent of Cabernet Franc grapes may be added to the wine, but this is rare. Other famous wine comes from the small areas of Pomerol and St. Émilion on the Right Bank of Bordeaux.

United States: California

The Merlot grape has become one of the most popular wines from California. Red wine has recently proven to have some health benefits when consumed in moderation. This new information and the mellow flavor of Merlot wine has made it one of the top-selling wines in the United States.

United States: Other States

Long Island, New York, and Washington State practice the Bordeaux tradition of growing Merlot grapes next to Cabernet Sauvignon. Vineyards in Colorado and Texas are also growing Merlot grapes on a smaller scale.

Figure 12.6 A Merlot label from the Sonoma AVA in California [Dorling Kindersley Images]

Italy

In Italy the Merlot grape also is replacing traditional grapes. Most of this is happening in Tuscany, which is located in the center of Italy. These new wines are being referred to as Super Tuscans.

Chile and Argentina

Merlot grapes, along with the Cabernet Sauvignon grapes, make up most of Chile's and Argentina's grape crops. Unlike any other region in the world, these two countries can claim old-world roots. Most vineyard roots were replaced worldwide during the *Phylloxera vastatrix* outbreak; for some reason, these countries have not had any (or at least very limited) problems with the parasite.

Merlot wine from both of these countries can be a wonderful bargain compared to many other Merlots.

Key Terms

Bordeaux
Left Bank

Right Bank
Baron Rothschild

The 1855 Classification
Warren Winiarski

Meritage
Robert Mondavi

Study Questions

1. What is the flavor and aroma profile of Cabernet Sauvignon wine?
2. What is the flavor and aroma profile of Merlot wine?
3. Do Cabernet Sauvignon or Merlot grapes have more tannin?
4. What is the difference between the Left Bank and the Right Bank of Bordeaux?
5. What is the 1855 Classification?
6. Why is the 1855 Classification so important?
7. What is the only change ever made to the 1855 Classification?
8. How many "first growths" are there in the 1855 Classification?

Chapter
13

Sparkling Wines, Dessert Wines, Fortified Wines, and Aperitifs

After reading this chapter, you will be able to:

❐ Explain the difference between sparkling wine and champagne.

❐ Describe the different origins of the bubbles in sparkling wine and how they are infused.

❐ Explain characteristics of sparkling wines from around the world.

❐ Discuss the grapes of the Champagne region.

❐ Explain the role of sweetness and color in champagne ranking.

❐ Explain the differences and similarities between nonvintage, vintage and prestige champagnes.

❐ Explain the difference between sweet and fortified wines and the methods that produce them.

❐ Discuss the characteristics of German sweet wines.

❐ Discuss and distinguish characteristics of French Sauternes and Barsac.

❐ Explain how and why wine is fortified.

❐ Discuss the different types of Port.

❐ Discuss Madeira production and classifications.

❐ Explain Marsala's "Triple Trinity."

❐ Discuss sherry production and classification.

❐ Explain the *solera* system.

❐ Distinguish between Finos and Olorosos.

I drink it when I am happy and when I am sad. Sometimes I drink it when I am alone. When I have company I consider it obligatory. I trifle with it if I'm not hungry and I drink it when I am. Otherwise I never touch it . . . unless I'm thirsty.

— Madame Lilly Bollinger, on champagne

While most people may not imbibe as frequently as Madame Bollinger, sparkling wine creates a mood of revelry that sets a moment apart or makes an event special. The sound of corks popping at weddings, victory celebrations, and, of course, New Year's Eve, mark the events as out of the ordinary. What is it about this drink that intoxicates the soul as well as the body?

Sparkling wine can be produced from any number of grape varieties and vintage years. But when most people think sparkling wine, they think of champagne, and when they think of champagne, they think of bubbles. Those tiny bubbles are what make sparkling wine different from still wine. The pressure from those bubbles causes the cork to fly from the bottle and allows the foam to come gushing out. It is the bubbles—from the addition of carbon dioxide—that give the wine its sparkle.

Figure 13.1 Celebrations and sparkling wine go together. [Dorling Kindersley Images]

Figure 13.2 A glass of sparkling wine. [Dorling Kindersley Images]

Sparkling Wines

A Rose by Any Other Name . . .

In Shakespeare's *Romeo and Juliet,* Juliet, upon learning that Romeo is from a rival family, says, "A rose by any other name would smell as sweet." When it comes to sparkling wines, however, the name makes a world of difference. Learning the laws, rules, and processes of naming and producing sparkling wines will give the novice a better understanding of wine.

Most people think that champagne is sparkling wine. This is true, but not all sparkling wines are champagne. As a matter of fact, the only wine that truly can be called champagne accounts for only 10 percent of the world market of sparkling wine. True champagne only comes from the Champagne region of France.

How Champagne Is Different from Sparkling Wine

Champagne has tradition and mystique that other sparkling wines do not share. The area of Champagne, France, basically has a monopoly on the name *Champagne;* even other areas in France cannot call sparkling wine champagne. Most countries have trade agreements with France that enforce this name monopoly. Any wine, perfume, soap, and even clothing line that uses the name and does not have prior approval from the Champagne region can be shut down because of this agreement. Only the United States and Russia do not have such an

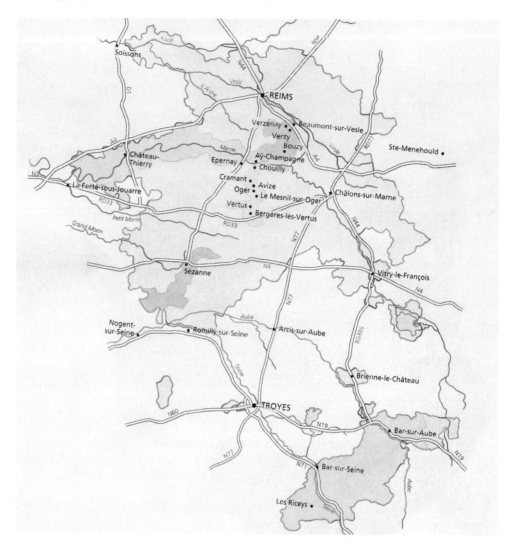

Figure 13.3   The Champagne region in France. [Dorling Kindersley Images]

agreement. In these countries, the word *champagne*, with a lower case *c*, can end up on a sparkling wine label.

The Grapes of Champagne

Champagne distinguishes itself from the rest of the sparkling wines in many ways. One of the most important ways is the type of grapes allowed in Champagne production. In the Champagne region, only three grapes can be used: Pinot Noir, Pinot Meunier, and Chardonnay. Because most Champagne is clear,

Chardonnay grapes are an obvious choice for Champagne production. Chardonnay is, of course, a white grape, but what about the Pinot Noir or the Pinot Meunier? Both of these are red grapes, so how could they be used to make a white champagne? The insides of the grapes are white or clear. White wine can be made from red grapes by skimming the skins off quickly when the red grapes are crushed. White grape juice comes from red grapes that have the skins removed. If 100 percent red grapes are used, the wine is known as Blanc de Noir, a white wine from red grapes. If, however, the winemaker uses 100 percent Chardonnay grapes, the wine is known as Blanc de Blanc, a white wine from white grapes.

The idea of sparkling wine did not start in France, but the names associated with good sparkling wine are associated with France: Veuve Clicquot, Taittinger, Moet and Chandon, Dom Perignon, Pommerery, and Laurent-Perrier are all historical names related to the area and production of champagne. Sparkling wine started in the abbeys of the Roman Catholic church. Some sources say these abbeys were located in Spain; others say they were in Italy. In the end, the knowledge of how to add bubbles to wine came to rest in northern France.

Other Sparkling Wine Regions

The Champagne area is not the only area to produce wine with carbon dioxide bubbles. Many other areas have made a splash with sparkling wines. Spain, Italy, Germany, Australia, South Africa, California, New York, Hawaii, Oregon, and

Figure 13.4 Ornate art from the Champagne region of France. [Dorling Kindersley Images]

Figure *13.5* A bottle of Taittinger Champagne.
[Dorling Kindersley Images]

even New Mexico all offer sparkling wines. Each area has something to offer that is distinct.

One of the qualities they all have in common, however, is the price. The prices of these wines may be similar due to their similar reputations. If the sparkling wine comes from Champagne, France, the price seems to skyrocket. If a sparkling wine does not have the word *Champagne* on the label, it does not mean that it is not a "champ" in its own right, or at least a world contender.

While reputations and price may be similar, these sparkling wines can have some differences. A more northerly growing location means more acid in the grapes. Grapes grown further south will have more fruit flavors. Therefore, Champagne from the Champagne region has a higher acid level than a sparkling wine from California because of differences in climate. California has much more sun and warmth than Champagne, France. This extra sun and warmth allows the grapes to ripen more quickly. During the process of ripening, acid is lost and the sugar is gained. This gives the grapes a sweeter and fruitier taste.

Sparkling wine is produced all over the world, including other regions in France. Sparkling wine goes by different names depending upon where it is made. See Table 13.1 for names of sparkling wines and their regions of origin.

Many of the houses that produce sparkling wine outside of Champagne, France, use grapes that are classic to Champagne. One of the benefits of growing grapes outside of Champagne is that the producer is not locked into any particular grape variety. Many grape varieties that are not classically used in Champagne make outstanding sparklers.

Figure 13.6 Not Champagne . . . a sparkling wine from the Loire Valley. [Dorling Kindersley Images]

Nonvintage, Vintage, and Prestige

Nonvintage accounts for the majority of Champagnes on the market; however, the bottle will rarely be marked *nonvintage*. Nonvintage means the grapes are not from a single year. Most people think that this denotes a flaw in the wine, but the wine may have been improved by blending with other years. This is the way that Champagne used to be made, and it is part of the reason producers have started to call nonvintage champagne *Classic Champagne.*

By law, Champagne producers must set aside 20 percent of each year's wine production for nonvintage use. Many producers set aside much more than that; sometimes they set aside as much as 50 percent. Most champagne houses mainly

Table 13.1 Sparkling Wines and Their Regions of Origin

Origin of Production	Name
France, Champagne	Champagne
France, outside Champagne	Mousseux or Cuvee
Italy	Spumante
England	Moussec
South Africa	Cap Classique
German and Austria	Sekt or Schaumwein
Spain	Cavas or Espumosa
Bulgaria	Champanski
Yugoslavia	Sampanjac
Australia	Sparklers

Figure 13.7 Two examples of Australian 'sparklers' that compete against Champagne. [Dorling Kindersley Images]

focus where the money can be made. Every year cannot be a good vintage, so blending grapes into nonvintage champagnes makes business sense.

Vintage refers to wines that are made from grapes grown in the same year. Vintages can be good or bad, but in the Champagne region of France, vintages are attached to wines only if they are of high quality. Vintage years are rare in Champagne because the growing season is so short in this northern region. This means that the grapes usually have high acidity, and they don't mature the way they could if they were grown in southern France. To have a season in which the grapes are the best they can be is rare, and even when they can declare a vintage, some houses don't. The production house does not want the style of wine that very ripe grapes would produce.

To achieve the status *prestige cuvée,* all of the wine has to be from the same vintage, and there are longer aging requirements than the twelve-month minimum. For example, the famous Dom Perignon champagne is aged for six to eight years.

How Sweet Is It?

A sparkling wine's sweetness partially is determined by the *dosage.* Dosage is the addition of a mixture of sugar syrup, grape concentrate, and/or brandy to champagne or sparkling wine before it is recorked. This is also known as *Liqueur d'Expedition.* This establishes the level of sweetness in the finished product. The mixture is added to sweeten wine, but it also tops off the bottle after disgorging, or removing, the sediment.

Figure 13.8 A worker adds the dosage to a bottle of Champagne. [Dorling Kindersley Images]

Determining the sweetness of sparkling wine or Champagne can be confusing. People have different tastes; one person might like dry Champagne, whereas others might like a sweet drink. The food the drinker is eating also influences the level of sweetness desired. There are six levels of sweetness in Champagnes and sparkling wines. The sweetest level is Doux. However, the term *Doux* is rarely used today. The next two levels are Demi-Sec and Sec. *Demi* means half and *Sec* means dry. Therefore, if a wine's label says Demi-Sec, it will be semi-dry; if Sec is on the label, it will be dry. There is still residual sugar in wines labeled Demi-Sec and Sec, however. As a matter of fact, to most tasters, Demi-Sec is quite sweet, and Sec is medium-dry.

The next level of sweetness is Extra Sec or Extra Dry, which means mostly dry or "off-dry." The last two levels are Brut and Extra Brut. Both of these levels range from a little residual sugar to totally dry.

Table 13.2 lists the levels of sweetness in Champagne and sparkling wine.

Table 13.2 Levels of Sweetness in Sparkling Wine and Champagne

Doux	Very sweet
Demi-Sec	Sweet
Sec	Semi-sweet
Extra Sec or Extra Dry	Bitter-sweet
Brut	Dry
Extra Brut	Totally dry, no sweetness

The Color

Regardless of what it is called, "bubbly" can be made using almost any grape. Two of the three grapes that are "Champagne grapes" are red. So, how does Champagne get the clear or yellow white wine color? Its color is the result of several factors. The most important factor is how long the macerated skins stay in the grape juice once it is squeezed. The longer the skins stay in contact with the juice, the more color the juice will have.

In recent years, rosé Champagne has been the rage. Allowing some skin contact with the grape juice creates the wine's pink to salmon color. The contact is kept to a minimum so that the sparkling wine does not turn red. This color does not mean that the resulting wine is going to be sweet; the level of sweetness is based on the residual sugar in the grape juice after fermentation and the dosage.

All About the Bubbles

Different sparkling wines have different qualities, but one thing that all sparkling wines have in common is bubbles. The bubbles are simply the carbon dioxide (CO_2) gas created during fermentation; the makers of the sparkling wine do not let the gas float away, as with still wines (For more information about carbon dioxide created during fermentation, see Chapter 6). As the carbon dioxide builds up in the bottle, it is measured in atmospheres (atms), normal air pressure at sea level, which is 14.7 pounds per square inch. Sparkling wine ranges from 2 atms to 6 atms (between 29.4 pounds per square inch to 88.2 pounds per square inch). This is roughly three times the pressure in your automobile tire. (Because of the amount of pressure behind the cork, a bottle should always be pointed away from people when opening. The person opening the bottle also should take care to open it very carefully, slowly easing out the cork. If the person opening the bottle does not take care in doing this, the gas and bubbles will be lost when the bottle is opened. (For more information on how to open a sparkling-wine bottle, refer to Chapter 17.)

The carbon dioxide bubbles are infused into sparkling wine and Champagne in one of four ways:

1. *Méthode Champenoise.*
2. Transfer Method.
3. Charmat Process.
4. Carbonation Method.

Méthode Champenoise   *Méthode Champenoise* is the classic and original way to add bubbles to sparkling wine. The method dates back to a time well before the famous monk Dom Pierre Perignon arrived at the Abbey of Hautvillers in 1668. However, most experts agree that Dom Perignon did perfect the process of blending and bottling sparkling wine before his death in 1715 at age 77. Even though this process cannot be attributed to a single person, it was most likely developed in a Catholic monastery. Some experts say this monastery was in Spain.

The production method for sparkling wines begins just like any other wine production. The producer of the wine picks the grapes that they want to use and presses or squeezes them to extract the juice. The juice is then moved to oak barrels or stainless steel vats for fermentation. Once the wine has fermented, it is cold stabilized and blended. The cold stabilization helps prevent the formation of tartrate crystals or any other unwanted reaction. The blending is an optional step. The producer may or may not add the juice of different grapes to the blend. After the wine is blended, the *liqueur de triage*, a sweet liquid made from liquid yeast and sugar, is added to encourage secondary fermentation. At this point the bottle is capped.

The wine is then laid on its side in a cool, dark cellar. Once the secondary fermentation has taken place, it is important to clarify the wine. This is done by gradually rotating and tilting the bottle so that eventually it stands on its end, a process known as *riddling*. This also allows the *lees*, or sediment, to be mixed into the wine, giving it better and more complex flavors. The riddling process has been simplified in the New World with a large machine known as a VLM (very lage machine). The VML can riddle many bottles in a fraction of the time it takes human hands to do the same. Once the yeast has settled, the sparkling wine is allowed to mature for up to five years. By that time, the sediment is all in the neck of the bottle.

With the sediment in the neck of the bottle, the producer freezes the neck in a very cold bath. The bottle cap is removed and the carbon dioxide forces the frozen sediment plug out of the bottle. The bottle is topped off with wine, and sometimes liquid sugar, then recorked and packaged for sale with a label that reads, "fermented in this bottle."

Figure 13.9 A worker disgorges a bottle of Champagne, preparing the bottle for sale. [Dorling Kindersley Images]

Transfer Method   This method is very similar to *Méthode Champenoise*. However, after the second fermentation, the bottled wine passes through a large filtering system to remove the sediment. This makes the riddling and disgorgement steps unnecessary. The label reflects this process by being marked "bottle fermented," "fermented in the bottle," or "transfer method."

This method produces many high-quality sparkling wines and reduces the labor put forth by the producer in making the wine. The final product tends to be less expensive than its *Méthode Champenoise* counterpart.

Charmat Method   Frenchman Eugene Charmat developed this method, which was identified with cheap sparkling wine in 1910. The method is much faster and lower in cost than either *Méthode Champenoise* or the transfer method. The use of pressurized tanks throughout the process keeps the carbonation in the wine. The carbonation is already there as a by-product of fermentation; it is just not allowed to escape. In this process, the wine is not bottled until after it is carbonated.

This process does not yield bubbles that last long; however, some of the wines can be good. They are identified on the label with the cheaper process, and sometimes are not as highly thought of because of the disappearing bubbles. The bottles may be marked "bulk process" or "Charmat process." The French call this process *cuve close*. The Italians refer to it as *metodo charmat* or *autoclave*. Spanish bottles will be marked *granvas*, whereas in Portugal it is called *metodo continuo*.

Carbonation Method   This is the same method that is used when making soda: carbon dioxide is injected into a still wine. The bubbles are large, and the wine loses them quickly. The method is the least effective in adding carbonation to wine and is always associated with the least expensive of the wines. The wines are labeled "carbonated" in the United States. This method is called *gazeifié* in France.

Drink It or Store It Well

Most of the sparkling wine bought in the store is ready to drink. However, if you are looking to store sparkling wines, there are several things that you should take into consideration.

First, keep the bottle away from light and heat, but do not put it in the refrigerator until that special occasion. Keep it in a proper cellar and make sure the following conditions exist:

1. Make sure that the temperature is anywhere from the low 50°F. range to the low 60° F. range. Any temperature lower or higher or a constant fluctuation in temperature can be bad for the wine.
2. Keep the bottle away from the light.
3. Make sure that there are no vibrations that will damage the wine.

4. The humidity also should be between 50 and 60 to 65 percent. Lower humidity will cause the cork to dry out which could damage the wine. Higher humidity levels will cause the cork to mold.

Sparkling Wine and Food Pairing

The first things to consider when pairing sparkling wine or champagne with food are the wine's sweetness and body. The body refers to the overall flavor or the weight of the wine in the mouth. Something that pairs well with a sweet, sparkling wine does not necessarily pair well with a Brut or Extra Brut. The body of the food needs to be considered as well.

The sweeter sparkling wines go with sweet desserts while the dryer sparkling wines will pair with various cuisines. For example, a Sec or Demi-Sec sparkling wine would pair well with foie gras or with a dessert because the sweetness of the wine compliments the richness of the food. An Extra Brut or Brut might pair well with a Caesar salad, caviar, or a blue cheese appetizer. The boldness of the wine's flavor pairs well with the boldness of these dishes. A Brut Rosé sparkling wine would pair well with a spinach salad due to the flavors of strawberry and raspberry. Rosé sparkling wine is well known for the strawberry and raspberry flavors.

Dessert Wines

There are numerous types of dessert wines, including those that are sweet or fortified. The most notable sweet wines include the German sweet wines, the French Sauternes, and Barsac. Fortified wines are Porto, Madeira, Marsala, and Sherry.

The processes used to produce these wines help define them. Many of the sweet wines discussed in this chapter are wines that have *residual sugar*, or sugar that is left over after the fermentation process. Grapes used for sweet wine production are specifically picked for degrees of ripeness or overripeness and, after fermentation, these grapes can be infused with a sweet, nonalcoholic liquid.

German Sweet Wines

Sweet German wines are made at the end of the growing season in Germany from grapes that are harvested late in the season. The later in the season the German grapes are picked, the sweeter and more concentrated the sugar becomes. The German terrain is so hilly that the harvest is mostly done by hand, which allows the German growers to pick through their grapes to select the ripest ones. There are five German classifications that denote how sweet the wine will be. This classification is easy to remember because the German category names describe the wine exactly; the person reading the wine label just needs to know a little German.

1. *Spätlese*—These wines come from late-picked grapes. In German *spät* means late and *lese* means picked. These grapes are usually picked at least seven days after the normal growing season; the commissioners in each of the villages define the normal growing season, so harvest time can vary from town to town. These wines are fuller in body and more intense in flavor than Kabinett (the least expensive and driest wine in the German classification system) and Qualitatswein (quality wine), mostly as a result of extra days on the vine.

2. *Auslese*—Growers painstakingly go through the field, picking out bunches of ripe grapes that will make this wine. In German *aus* means out. *Lese* means picked, so the grapes are "out picked." Auslese wines tend to be sweeter and have more body than Spätlese wines, but because of the extra harvesting labor, they also are more expensive.

3. *Beerenauslese*—For Beerenauslese, individual berries are picked out and made into wine. The wine is sweeter than Auslese and Spätlese wines and much more expensive. A factor that drives up this wine's price is how rarely it is made, which is usually only two or three times in a decade.

4. *Eiswein*—This wine is made from Beerenauslese-quality grapes, but the grapes are left on the vine until the vines freeze. The grapes are gathered and pressed while they are still frozen. This process gives the wine its name. *Eis* means ice, and *wein* means wine. This is a very rare wine. It is very sweet, very concentrated, and very expensive.

5. *Trockenbeerenauslese*—This is the rarest, sweetest, richest, and most expensive class of German sweet wines. The grapes are picked out the same way they are for Beerenauslese wines, but they also are *trocken,* or dried, so the sugar is very concentrated.

Sometimes German grapes are affected by the mold called Noble Rot. This mold withers the grape, which helps to concentrate the wine's sweetness through the evaporation of water. This mold is more commonly used in France to make Sauternes and Barsac. The Germans do not rely on Noble Rot alone for sweetness. Unless the wine is marked *trocken,* German wines always have a little extra sweetness because of the addition of süssreserve. The süssreserve is unfermented grape juice that is added at the end of fermentation to add sweetness to a wine that is already high in acid. (Many of the German wines are high in acid.) Producers do not add süssreserve to regular German table wine, but they do add it to everyday German wine (see Chapter 7).

Some wines from other parts of the world are made in the general style of these great German wines, but they have other distinct characteristics. For example, a producer in California might make ice wine using some of the same techniques used by the German producers. However, the weather in California is not like the weather in Germany; therefore, the growers may need to employ other methods to achieve the same result, such as using a commercial freezer rather than leaving the grapes on the vine to freeze.

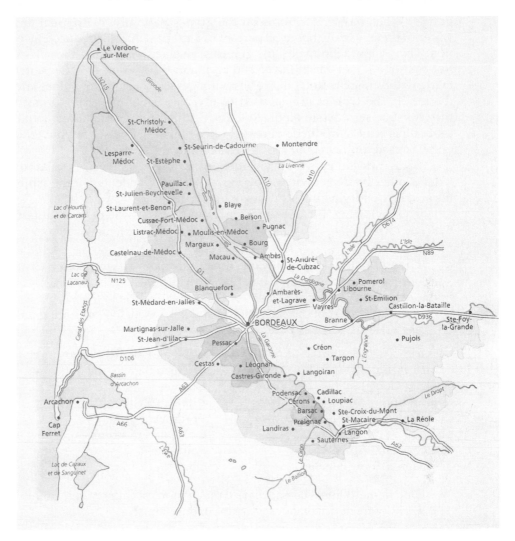

Figure 13.10   The Sauterne area in Bordeaux, France, is known for very sweet wines. [Dorling Kindersley Images]

Sauternes and Barsac

Sauternes and Barsac are wines that come from the Graves area of the Bordeaux region of France. These small tracts of land are located across from each other on the Ciron River where the Ciron River merges with the Garonne River. The Garonne River is cooled by the Ciron, creating a humidity that causes the grapes to be damp in the morning. The Sauternes area is located to the southeast and Barsac is located to the northwest. Part of the reason that these golden wines are sweet is their location, but a mold, *Botrytis cinerea* (Noble Rot), also grows on the grapes. When Noble Rot forms on the grapes naturally, the normal amount of water in them, usually about 90 percent of a grape's mass, is reduced by evaporation. This evaporation makes the grapes shrivel, concentrating the sugars. Noble Rot creates a honey-raisin flavor and aroma in these grapes. Some Sauternes are made without Noble Rot, but the best vintages are those using grapes affected by the mold. The type of grapes used to produce Sauternes is important because they must be sensitive to Noble Rot. The Sémillon grape makes up about 80 percent of this wine's production because of its high sensitivity. The Sauvignon Blanc grape is used for the remaining 20 percent.

Sauternes and Barsac are included in a rating system very similar to the system for other Bordeaux wines. This system was implemented at the same time as the system classifying the Bordeaux wines in 1855.

The following list presents the classification system for Sauternes and Barsac.

Grand Premier Cru—Only one house can claim this top honor: Château d'Yquem. All others fall in the first growth, second growth or unclassified/regional Sauternes. This wine is made in the Sauterne region.
Premier Cru—This classification is still very exclusive, including only eleven houses from five areas:

Barsac
Château Climens
Château Coutet
Bommes
Château Clos Haut-Peyraguey
Château de Rayne-Vigneau
Château Lafaurie-Peyraguey
Château La Tour-Blanche

Château Rabaud-Promis
Château Sigalas-Rabaud
Fargues
Château Rieussec
Preignac
Château Suduiraut
Sauternes
Château Guiraud

Deuxièmes Crus—Barsac plays a much more prominent role in this class. Eight of the fourteen houses are located in Barsac.

Barsac
Château de Myrat
Château Doisy-Daene
Château Doisy-Vedrines
Château Doisy-Dubroca
Château Broustet
Château Nairac
Château Caillou
Château Suau

Fargues
Château Romer-du-Hayot
Preignac
Château de Malle
Sauternes
Château d'Arche
Château Filhot
Château Lamothe-Despujols
Château Lamothe-Guignard

Most Sauternes and Barsac can be found for sale in the United States. Sauternes usually cost more than Barsac wines because of their reputation. Both of these will cost more than most other wines because of the intense labor and low yield in the vineyard. By French law, producers and growers in Sauternes may only produce about 267 gallons of wine per acre. This is astoundingly low; in the rest of Bordeaux, producers and growers are limited to almost 588 gallons per acre. In addition to this low yield, the law also requires that the alcohol level be 12.5 percent and the sugar level be about 7¾ ounces (by weight) per quart.

Fortified Wines and Aperitifs

Fortified wines are those that are manipulated primarily after fermentation by the addition of other types of alcohol to achieve a bolder taste, a higher alcohol content, and a longer shelf life. An aperitif can be made the same way as sweet fortified wines, but an aperitif is consumed before the meal to stimulate the appetite. Some of the wines in this chapter are appropriate served as an aperitif as well as after meals.

One way wine can be made sweet is by stopping fermentation and allowing the residual sugar to remain. One of the easiest ways to stop fermentation is to raise the alcohol level so high that the yeast cannot function anymore. This can be achieved by adding a neutral grape brandy to a wine, which raises the alcohol level to between 18 and 24 percent. This unaged brandy also preserves the wine.

Figure 13.11 Port wine is ferried down the Douro River to the city of Oporto. [Dorling Kindersley Images]

Porto (or Port)   Porto is named for the city of Oporto, Portugal, a port city at the end of the Douro River. Porto grapes are grown in the Douro River area. Over forty different varieties of grapes can be used when making Porto; however, the main grapes used to make red ports (ruby and tawny) are Tinta Barroca, Tinta Cao, Tempranillo (which is better known as Tinta Roriz in Portugal), Touriga Francesa, and Touriga Nacional. When the producers make white port, they use white grapes such as Esgana—Cao, Folgasao, Malvasia, Rabigato, Verdelho, and Viosinho. The producer's aim is to make this wine a strong—about 18 to 22 percent alcohol—sweet drink. The alcohol level was originally increased with brandy to help preserve the wine during long voyages from Portugal to England.

Here are the various types of Port that can be produced:

Ruby Port—Lower-quality wine is made into Ruby Port and aged in wood for approximately three years before being released for sale. These Ports are, as the name suggests, very red. The flavor displays the fruity characters of a young wine, and it is meant to be drunk young. Ruby Port is usually consumed in the winter months, and it is the least expensive of the ports.

Vintage Character Ports—These Ports are high-quality Ruby Port blended from several vintages and aged in wood. They are the lightest and fruitiest of all the Ports.

Late Bottled Vintage Port (LBV)—This is a very high-quality Ruby Port. It must be aged in wood for at least four, but no more than six, years. If the Port produced from a single year's grape production is of high quality, the

Figure 13.12   Seven glasses of different styles of Port. [Dorling Kindersley Images]

shipper can declare it to be "late bottle vintage." Late Bottled Vintage Port is usually made in years that were not declared "vintage." This port is ready to drink after it is bottled and does not have the aging potential of vintage port.

Crusted Ports—Crusted Ports have been, for the most part, replaced by LBV Port. Crusted Ports claim their name from the sediment (crust) that forms during the aging process. They differ from LBV Port in that Crusted Port is a blend of two or three vintages, which is aged for three or four years before bottling.

Tawny Port—Tawny Port takes its name from its color. This port is a blend of several vintages that have been aged in wood. The aging can last for almost forty years; however, most are aged closer to the six-year minimum. Tawny Port, which is usually consumed during the summer months, is lighter and more delicate with a distinct nutty aroma when compared with Ruby Port. Most of the Port made, about 60 percent, falls into the category of either Ruby or Tawny Port.

Colheita Port—The word *colheita* means "vintage" in Portuguese. This Port is also called Dated Port. It is similar to LBV, but it is a Tawny Port. This Port is aged for a minimum of seven years before it is bottled. The date on the label, however, refers to the date the Port was bottled rather than the vintage year. Colheita Port is ready to drink when it is bottled, just like LBV.

Vintage Port—This is considered by most to be the best Port available. Only the best grapes from the best growing site make up this wine, but it is made only during the best years. A vintage is not declared every year because of all these factors: Vintage Port makes up only 2 percent of all port production, and it must be bottled within 2 years of being made. After bottling it can age up to fifty years. A Port's aging ability is due to the amount of tannin in a young bottle of Vintage Port. Because of the care taken in producing this highly selective wine, the cost also will be high.

Second Label Vintage Ports—When a firm feels that their Port is very good but not vintage, they will call it a Second Label Vintage Port. It is made the same way as Vintage Port.

Single Quinta Ports—This Port is similar to high-quality estate, château, or single vineyard reserve wine. All of the wine is from a single estate, usually labeled as such, in nonvintage years to establish the vineyard's claim of a superior Port. Today some firms also are doing this during declared vintage years. The qualities of Single Quinta Port can range from house to house.

White Port—This Port is made from white grapes. The producers make White Port using the same methods as for those making Ruby or Tawny Port, but they allow the white wine to ferment a little longer. This makes for a dryer finished product. White Ports range from medium sweet to almost dry, and mainly are served as an aperitif.

Madeira Madeira comes from the Island of Madeira, which is located in the Atlantic Ocean off the coast of northwest Africa about 350 miles from Morocco.

Joao Goncalvez, a Portuguese explorer, discovered the island in 1418. The island was dubbed *Madeira*, the Portuguese word for "Island of Wood" because the island was thick with trees. To this day Madeira is partially ruled by Portugal. The island served as a port for ships sailing to the East Indies and Africa and later the West Indies and the Americas. The wine was very popular in Colonial North America; General George Washington used it to toast the signing of the Declaration of Independence.

Brandy is added to wine to make Madeira just as it is added to wine to make Port. Unlike Port, however, Madeira is then exposed to air and heat, two things that would ruin any other wine. In the nineteenth century, Madeira shippers would find that the wine was better when it arrived at the destination then when it left the Island of Madeira. This difference was caused by the exposure to the heat and air the wine received on board the ship. Madeira producers began creating this airflow and heat in little huts they call *estufas*. In the *estufa*, wine is allowed to reach temperatures of 120° F. The oxidation and the heat cause the wine to take on a nutty, caramel quality.

Unlike Port, Madeira is not always sweet. There are five levels of Madeira; four of the five levels claim their names from the grape varietal used in production. Even though these grapes often are no longer used in the wine's production, the styles are still named for the grapes that were originally used.

1. *Malmsey*—This Madeira is named for the grape varietal Malvasia, which came to the island very shortly after the island was found. Malmsey has a honey flavor with overtones of chocolate and figs. It is the sweetest of the five levels.

Figure 13.13 Bottles of Vintage Madeira in storage. [Dorling Kindersley Images]

2. *Bual*—This Madeira comes from a grape variety closely related to the Pinot Noir. The grape is also known in Portuguese as *Boal.* The wine is medium-sweet to sweet and is distinctive because of the fruit and butter flavor.
3. *Rainwater*—This is the newest style of Madeira. It is a blend of Negra Mole and Verdelho grapes. It was first made by accident when a shipper's Madeira became "waterlogged" in heavy rain from the island to the Americas.
4. *Verdelho*—This is a medium dry or semi-dry Madeira. It is believed that the Verdelho grape is a cross between the Pedro Ximenez grape (a grape also used to make sherry) and the Verdea grape. The wine has a gentle, smooth, smoky flavor and is great for use in cooking.
5. *Sercial*—This is the driest style of Madeira, which has been compared to Fino Sherry. The sercial grape is hard to grow, but it produces a highly acidic, dry wine. Even though the original grapes are still used, today this style of wine often is made with the Tinta Negra Mole grape.

In recent years, there has been an effort to go back to the original grape varieties used to produce Madeira because of laws related with the European Union and Portugal. According to these laws, a wine only can be marked with the name of a varietal if it has 85 percent of that varietal in the bottle.

Vintages for Madeira are not declared until the wine has aged for twenty years in the barrel and two in the bottle. The twentieth century only produced

Figure 13.14 Madeira wine ages in an estufa. [Dorling Kindersley Images]

about two or three vintages a decade, making the total number well under forty. Madeira has a reputation for growing old gracefully. It is not uncommon for a good vintage Madeira to have the staying power of well over a full century. These wines tend to be moderately expensive.

Other Madeira can be labeled with information on how many years it was aged in wood. If the wine is labeled "Finest," it was aged for three years. If it is marked "Solera Madeira," it was made using the *solera* system (see the section on Sherry in this chapter). These Madeiras are becoming more and more rare, but nineteenth century Solera Madeira can be found at auction.

Marsala   Marsala is the youngest of the major fortified wines. It was first produced in the 1760s. Even though it is an Italian wine that is made with a blend of grapes indigenous to Sicily, it is the brainchild of an Englishman, John Woodhouse. The name of the wine is taken from the port city of Marsala, which is on the western tip of Sicily. Sicily is said to come from Arabic, meaning "harbor of God" or "Marsah-el-Allah." Marsalas are classified according to three characteristics. Each of these characteristics has three manifestations; therefore, these characteristics become a "Triple Trinity." The first characteristic concerns the level of sweetness, the second concerns color, and the third concerns class, or ranking.

Marsala has three levels of sweetness: *secco, semisecco,* and *dolce.*

1. **Secco**—This designation indicates that the Marsala is dry. The wine can contain no more than 4 percent residual sugar to be classified as *secco.*
2. **Semisecco**—This category indicates that the Marsala is semi-dry. The wine can contain no more than 10 percent residual sugar.
3. **Dolce**—This indicates a Marsala that is sweet. The wine contains more than 10 percent residual sugar.

Marsala's three color classifications are *oro, ambra,* and *rubino.*

1. **Oro**—*Oro* translates as "gold." White grapes such as Catarratto, Inzolia, Grillo, and Damaschino are used for this classification of Marsala.
2. **Ambra**—*Ambra* means "amber." The same white grapes are used for *ambra* as for *oro.* Unlike *oro* Marasala, however, a *catto* or *musto catto* is added to *ambra* Marsala. *Catto* is a reduction of wine. The wine is reduced to one-third of its original volume, which gives the Marsala its cooked taste. A *sifone* (a mixture of semi-dried grapes and alcohol) also is added to the wine; the *sifone* is responsible for the wine's sweetness.
3. **Rubino**—This term means "ruby." Red grapes are used to make this wine and provide its color. Grapes such as Perricone, Calabrese, and Nerello are used for *rubino* Marsala. These grapes can be mixed with white grapes, but the white grapes cannot exceed 30 percent of the total grapes used.

The third part of the trinity refers to Marsala's quality ranking. The three classifications are Marsala Fine, Marsala Superiore, and Marsala Vergine (also known as Vergine Soleras).

1. **Marsala Fine**—This Marsala can have any of the sweetness or color rankings. It must be aged at least one year in wood and have an alcohol content of at least 17 percent. Sweet Marsala Fine wines are good to serve as dessert wines while the drier ones are good as aperitifs.
2. **Marsala Superiore**—This Marsala can come in any color and level of sweetness. The wine must be aged for at least two years in wood and have at least 18 percent alcohol. If the wine is aged for a total of four years in wood, it can add the word *riserva* to the label. In addition to this, Marsala Superiore may have one of the following designations on the label:

   L.P.—London Particular

   S.O.M.—Superior Old Marsala

   G.D.—Garidaldi Dolce. Sweet G.D. Marsala Superiore wines are good to serve as dessert wines, while the drier ones are good as aperitifs.
3. **Marsala Vergine (Vergine Soleras)**—This Marsala can come in any color, but it is limited to *secco* in its level of sweetness. This is the best Marsala made. It is aged in wood for five years and has at least 18 percent alcohol. In addition, this level of Marsala cannot have any *catto* or *sifone* added. If the Marsala is aged for ten years, it can add the word *stravechhio* or *riserva* to the label. This level is made using the *solera* system (see the discussion on sherry). It should always be served as an aperitif.

Sherry   Sherry is Spain's addition to the ranks of fortified wine. Like other fortified wines, sherry has several levels that are categorized in various ways. There are only two grape varieties used to produce sherry: Palomino Fino and Pedro Ximenez. The Palomino grapes make up about 90 percent of the grape production for sherry. These grapes are all grown in an area within three towns: Jerez de la Frontere, Puerto de Santa Maria, and Sanlucar de Barrameda. Once the wine has been made, it always is aged in American white oak barrels.

Sherry is a blended fortified wine that usually has between 17 and 22 percent alcohol by volume. It is made using the *solera* system, a system of combining several vintages (in some cases ten or more) of sherry to allow flavors to combine and heighten.

The *solera* system is a blending process that helps age and mature sherry in a way that allows the producer to maintain the same style from year to year. A row of barrels is lined up. The first is filled with the first year's wine production. During the second year, about one-third of the first year's production is taken out and the wine is replaced with the second year's production. This continues for several years, allowing many years of sherry to be mixed and the flavors to blend for consistency. The date of the sherry indicates the year the *solera* started. Some of

Figure 13.15 The solera system allows different vintages of sherry wine to be mixed during the aging process. [Dorling Kindersley Images]

the wine in the bottle comes from that year's production, but most of it comes from later years.

Oxidation is an important part of Sherry's production process. There are several ways the producers ensure that oxidation happens. One way is to store the wine in an above-ground cellar called a *bodega*. The second is to make sure the barrels are not filled to the top, leaving an air gap so that the wine is exposed to the air. Barrels are only filled two-thirds full and the bung (cork) is not completely shut; this allows air to circulate.

There are seven styles of sherry and each has a different character that makes it unique. All seven styles can be divided into two main categories: Fino and Oloroso. These two categories have seven subclassifications: (1) Fino, (2) Manzanilla, (3) Amontillado, (4) Oloroso, (5) Palo Cortado, (6) cream sherries, and (7) PX.

Finos

1. **Fino**—These are the lightest of the sherries. They are pale and dry, but fragrant, refreshing, and tangy. They should not be aged because they will decline with age rather than improve. To be classified as a Fino, a thick yeast blanket has to form on top of the sherry. This blanket is referred to as *flor*. The flor gives the Sherry a flavor of yeast. A Fino should be served chilled, and it makes a wonderful aperitif.
2. **Manzanilla**—This sherry has a hint of saltiness, which may have something to do with where it is produced. It is made in the Sanlucar de

Barrameda region, which is close to the sea. Manzanilla also is classified as a Fino because of the growth of the flor. Like Fino, it should be served chilled and makes a wonderful aperitif.

3. **Amontillado**—This Sherry also is classified as a Fino, but the flor that develops is thinner than that of other Finos. Amontillado has a little more age to it and tends to be dry unless it is blended. These should be served at room temperature or with ice.

Olorosos

1. **Oloroso**—Some Oloroso sherries can be aged for many years; in some cases, they can be aged a full century. The flavors of this type of sherry vary greatly. Some need to be blended to enjoy, while others are good to drink as they are. Oloroso sherries tend to be higher in alcohol than Finos, which helps to hinder the development of the flor. Drier Oloroso should be served at room temperature or with ice, and sweeter Oloroso sherries should be served at room temperature with fruit or pastry for dessert.
2. **Palo Cortado**—These sherries tend to develop like an Oloroso, but they are lighter in flavor. This style varies from producer to producer.
3. **Cream Sherries**—This class of sherry has given the other styles a bad name, even though some cream sherries can be quite good. A cream sherry is a sweet oloroso.
4. **PX**—This group of sherries is small and hard to find. The Pedro Ximenez grapes are used to produce PX sherries, but they are somewhat dried before the crush, allowing the sugars to concentrate. These are very sweet sherries and can be used to top ice cream or to blend with other sherry such as Fino or Oloroso.

Key Terms

Atmospheres (atms)	Classic Champagne
Auslese	Demi-Sec
Barsac	Deuxièmes Crus
Beerenauslese	Disgorging
Blanc de Blanc	Dosage
Blanc de Noir	Doux
Bottle Fermented	Eiswein
Brut	Extra Brut
Bual	Extra Sec
Carbonation	Fino
Champagne	Fortified Wine
Charmat Method	Grand Premier Cru

LBV
Liqueur d'Expedition
Liqueur de Tirage
Malmsey
Mousseux
Méthode Champenoise
Noble Rot
Nonvintage
Oloroso
Premier Cru
Quinta
Rainwater
Riddling
Ruby Port

Sauternes
Sec
Sercial
Sparklers
Sparkling Wine
Spumante
Spätlese
Tawny Port
Transfer Method
Triple Trinity of Marsala
Trockenbeerenauslese
Vintage Blend
Vintage Port
VML

Study Questions

1. What is the difference between champagne and sparkling wine?
2. What is the difference between Blanc de Noir and Blanc de Blanc?
3. Who perfected the production of champagne?
4. What is the difference, if any, between vintage champagne and classic champagne?
5. Of the six sweetnesxs levels of champagne, which is the sweetest and which is the driest? What makes a sparkling wine sweet or dry?
6. What are the differences between German Sauternes?
7. What is the Triple Trinity of Marsala?
8. What is Eiswein and how is it made?
9. What is Noble Rot and why is it important?
10. What is the difference between Vintage Port and Late Bottle Vintage Port?
11. What is the difference between Ruby Port and Tawny Port?

Chapter 14

Beer:
Ales and Lagers

After reading this chapter, you will be able to:

❑ Talk about the ingredients used to make beer.
❑ Explain the brewing process.
❑ Discuss the difference between lager and ale.
❑ Discuss the production and marketing of beer.
❑ Identify general varieties of lagers and ales.
❑ Justify an argument for classifying sake as a wine or a beer.

I have fed purely upon ale; I have eat my ale, drank my ale, and I always sleep upon my ale.

— George Farquhar, 1678–1707

Mmmmm . . . beer.

—Homer Simpson

Figure 14.1 A horse drawn cart carries beer barrels. [Dorling Kindersley Images]

Beer is a fermented alcoholic beverage made from water, malted grain, hops, and yeast. Brewed beverages such as beer are all heated; thus, the water is sterilized before the beverages are fermented. Brewed beverages also all use grains or honey as the sugar in their fermentation. This produces alcohol contents that vary up to 15 percent alcohol. Sometimes a flavoring agent is added to enhance the flavor of the final beverage as well.

There are two primary types of beer: ales and lagers. Both ale and lager are made using the same basic process. The color, flavor, alcohol content (which can range from almost nothing to 15 percent but usually hovers at about 5 percent), and aroma can all be the same or similar regardless of whether the beer is an ale or a lager.

The Brewing Process

To make beer, malted grain and hops are added to water and this mixture is brought to a boil. During the boil, more hops may be added to help create different flavors and aromas. The mixture of malted grain and hops is heated to combine the sugar, color, and flavors of the grain and the hops. After the mixture has been boiled one to three hours, the liquid is strained of malt and hops. The resulting liquid is called *wort*. The wort is cooled and yeast is added. The yeast converts the sugar from the malted grain into alcohol and carbon dioxide. Once the desired alcohol content has been achieved, or the yeast runs out of sugar, the fermentation stops. Carbon dioxide is added and the brew is bottled. Carbon dioxide is added by one of two methods. The first method consists of adding a little more sugar to the brew before bottling. This allows a secondary fermentation to occur, converting the new sugar into alcohol and carbon dioxide. The carbon dioxide is unable to escape because it is locked in the bottle by the bottle cap. This method allows for a little yeast, called *lees*, to be left at the bottom of the bottle. The second method consists of injecting the wort with carbon dioxide. After a little sugar has been added or the carbon dioxide has been injected, the altered wort is bottled and sealed with a bottle cap. This captures the extra carbon dioxide, keeping it in the bottle.

Fining and Clarifying

Fining and clarifying agents often are used in brewing because the yeast and some of the residue from the grains are left in the beer, making the beer cloudy. This cloudiness does not affect the taste or wholesomeness of the beer, but it does affect the appearance. A clarifying or fining agent is used to remove this sediment, and a crystal-clear beer is the result.

Traditional clarifying agents such as Irish Moss and gelatin are still used today, but modern filters are now used to clarify commercially produced beer.

Aging

After fermentation, the beer, which is known as *green beer*, is placed in an aging tank, barrel, or bottles, and it is aged for up to two months. Beer is aged for several reasons. First, aging permits the newly fermented beer to mature and develop smooth, desirable flavors. Ales generally need to age at least ten to fourteen days, whereas lagers need a minimum of 21 days. Smaller breweries and home brewers sometimes allow the green beer to age in the bottle, which is why this beer has sediment at the bottom. Beer that has sediment in the bottle is referred to as beer "resting on the lees."

Packaging

Beer generally is packaged in bottles, cans, kegs and barrels. Bottles come in all shapes and sizes. Most are similar to a small wine bottle with a bottle cap, but some bottles may even be closed with a cork. Beer bottles with corks are opened the same way sparkling wine bottles are opened (see Chapter 17). Cans look similar to old soda cans that had pull tabs on top. There is no international standard

Figure 14.2 Barrels are used to age beer as well as package beer for transport. [Dorling Kindersley Images]

size for cans. United States beer producers most often use 12-ounce cans, but they use 16-ounce cans as well. Other countries can beer in Imperial pints (20 ounces). Some of these beers are imported into the United States.

Barrels and kegs (also known as half-barrels) are nothing more than very large cans of beer. A barrel holds 31 gallons of beer, and a keg holds 15.5 gallons. They can be *tapped*, or opened, so that many people can enjoy beer in glasses or cups. Kegs usually have a manually controlled spout that can open and close at the touch of a button. Kegs are very popular with large groups because they are safer and more convenient than bottles or cans, and they are less expensive than purchasing individual beers. There is also less waste because the beer in the keg is not exposed to air, allowing it to stay fresh longer.

Regardless of the packaging, beer is usually enjoyed from a glass so the drinker can enjoy the aroma of the beer. In addition, when beer is drunk from a bottle or can, the beer sloshes back and forth each time the drinker tips the vessel to take a drink. Each time this movement happens, the beer loses quite a bit of the carbon dioxide. By the time the drinker gets to the bottom of the bottle or can, the remaining beer has gone flat. While beer does slide in a glass, beer in a glass is less disturbed and retains its fizz.

Brewing Ingredients

The ingredient that determines whether beer is lager or ale is the type of yeast used in the fermentation process. A brewer could mix a wort, split it in half and make ale out of one half and a lager out of the other half simply by using different yeast.

Yeast

Ale yeast (*Saccharomyces cerevisiae*) is referred to as *top fermenting* because the yeast works at the top of the fermentation tank. Ale is fermented between 55° and 75°F. because cooler temperatures will stop the fermentation process. Ale yeast is the same kind used for making bread.

Lager yeast (*Saccharomyces uvarum*, formerly known as *Saccharomyces carlsbergensis*), on the other hand, is referred to *bottom fermenting* because it works at the bottom of the fermentation tank. Lager yeast functions at lower temperatures than ale yeast, between 32° and 55°F. It is possible to create a beer with lager yeast at higher temperatures with good results, but the "smoothness" expected from a lager is hard to achieve without the lower temperatures.

Yeast strains vary somewhat from one area to another. The yeast found in France, for example, is not exactly like the yeast found in the United States, New Zealand, or Japan. The differences in regional yeast is very slight, but the minor differences in yeast can cause major differences in the final product. The yeast

Figure 14.3 Beer is composed of water with flavoring, alcohol, and carbon dioxide. [Dorling Kindersley Images]

used to make Pilsner comes from Eastern Europe, but brewers in the United States can order and use this yeast to produce their beer. The result will be a beer that has many of the characteristics of a classic Pilsner made in the town of Pilsen in the Czech Republic.

Water

Even though yeast determines whether the beer is an ale or a lager, water is the most important element of beer, simply because beer is approximately 90 percent water. Water is a molecule string of two hydrogen and one oxygen molecule (H_2O). In one sense, water is a simple molecule, but it is complex because it carries minerals that can benefit or harm the final product. The types of minerals or flavors water carries is dependent on the water's source. According to *Fearless Brewing: The Beer Maker Bible*, if the water is safe for human consumption and free of metal, iron, and chlorine flavors, the water is good for making beer.

Water with a high mineral content is called "hard," while water with low mineral content is called "soft." Each type of water is good for making a certain style of beer. If certain minerals exist in the water, the minerals can make it more conducive to certain types of beer production. For example, if a high amount of gypsum (calcium sulfate) is present, the water would be good for producing Pale Ale. If the gypsum content is low, the water would be good for Pilsner. If the gypsum content falls somewhere between these two levels, the product would be similar to a standard American or German beer. However, there are other minerals to consider when making beer. Chloride, for example, accentuates the malty character in the flavor of beer. Another important mineral in brewing beer is calcium. Calcium has three functions: (1) it helps extract sugar from the grain which helps with fermentation, (2) it discourages color transfer from the grain to the wort in lighter beers, and (3) it discourages tannin transfer from the grain to the wort. If a brewer does not have the correct type of water to make a specific type of beer, the brewer needs to add minerals to the water to achieve the desired result.

Malt

Malt refers to a kernel or seed of grain that has been exposed to water. When the grain is exposed to water, the natural growth process begins, and the starches in the seed convert to sugars. These are the sugars that are used by the yeast during fermentation to produce alcohol. When the seed begins to sprout, its growth is stopped by applying heat, which is a process known as *roasting*. A malted grain can be roasted for as long as the brewer desires. It can be roasted just enough to stall the growth of the seed, which is called a *pale malt*, to a dark, almost burned, color called *black malt*. When the roasting continues past pale malt to produce golden brown malt, it is called *crystal malt*. The roasting can continue longer to produce *chocolate malt*, and, finally, *black malt*. The choice of particular malt gives the beer its color and some of its flavor. It is a misconception that all lagers are pale and that all ales are dark; malts can be combined in varying amounts to achieve endless combinations of color and flavor profiles.

The only roast that does not add flavor to the final beer is black malt. It is used chiefly for coloring the beer. As its name implies, black malt is roasted to a dark brown that is almost black. Black malt is used sparingly because in larger doses it can contribute a burned flavor to the beer. The difference between black malt and chocolate malt is that chocolate malt is not roasted quite as long. This allows the chocolate malt to add a sweet, almost chocolate flavor to the beer.

The malt used in beer making can be produced from any grain, including wheat, rye, and oatmeal, but barley is usually the grain of choice. Some of the malts brewers use include Dextrine (Cara-Pils) Malt, Mild Malt, Vienna Malt, and Munich Malt. Dextrine Malt gives the final product a light color, but it does not help with head retention on the beer. Mild Malt, Vienna Malt, and Munich Malt all give an amber color to beer. Vienna Malt and Munich Malt both are German-style malts that contain *enzymes*—small organic proteins—that act as catalysts in increasing the rate of chemical reactions. A single enzyme can process up to a million reactions a second. Crystal malt, chocolate malt, and black malt do not contain enzymes.

Crystal malt gets its name from what happens to the sugar in the malt upon drying. Warm sugar is in a liquid state, but as it cools, the sugar crystallizes. Most people think of crystal as clear or white, but crystal malt is actually produced in three different shades: light, medium, and dark. Crystal malt is made from *green malt*, or malt that has germinated but not roasted. Crystal malt is not dried the same way as most other malts. It will give beer a gold to red color in the final product and with the head retention of the beer.

Hops

Hops, a cone-shaped blossom, comes from a climbing vine in the cannabis family. Hops give beer its bitter, dry, almost tannic taste. Hops are not necessary for the production of beer, but there are practical reasons that brewers add hops. Hops balance the sugar in a beer's flavor and act as a preservative and an antiseptic, allowing a beer to survive many months beyond its natural shelf life. Hops also are used to add flavor and aroma to beer.

Hops, like apples or wheat, come in many varieties, and each variety gives a different taste and quality to the brew. Hops are divided in two main groups: (1) boiling, or bittering, hops and (2) finishing, or aromatic, hops. These two types of hops are applied at different times during the production process, depending on what type of beer the brewer is trying to produce.

Boiling, or bittering, hops are added during the first boil of the wort (beer stock) and are boiled to release resins, which give beers their bitter flavor. Finishing, or aromatic, hops are added at the end of the boil when the wort is still warm. These also are known as aromatic hops because these they give beer its distinctive aroma.

Figure 14.4 Hops on the vine. This flower-like plant is used to flavor as well as preserve beer. [Dorling Kindersley Images]

Adjuncts

Adjunct grains are highly fermentable grains containing a great deal of starch that is converted to sugar during the brewing process. Adjuncts are unmalted grains that produce both the milder flavor and lighter color preferred by the American public. The large companies that produce American-style lagers use adjunct grains to achieve a beer with milder flavor than European imports. The two most common adjunct grains are rice and corn, but wheat and barley also can serve as adjuncts.

Figure 14.5 Roles are reversed in the Garden of Eden with Adam offering Eve a beer. This ale was almost banned when it was first imported into the United States because of the suggestive nature of the label. [Dorling Kindersley Images]

Pilsner Malt. [Dorling Kindersley Images]

Vienna Malt. [Dorling Kindersley Images]

Munich Malt. [Dorling Kindersley Images]

Crystal Malt. [Dorling Kindersley Images]

Roasted Barley. [Dorling Kindersley Images]

Chocolate Malt. [Dorling Kindersley Images]

Oats. [Dorling Kindersley Images]

Rye. [Dorling Kindersley Images]

Wheat. [Dorling Kindersley Images]

Green hops, a twining peren-
nial with heart-shaped leaves.
[Philip Dowell/Dorling Kindersley Media Library]

The Harveys brewery, in Sussex, England, takes
pride in using hops from its own county's tiny out-
put, as well as those from across the line in Kent. Here
different kinds of hops are displayed/stored in sacks.
[Dorling Kindersley Media Library]

In the process of making beer, hops are added to
the brewkettle. In this instance, pressed "blossom" or "leaf" hops are being used, as opposed
to pellets or the jam-like extract. [Dorling Kindersley Media Library]

The Two Types of Beer

In the beer family, there are two main branches: ale and lager. The colors, flavors, and aromas of beer can be the same regardless of whether the beer is an ale or lager, but the yeast in the products is different. Ale yeast is a top-fermenting yeast, and lager yeast is a bottom-fermenting yeast. Within the two major classifications of beer, there are minor classifications. Each of these minor classifications has a specific quality that makes the beer unique.

Ale

While not always true, ale generally comes from countries that have moderate to warm weather, such as France, Great Britain, and Belgium. Some of the beers that fall into this category follow:

Abbey Beers—Abbey beers are strong beers that were brewed by Cistercian monks in Belgium for many years. These beers are now brewed by commercial companies under license from religious communities. The beer usually is named for a church or a saint. Everything about this beer varies from producer to producer.

Altbier—*Alt* is the German word for "old" or "traditional." This ale is brewed in the old German style. Altbier is heavy in hops and barley and has a bitter flavor and a reddish-brown or copper color. Altbier contains about 4.5 percent alcohol.

Figure 14.6 Kwak is an ale that was masterfully marketed by the producers. It is always served with a wooden stand in a glass that will not stand up by itself (not shown) so other patrons in the bar will notice the beer being served. [Dorling Kindersley Images]

Figure 14.7 Three different bottles of beer. [Dorling Kindersley Images]

Barley Wine—This beer, once known as "Stingo," is very high in alcohol. (Barley wine is technically beer because it is made from grain and not fruit.) Barley wine almost rivals wine in alcohol content, ranging between 10 and 14 percent alcohol.

Bière de Garde—Made in northwest France, this beer was originally produced in farmhouses. Many are sealed with corks, and they tend to be bolder in flavor than most ales and higher in alcohol.

Bitter—Bitter is British pub ale found in England and Wales. Hops and barley help make this ale bitter. It usually has a red or amber color and its alcohol level ranges from 3 to 5 percent, unless it is marked "Best" or "Special"; a higher alcohol range can be expected in these beers.

Brown Ale—Brown Ale has a sweet to bittersweet taste with undertones of malt. Belgium makes sweet and sour brown ale by slowly simmering the wort and adding special yeast. As its name suggests, this ale has a dark brown color and has become known as "Nut Brown Ale." It is low in alcohol compared to some other ales.

Cream Ale—This beer is an ale that is trying to mimic a pilsner-style lager beer. It looks like a pilsner and tastes like a pilsner, but it is ale. Sometimes this effect is achieved by mixing ale and lager. Cream ale is usually high in carbonation.

Duppel/Double—This is an example of an abbey beer from Belgium. The term is used to describe a dark beer with medium strength that can have up to double the alcohol content of most ales (about 7.5 to 8 percent).

Export—This is a term used to describe better quality beers that are sold in countries other than the one that produced the beer. When the term is used in Scotland, it refers to premium ales.

Faro—This is rarely produced today. Faro is a Belgian lambic-style beer (see below). It is often sweetened with fruit or sugar and/or seasoned with spices.

Framboise—Framboise is a raspberry-flavored lambic from Belgium. It has the character of a pink sparkling wine. This beer was very popular with Napoleon's army when they invaded Belgium on their way to Russia.

Gueuze—This is a blend of old and new lambic. Traditionally, Gueuze is not sweetened, filtered, or pasteurized. It should be rather sour in flavor with the aromas of apples and rhubarb. Many times, however, commercially produced Gueuze is all that it should not be: sweetened, filtered, and pasteurized.

Imperial (Russian) Stout—First made in England during the eighteenth century, this beer claimed the Imperial status because it was a favorite beer of Catherine the Great, the Empress of Russia. Imperial Stout is a very strong beer.

India Pale Ale (IPA)—This ale was originally made in England, most notably on Burton-on-Trent, and shipped to India. The only way that this beer would make the long journey was for the producer to add an abundance of hops. It became a favorite both of British troops in India and of their loved ones in the British Isles.

Irish Ale—Irish ale is a red ale that has its origins in Ireland. It is soft, very drinkable, and is also made as a lager. It was known as "ruby ale" when George Killian Letts brewed this special beer. Irish ale generally has about 4.5 percent alcohol.

Kolsch—This beer is very much like a pilsner, but its fruity taste reveals it is ale. It is made in Cologne, Germany, and has an alcohol level of about 5 percent.

Kriek—This is cherry-flavored beer, which gets its flavor from a secondary fermentation that is stimulated by the addition of cherries. It is named for a small cherry grown near Brussels. A brand name called Mort Subite, or "Sudden Death," has about 4.5 percent alcohol and is supposed to be for women only because of the light, sweet taste.

Lambic—*Lambic* is a general term for a Belgian beer that relies on a wild yeast for fermentation. These beers spontaneously ferment in the open air. Because of the addition of fruit, they have various fruit flavors, most notably raspberry and cherry.

Light Ale—*Light ale* is a British term indicating a weak beer that is light in strength and/or light in bitter.

Milk or Sweet Stout—The name *milk stout* was banned in Britain in 1946 because it implied the addition of milk. This is dark-colored beer with a medium-sweet flavor. It is high in lactic acid—thus the name milk stout—but low in alcohol.

Oatmeal Stout—Oatmeal is added to the roasted malt to make this stout. It is very dark in color and rich in flavor.

Old Ale—This is English beer that has been aged longer than traditional ales. It usually has a high alcohol content.

Oyster Stout—Some claim that this stout is the perfect accompaniment to oysters. Some brewers achieved this notoriety by actually adding oysters to the mash or the brew.

Porter—Invented in 1722 by Ralph Harwood, this ale is named for the porters who enjoyed drinking it. Porter has a deep color and a rich, bittersweet taste with a distinct bouquet of smoke and fruit. Porter is lower in alcohol than stout at only about 4.5 to 5.5 percent.

Real Ale—This name was devised by a British drinkers' consumer organization to describe ale that is not filtered or pasteurized. It is cask-conditioned and matured in a pub cellar.

Scotch Ale—Produced in Scotland, this rich, full-bodied ale is maltier in flavor than its English counterpart. Ale brewed in Belgium also is referred to as Scotch ale. It is powerful, rich ale with alcohol levels reaching about 7 to 10 percent.

Stout—Stout is a general term used to describe a dark, almost black-colored ale. The color comes from the malt, which is roasted until almost black. The malt produces several different types of stout, including imperial stout, milk or sweet stout, oatmeal stout and oyster stout.

Trappist—Five beers are made only by monks of the Trappist Order in Belgium. Theses beers are Chimay, Orval, Rochefort, Westmalle, and Westvleteren. These beers tend to be complex and spicy with a high amount of

Figure 14.8 Chimay, a beer made by Trappist Monks in Belgium. [Dorling Kindersley Images]

alcohol (about 7 to 10 percent). Some of these beers are dubbed *dupple* and *tripel* because of their high alcohol content.

Triple/Tripel—This is a term related to Belgian beer—specifically, abbey beer or Trappist beer. The term refers to the strongest beers in their class; the alcohol levels can be up to about 10 percent.

Weisse or Weizen (Wheat Beer)—This beer is made almost entirely from wheat malt. Wheat beer has about 5 to 6 percent alcohol. Generally *weisse* comes in *kristall* or *dunkel* (clear or dark).

Witbier—White wheat beer from Belgium was first produced in 1543. Brewers use about 50 percent wheat malt and add a variety of spices. The alcohol level varies between 5 and 7 percent.

Lager

Lager beers are brewed at lower temperatures than ales and the yeast ferments on the bottom of the fermentation tank. Lager beer traditionally is brewed in places that have relatively cold weather such as Germany, the Czech Republic, Wisconsin, and Colorado. The word *lager* comes from the word *lagern*. In German *lagern* means "to store." Lagers are best served cold between 38° and 45°F. These beers were introduced to the United States in 1840 by the Germans who developed them in the seventh century. Today lager makes up more than 90 percent of the beer produced in the United States.

The following section lists the main types of lagers.

Black Beer (Dark Beer)—Black beer is a dark lager that may have a bitter chocolate flavor. Black beer should not be confused with stout, which is ale.

Figure 14.9 A bottle of triple-fermented beer. [Dorling Kindersley Images]

Figure 14.10   A bottle of wheat beer. [Dorling Kindersley Images]

The malt is roasted darker than stout or other lagers to give color and flavor to the beer. Black beer has an alcohol level between 5 and 6 percent. **Bock**—*Bock*, or "billy goat" in German, is best served between 45° and 50°F. Bock was first produced in Einbeck, Germany (Lower Saxony), in about A.D. 1200. This beer is known for a full-bodied flavor and the sweet

Figure 14.11   A bottle of wheat beer. [Dorling Kindersley Images]

aftertaste of malt. Bock is strong beer with an alcohol level between 6.5 and 10 percent.

Dopplebock—Dopplebock is very similar to bock, but it has a higher alcohol content (not double as its name would indicate, however). An easy way to find these beers in the stores is to look at the names. Dopplebocks always end in *ator*. Examples of dopplebock include Celebrator, Fortunator, Kulminator, and Salvator. This beer's alcohol level ranges from 7.5 to 9 percent.

Dortmunder Beer—This beer was named for the town in which it originated: Dortmund, Germany. Known for high levels of malt and hops, dortmunder is golden in color. The beer is full-bodied with an alcohol level of about 5.5 percent.

Dry Beer—These lagers seem dry to the palate and have no aftertaste. Dry beer is produced so that most or all of the sugar is turned to alcohol; therefore, the beer has a high alcohol level. It was first produced in Germany for people with diabetes under the name *diat pils*. The Asahi Brewery in Japan first brewed it under the name *dry beer* in 1987.

Dunkel—This is a soft, brown, malty, German beer with about 4.5 percent alcohol.

Festbier—Festbier is a German beer made for festivals and includes many styles.

Eisbock (Ice Beer)—Eisbock, or "ice bock," is an extra potent bock. This beer is higher in alcohol than most bocks because the beer's temperature is lowered below 32 degrees Fahrenheit. This allows some of the water in the beer to form ice crystals, which are then skimmed off, leaving the alcohol. Alcohol levels range between 5.5 and 10 percent.

Kulmbacher Beer—This lager is named for the city in which the beer is produced: Kulmbach, Germany. Kulmbacher is best served between 38° and 45°F. It can have as much as 14 percent alcohol by volume.

Light Beer—This beer has a lighter taste and is lower in calories than "regular beer." A 12-ounce beer usually contains between 135 and 170 calories. Light beer has under 100 calories. This beer can be made by two methods: (1) by adding enzymes that lower the calories and alcohol content of the beer, or (2) by diluting regular beer that was fermented dry.

Mailbock—Mailbock is a bock beer that is used to celebrate the arrival of spring in Germany.

Malt Liquor—This is an American term for lager beer that has a high alcohol content. The malty flavor gives the lager its name. It tends to have some sweetness with overtones of bitterness. Malt liquor usually has between 6 and 8 percent alcohol by volume.

Marzenbier—"March beer" is brewed in March. This amber-colored brew usually is consumed by October or during Oktoberfest. It contains about 6 percent alcohol.

Munich—This beer is slightly darker in color than pilsner, but it is lighter and less bitter than most German beers. It originally was produced in Bavaria.

Oud Bruin—Oud bruin is a light, sweet Belgian lager.

Pilsner—First produced in 1842, Pilsner has become the most popular style of beer in the world. Pilsner is golden in color and contains high levels of hops. The flavor is crisp and clean. Generally a dry beer, pilsner usually contains about 5 percent alcohol. It is named for the Bohemian Czech town, Plzen, or "Pilsen," in German.

Rauchbier—Beechwood smoked malt is used to produce Rauchbier, which makes it different from all other beers. Rauchbier is amber to dark in color. The alcohol level ranges between 4.5 and 5.5 percent.

Steam Beer—Even though this is made with lager yeast, steam beer is fermented at ale temperatures. Brown-gold in color and almost sweet and sour in taste, steam beer has the flavors of orange peels, peaches and cloves. Steam beer's taste is similar to an ale. It was first made in San Francisco, California, during the Gold Rush of 1848. Only one brewery, Anchor Brewery, makes steam beer today. The alcohol level is 5 percent.

Ur-Bock (Urquell)—*Urquell* is German for "original source" and refers to the first in a style. Urquell is darker in color and fuller in body than bock beer; the alcohol level ranges from 4.5 to 7 percent.

Vienna Beer—Vienna beer was named for an amber-colored beer once brewed in Vienna. Anton Dreher, an Austrian brewing pioneer, was instrumental in founding this style. Vienna beer has a medium body with a forward malt flavor.

Figure 14.12 A stein of Pilsner.
[Dorling Kindersley Images]

Large-Scale Breweries

The Institute for Brewing Studies defines a large brewery as one that has sales that exceed 500,000 barrels a year. Since a barrel holds 31 gallons of beer, a large-scale producer sells in excess of 15,500,000 gallons of beer per year. Some well-known examples of large-scale breweries in the United States include:

Anheuser-Busch—California, Colorado, Florida, Georgia, Missouri, New Hampshire, New Jersey, New York, Ohio, Texas, Virginia.
Miller Brewing Company—California, Georgia, New York, North Carolina, Ohio, Texas, Wisconsin.
Coors—Colorado, Tennessee, Virginia.
Strohs Brewing Company—Florida, Michigan, Minnesota, North Carolina, Pennsylvania, Texas.
G. Heileman Brewing Company—Illinois, Maryland, Texas, Wisconsin.
Genessee Brewing Company—New York.
Blitz-Weinhard Brewing Company—Oregon.
Pittsburgh Brewing Company—Pennsylvania.
Latrobe Brewing Company—Pennsylvania.
Pearl Brewing Company/Pabst Brewing Company—Texas.
Pabst Brewing Company—Washington, Wisconsin.
Rainier Brewing Company—Washington.
Cerveceria India Inc.—Puerto Rico.

The beers that these major producers brew all fall within the same flavor profile, which is designed to appeal to a wide North American audience.

Microbrewers

Microbreweries became very popular in the late twentieth century. The first microbreweries set the stage for designer beer, and a few people who wanted to offer something different to American consumers took brewing to an art form. The beer these smaller producers make is based on many different flavor profiles that are as varied as the producers and the states in which they are found. The American public responded in a positive way, and, suddenly, small breweries were popping up all over the country.

The Institute for Brewing Studies listed more then 550 microbrewing companies making beer in the *1995–1996 North American Brewers Resource Directory*. This figure is up from only 40 in 1980. All fifty states, the District of Columbia, Puerto Rico, and the Marshall Islands now boast a regional brewery, microbrewery, brewpub, or contract brewer.

The Institute for Brewing Studies defines a regional brewer as one that has annual sales of between 15,000 and 500,000 barrels. A microbrewery has sales of less than 15,000 barrels. A brewpub is a brewery that sells at least 50 percent of its product on site. A contract brewer is one that has beer produced for it by another brewery.

Other Types of Brewed Beverages

Sake

The word *sake* means "the essence of the spirit of rice" in Japanese. Sake is a brewed beverage that is fermented from rice. It does not fall into the ale or lager category, but many still place it in the beer category. There are two camps of thought on what sake really is. Some think is a rice beer based on its ingredients and production process. The United States government, however, defines sake as wine that is from a source other than fruit. This also makes sense because the alcohol content of sake usually is between 12 and 17 percent, which is more like wine. With the exception of Nigori, sake does not contain carbon dioxide, which is integral to its ale and lager cousins. This lack of effervescence allows sake to be stored in the refrigerator for up to six weeks after opening. In addition, sake, unlike either beer or wine, traditionally is served between 100° and 110°F. Sake also can be served at room temperature or on the rocks, depending on the style and grade.

Sake comes in several styles and grades:

Futsu-shu—This is the most commonly consumed sake; it is also the lowest grade. It is best if served warm.

Honjozo-Shu—This sake is a step up from Futsu-shu in grade, flavor and body. It may be served warm or cold.

Junmai-Shu—This sake is named "pure rice" because it is made from only rice, water, and yeast. Being of higher quality, it should be served at room temperature or cold.

Koji-Shu—This grade is usually served as an aperitif because it is very rich and sweet. The sweetness is achieved by the brewer substituting some of the water used in the brewing process with sake.

Mirin—This style of sake is used for cooking. The name means "taste sweet."

Toso—This style is used for celebrating the New Year. It is aged in wooden barrels and has a spicy sweet flavor. It is full in body and darker in color than other sakes.

Genshu—Most sake is best served diluted with water. This sake, however, is best served on the rocks because of its high alcohol content, which is 18 percent.

Nigori—This style of sake is semi-refined and may or may not be filtered. This style is often served after meals; it is sweet and usually sparkling.

Namazake—This is unpasteurized sake. When you open the bottle, plan to drink it within several days because it will turn quickly. The flavor is tart and fresh.

Seishu or Ama-Kara-Ping—This name means "sweet, lightly bitter, with a delightful effect."

Ginjo—*Ginjo* means "superior" and refers to some of the highest grades of sake.

Dai-Ginjo—*Dai-Ginjo* means "super premium" and refers to sake of the highest grade.

Mead

Mead is honey wine or a beverage fermented from honey water. Mead is brewed just like beer or sake, but it falls into the wine category because of its higher alcohol content. Mead usually ranges between 8 and 12 percent in alcohol, but the alcohol level can be as high as 14 percent. The color can range from clear to golden, and flavors range from very sweet to very dry. Mead could have been one of the first fermented beverages produced by man. This drink definitely dates back to the ancient Greek, Egyptian, Inca, and Aztec cultures.

Mead was an important and popular drink during the fifth and sixth centuries. According to Charlie Papazian in *The New Complete Joy of Home Brewing*, during this time, the custom of the honeymoon was started. The newlywed couple would be offered a month's—a moon's—supply of mead. It was believed that if the couple consumed the mead for a month after the wedding, it would help produce a male child, which was an important factor in carrying on the family name.

Key Terms

Lager	Yeast
Ale	Water
Sake	Hops
Top fermenting	Malt
Bottom fermenting	

Study Questions

1. Is sake wine or beer? Justify your answer.
2. Why is water so important in beer making?
3. What are hops and why are they important to beer making?
4. What is malt and how is it produced?

Chapter
15

Distillation and Distilled Spirits

After reading this chapter, you will be able to:

❐ Explain the process of distillation.
❐ Explain how different ingredients react to distillation.
❐ Discuss the science of distillation.
❐ Explain how different alcohols are distilled.
❐ Explain the meaning of double and triple distillation.
❐ Discuss the differences between clear and brown distilled spirits.
❐ Discuss clear spirits such as fruit brandy, aquavit, arak, marc, gin, mescal tequila, rum, and vodka.
❐ Discuss aged spirits such as brandy and whiskey.
❐ Discuss liqueurs.

The Arabs produced a cosmetic through distillation, which harem women used as eye makeup. This was called al-kohl *from which the word alcohol is derived.*
—Mr. Boston, in Official Bartender's and Party Guide

Yeast and fermentation can only go so far in the production of alcohol from a starch or sugar filled liquid. Yeast will only produce about 10 to 15 percent alcohol by volume if all of the conditions are right. After that, the yeast is spent and alcohol production ceases. Therefore, another process must come into play to produce beverages with a higher alcohol content. This process is distillation.

Distillation

Distillation is simply a reduction. A *reduction* is a liquid that has been boiled until the volume is reduced by evaporation. Distillation will not change the flavor of a liquid; it concentrates it and increases the alcohol content. Many distilled spirits derive their name from the Latin phrase *aqua vitae*, meaning "water of life." Examples include the French drink *eau de vie*, the Scandinavian *aquavit*, and even whiskey.

The distillation process begins by placing an alcoholic liquid, such as wine or beer, into a still. A still is basically a large cooking pot that has a cylindrical at-

Figure 15.1 Alcohol boils at 173.1°F. This still has a place for a fire to be built to bring liquid inside up to at least 180°F. The alcohol steam flows up the tube and then cools on its way down into a container that catches the concentrated alcohol. [Dorling Kindersley Images/The Welcome Institute/The Science Museum London]

tachment on the top with a tube running out of the cylinder. The liquid in the still is heated to a temperature between 180° to 190°F. because alcohol changes to a vapor at temperatures over 173.1°F. (Water doesn't change into a vapor or steam until it reaches 212°F.) The vapor from the alcohol rises and is forced up the cylindrical lid and into the tube. The alcohol vapor cools as it travels through the tube away from the still and it condenses back into liquid alcohol. Some water, as steam, also makes the trip from one side of the still to the other. During the first distillation, the alcohol level of the liquid at least doubles. If, for example, a fermented beverage is 12 percent alcohol before it is distilled, the distillation concentrates the alcohol to approximately 24 percent alcohol.

The process can be repeated many times over to achieve very high levels of alcohol and smoothness in the palatability of the alcohol. Most of the time, the bottle will be marked "double distilled" or "triple distilled" if the alcohol was distilled more than once.

All distilled spirits begin as the clear distillation or concentration of alcohol from a fermented liquid such as wine or beer. The finished spirit may remain clear, or it may become gold to golden-brown in color, depending on how it is aged or treated after distillation. Clear spirits, such as vodka and rum, can be bottled right after distillation. Spirits with a gold to golden-brown hue are aged in a charred wood barrel.

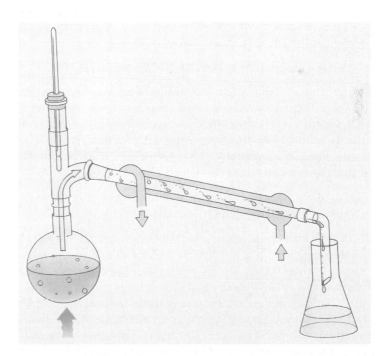

Figure 15.2   The distillation process. [Dorling Kindersley Images]

Distillation of Beer

If a grain or combination of different grains are mashed together, allowed to ferment, and then distilled, the resulting product is concentrated alcohol. How the liquid is handled after distillation will determine the type of alcohol it becomes. In the early stages, grain mash is processed as if it were beer. The mash takes about three to five days of fermentation to achieve approximately 8 to 9 percent alcohol, then it is distilled. The alcohol that results from the first distillation is called *low wine*. The low wine is distilled again, which results in *high wine*. The high wine is crystal clear and ready to be put in toasted oak barrels if the product is going to be aged. In the case of whiskey, only once the high wine has been aged in oak can the alcoholic beverage be called whiskey (with the exception of corn whiskey). If the distilled product is not going to be aged, it is ready for bottling.

Distillation of Wine

Some of the most famous spirits are distillations of wine. Cognac, possibly the most famous brandy, is made from Trebbiano wine in the Cognac region in France. The older cousin to cognac, armagnac, is similar to cognac but has several characteristics that are unique, including being aged in a different type of oak.

Apple wine can be distilled into "Applejack" or apple brandy. Applejack is similar to Calvados, another apple brandy. Distilled strawberry wine is Fraise, and distilled raspberry wine becomes Framboise. These are just a few examples of the types of spirits that can be created from distilling wine.

Distillation of Other Fermented Beverages

Anything that contains sugar can ferment and become alcohol and then be distilled. Therefore, any starch or sugar item can, under the right conditions, become alcohol. Distillers have used many obscure mashes to make concentrated alcohol. Tequila is made from the fermented juice of a cactus-like plant called agave. Vodka is distilled from grain or the fermented juice of potatoes, and rum is distilled from fermented sugar cane juice.

Double and Triple Distillation

Sometimes it takes more than one distillation to achieve the desired alcohol content of a specific spirit. If a spirit goes through two or three distillations, the alcohol content can go up by 40, 50, and even 95 percent. Scotch, a type of whisky, is double distilled. Irish whiskey is distilled three times. The grain alcohol marketed as pure grain alcohol is distilled many times before reaching 190 proof (95 percent alcohol by volume). The 190-proof grain alcohol is the highest alcohol level available on the market and has very limited use because of the dangers involved with an alcohol that is so concentrated. A 100 percent pure alcohol level is achieved by evaporating all of the water from a liquid and can only be reached in laboratory

Need Proof...Here It Is ....

The term proof comes from Old English. If a buyer or seller wanted to prove the content of alcohol in a distilled beverage they would mix the beverage with gunpowder. Once lit, the gunpowder/alcohol mixture would burn a slow blue flame. The beverage that would do this was always 50 percent alcohol by volume, or 100 proof. If the alcohol content was lower, the gunpowder would have trouble burning. If the alcohol content was higher, the gunpowder would flame up. Currently the scale of proof tops out at 200 proof.

or industrial conditions. Even under these conditions the liquid will evaporate very quickly.

Distilling: An Environmentalist's Dream

The products and by-products of fermentation and distillation are environmentally clean, nontoxic, and pure. For example, the carbon dioxide produced during fermentation is natural and does not harm the environment. It can be collected and recycled for use to carbonate drinking water or soda. Leftover mash can be sold for cattle feed. Grape skins, stems and seeds can be used as mulch. Even the excess yeast can be used for various things currently produced that need yeast as an ingredient. The only product that might be seen as harmful is the alcohol itself, but alcohol is only harmful when it is used in excess.

Non-Aged Spirits

Non-aged spirits are fermented, distilled, and bottled without being aged in wood barrels. They are, with some key exceptions, less expensive than their aged counterparts because the producer does not incur the additional barrel and storage costs attached to aged beverages. However, this is beginning to change with vodka and gin, which are in high demand. Known as "clears" in the trade, this category includes gin, vodka, clear or colorless rum, and aquavit.

Several factors can increase the price of non-aged spirits. The cost of advertising is one such factor. This cost is passed along to the customer in the price of the bottle. Beverage producers may also limit the production of alcohol to small batches to increase the quality, and price. By limiting production, the producers increase the amount of time it takes them to make the same amount of spirits they would if they mass produced the drink. The cost of the additional labor is passed on to the customer in the price of the bottle.

With very few exceptions, clear spirits are distilled and sold at a minimum of 80 proof (40 percent alcohol by volume). This high proof allows the spirit to be chilled below 32°F. without freezing. In fact, many of the clear spirits are better if they are served this cold.

Aquavit

Aquavit is made with a potato mash and filtered in charcoal. Aquavit also goes by the name of schnapps, which comes from a Nordic verb, *snappen*. Snappen describes how aquavit traditionally is drunk: snatched or seized and downed in one gulp. Even though many think of schnapps as a sweet fruit or peppermint-flavored spirit, aquavit may also be flavored with aniseed, fennel, cumin, caraway, dill, or bitter orange. Aquavit is best served very cold.

Arak and Raki

Arak and *raki* are general terms used to describe a distilled spirit with up to 50 percent alcohol. Bottles labeled with either of these terms can contain spirits that are made with figs, dates, raisins, or plums. They should be sipped because of their strength, and they should be chilled like aquavit. Arak or raki, or something very similar to these, may have been the first distilled spirit and probably originated in India or China between 800 B.C. and 1000 B.C.

Figure 15.3 A bottle of Aquavit. [Dorling Kindersley Images]

Eau de Vie

Eau de vie is the general French term for fruit brandy. Eau de vie can be made from almost any berry and from pears or plums. The specific name of the spirit is determined by which fruit the spirit is produced from. For example, *eau de vie* made from raspberries is known as Framboise. If the drink is made from strawberries, it is known as Fraise. Pears lend their name to Poire, and cherry brandy is known as Kirsch. One of the most important things to remember is that *eau de vie* is made directly from these fruits; it is not a fruit-flavored brandy made from grapes.

Gin

Gin starts as a neutral spirit but takes most of its flavor from juniper berries, which are added after distillation. Its name comes from either the French word for juniper, genievere, or the Dutch word for juniper, genever. Each gin producer has a very different recipe for the final product. In addition to the juniper berries, producers also are known to add lemon peel, orange peel, fennel or anise, almonds, cardamom pods, coriander seeds, caraway seeds, angelica, and orrisroot.

Even though gin is associated most frequently with England, it was made first in Holland as a medicine by Franciscus de la Boe (1614–1672). He used gin to treat people with kidney and bladder problems. For this reason, gin traditionally can be found as both "Dutch gin" and "Holland gin" in addition to "London dry gin." The differences between London dry gin and Dutch gin are that (1) London gin is distilled to a higher proof than Dutch gin; (2) London gin starts with a mixture of grains that feature more barley than any other grain, while Dutch gin contains a mixture of barley, malt, rye; and (3) London dry gin is not as sweet as Dutch gin.

Today gin also can be flavored with various citrus flavors such as lemon, lime or orange. It is the main component of the Tom Collins, Gin Fizz, Gimlet, and the Gin Martini.

Marc

Marc is produced from the leftovers of a French vineyard. Once the grapes have been squeezed and the juice is on its way to becoming wine, the skins, stems, and seeds are set aside to ferment. The alcohol that is produced from these products is distilled into a beverage known as marc. Marc also is known as *grappa* if it is produced in Italy or California. Most of this spirit, regardless of the name, is non-aged and clear. If it is aged, it will appear golden to golden brown. Many times this spirit is consumed *neat*, or without ice or mixers, after a meal to aid digestion.

Rum

Rum is distilled raw sugar cane juice. Rum producers use as many different raw sugar products to make rum as sugar producers use to make sugar. Rum producers can use sugar cane, sugar cane syrup, or molasses. Once the juice of the sugar

Figure 15.4 A bottle of rum. [Dorling Kindersley Images]

plant is extracted, it is boiled to evaporate some of the water. The resulting juice is then fermented for several days and distilled twice to a very high proof. When rum is bottled, it sometimes has to be combined with distilled water to bring the proof down to 80 proof (40 percent alcohol) from 180 proof (90 percent alcohol).

Rum is aged for a minimum of one year in glass, stainless steel, or non-charred oak barrels for it to remain clear. Rum also can be aged in charred barrels, but then it falls into the category of an aged spirit. If rum is aged in wood, it takes on a golden hue. Rum is primarily a Caribbean liquor with many of the islands producing their own styles of the beverage. The Puerto Rican style of rum is the lightest in body and flavor. Puerto Rico produces both non-aged and aged rums. Jamaican and Cuban rums tend to be aged and full-bodied. Rum is also produced in Mexico, Canada, and Australia.

Many of the names of rum make reference to the British navy, which used this alcoholic beverage as a standard ration (a half pint per sailor, per day) until 1970.

Tequila

Tequila is an alcohol that comes from fermenting and distilling the cooked sap of the blue agave plant, which is a close relative to the aloe plant. In recent years, the price of tequila has risen because of the demand for this spirit and the inability of producers to keep up with production. The blue agave plant takes between eight and twelve years to mature, which makes the situation even more difficult for producers.

Figure 15.5 The sap from the agava plant makes the base for Tequila. [Dorling Kindersley Images]

The cooked sap, which is known to the producers as *aquamiel* (honey water), is gathered and allowed to ferment before it is double distilled. Tequila is the spirit used in Margaritas and, of course, Tequila Sunrises. It can have a golden hue, which suggests barrel aging, but Tequila that is barrel-aged makes up a very small part of the market.

Mescal and Tequila

Mescal is a close relative to Tequila, but Tequila is considered the superior beverage. Both are made from a form of the agave plant (Tequila is made from the superior blue agave plant while Mescal is mostly made from the green agave) and both are made in Mexico. While Tequila and mescal have these similarities, they also have several distinguishing qualities. For example, mescal can be distilled once while tequila is always distilled twice. Mescal also has a worm at the bottom of the bottle while tequila does not. In addition, mescal can be made anywhere in Mexico, but tequila is made in the region known as Tequila, Mexico. Unlike most tequila, mescal is sometimes aged in wood, which gives it a golden color.

Vodka

Vodka can be made from almost anything that will ferment. Some producers use grains such as corn, wheat, rye, or barley. They also can use potatoes, beets, grapes, or sugar cane. According to United States standards, the final product must be void of a "distinctive" taste, color, aroma or character. Vodka's lack of

Figure 15.6 The agave plant is harvested after 8–10 years. The agave plant produces only one harvest during its life, unlike the grapevine, which produces one harvest per year. The agave plant's sap makes the base for both Tequila and Mescal. [Dorling Kindersley Images]

Figure 15.7 Three bottles of Russian vodka. [Dorling Kindersley Images]

Figure 15.8 A bottle of flavored Russian vodka. [Dorling Kindersley Images]

flavor makes it a good spirit to mix with strongly flavored liquids such as orange, tomato, and cranberry juice.

Vodka is run through an activated charcoal filter to heighten its purity and lack of flavor. It usually is served very cold and bottles may be kept in a freezer or an ice mold. Once distilled, vodka is ready to be bottled and consumed. Vodka is identified with Poland and Russia, where it may have been invented by Italian monks sometime in the thirteenth century. Vodka also is made in Finland, Sweden, and the United States.

In recent years, vodka producers have added flavors to their products such as mandarin orange, lemon, and pepper. In addition, vodka has begun to be produced in small batches. These small batches are marketed as high quality, super-premium vodkas.

Aged Spirits

After the distillation process, a spirit is clear and looks similar to water. If the producer ages this clear alcohol in a wood barrel, the wood imparts color, flavor, and body to the spirit. Air also can impart color, flavor and body to alcohol. When alcohol is oxidized, it may cause wine and beer to spoil, but it can also mellow spirits.

The aging process for distilled beverages usually takes two years at the minimum, but it can last as many as twenty years or more. The bottle is usually marked as to how long the spirit was aged in the barrel, rather than when the beverage was produced. For example, a twelve-year-old bourbon might be fifteen years old because it has sat on a shelf for three years, then was aged for twelve years in an oak barrel.

The additional time this spirit sits in the barrel costs the producer money because the producer is unable to recoup the costs on its investment during that time. In addition, the producer incurs storage costs and product loss caused by evaporation. For these reasons, aged spirits can command a relatively high price. Another factor that can cause the price of aged spirits to rise is the reputation of the producer.

Brandy

Brandy is distilled wine. It is a sipping drink that usually is served in a short-stemmed, bowl-shaped glass called a *snifter*. The bowl of this glass is meant to be cradled in the hand, which warms the brandy slightly. The glass also can be swirled to help release the aroma.

Almost any country that makes wine makes brandy. Some good examples of clear brandy, such as Pisco, are found in Peru and Chile. This brandy is aged in wood, but the barrels are usually so old that they lend no color to the alcohol.

Most other brandies have the golden-brown hue of an alcoholic beverage aged in oak barrels. Some brandies even have a rating system that allows the customer to know what they are paying when the customer looks at the label. There are certain criteria a brandy has to meet to be included in each category. In France and the United States, brandy producers use letters to make quality statements about the brandies they are producing (see Table 15.1).

Spain and France (which has cognac and armagnac) are the only countries to have an appellation or region that controls the production of brandy. The Spanish government declared a denominacion especifica (DE) for Brandy de Jerez in 1987. There are three levels of this Spanish brandy: (1) Brandy de Jerez Solera, (2) Brandy de Jerez Solera Reserva, and (3) Brandy de Jerez Solera Gran Reserva. As the names indicate, the Spanish use the solera system for rating brandy.

Figure 15.9 A bottle of Brandy. [Dorling Kindersley Images]

Table 15.1 Cognac Labeling System

Letter Used on the Label	Meaning
E	Extra
O	Old
P	Pale
S	Special or Superior
V	Very
X	Extremely

Greece also makes brandy called *metaxa*. The Greeks use a star system to indicate the quality of metaxa. A rating of three, five, and seven stars indicate the best quality metaxa. Seven Star Metaxa, which is the best, is aged for up to fifty years in the barrel.

Cognac

The word *Cognac* refers to the area in which the brandy is made—in and around the city of Cognac in western France. The Cognac region is located above Bordeaux on the west side of France. This distilled wine starts with three types of grapes: St. Émilion, also known as Ugni Blanc and Trebbiano; Folle Blanche; and Colombard. These three grapes must make up 90 percent of the final product. The other 10 percent can come from five other grape varieties: Blanc Rame, Jurancon Blanc, Montils, Sémillon, and Select.

Figure 15.10 Two bottles of Cognac. [Dorling Kindersley Images]

The soil near Cognac is very chalky, which contributes to a high acidity level of the grapes as they finish maturing. The harvest comes when the grapes reach 17 percent brix. The wine produced from these grapes has about 8 percent alcohol. The wine then is distilled twice and placed in barrels made from limousine oak. A single distillation of Cognac is then blended with other cognac to achieve the final product.

Table 15.2 illustrates the various designations that may be found on a Cognac label.

Other designations indicate where the grapes were grown. For example, there are six growing regions in Cognac. A label may refer to Grande Champagne or Petite Champagne (these are considered the best growing areas). The terms used to describe these two growing regions should not be confused with the Champagne region which is located in northeast France about 90 miles from Paris.

Armagnac

First produced in 1422, Armagnac is the oldest type of brandy. Like Cognac, Armagnac takes its name from the region in which it is made. The grapes used to produce Armagnac are similar to those used for cognac. Armagnac producers use St. Émillion, Colombard, Folle Blanche, and Baco Blanc grapes. Armagnac also has a rating system very similar to that for cognac (see Table 15.3).

There are some significant differences between Armagnac and Cognac. For instance, Armagnac is made in one slow, continuous distillation process, and Cognac is made with two distillations. Another difference is that Armagnac is aged in black oak, whereas Cognac is aged in limousine oak.

Calvados

Calvados is a French brandy made from apples. Other apple brandies include Applejack (United States), apple brandy (United Kingdom), cider brandy (United Kingdom), and batzi (Switzerland). Calvados is produced in Normandy in northwest France as well as other regions such as Brittany. It was first made in Normandy by Gilles de Gouberville in 1553, but Calvados did not claim its name until 1588 when a Spanish ship, the El Salvador, sank off of the Norman coast. Calvados was named for the ship.

Table 15.2 Cognac Label Designations

Letters on the Label	Quality Rating	Minimum Age of Brandy in Blend	Average Age of Blend
VS	Three Star	2½ years old	5 to 9 years old
VO or VSOP	Four Star	4 years old	12 to 20 years old
XO*	Five Star	6½ years old	20 to 50 years old

*XO cognac also can be labeled with some of the following terms: extra, Napoleon, VVOSP, cordon bleu, vieille reserve, grande reserve, royal, and vieux.

Figure 15.11 Bottles of Armagnac. [Dorling Kindersley Images]

Calvados is produced when the apples are harvested in the fall. They are crushed and allowed to ferment in oak barrels until a hard cider is formed. The liquid is about 6 percent alcohol at this point; it then is distilled twice to about 80 proof. Calvados must be aged for no less than one year in limousine oak. A vintage is declared occasionally. When it is, a date appears on the label, which is the date of the year after the harvest.

Just as with cognac, Calvados uses letters and words as quality statements on the label so that customers can understand the level of quality they are purchasing.

Whiskey (or Whisky)

Whiskey is a general term referring to a distilled spirit that comes from grain. Most of the time the spirit comes from barley or corn, but whiskey also can come from wheat and rye or a combination of these grains. Essentially, whiskey is distilled beer that has been aged in oak barrels. Most of the time it is distilled twice

Table 15.3 Armagnac Label Designations

Letters on the Label	Rating	Minimum Age
VS	Three Star	3 years old
VSOP or VO	Four Star	4 years old
XO*	Five Star	6 years old
Hors d'Age	Five Star	10 years old

* Extra, Napoleon, and vieille reserve are also terms that are used on the label.

Table 15.4   Calvados Label Designations

Letters on the Label	Minimum Age of Calvados in the Bottle
Three Stars	2 years
Reserve or vieux	3 years
Vieille reserve or VO	4 years
Grande reserve or VSOP	5 years
Extra, Napoleon, or Hors d'age	6 years

before it is placed in the barrels. The aging process can last as little as two years, but it can also last for several decades before the whiskey is released for sale.

Whiskey includes Scotch, Bourbon, Tennessee whiskey, Irish whiskey, and Canadian whisky. Each of these types of whiskey has some quality that makes it unique. People who like one type of whiskey do not necessarily like the other types because of the distinctions in flavors among the different whiskies.

The word *whiskey* can be spelled two different ways. *Whiskey* refers to bourbon and Irish and Tennessee whiskey. *Whisky* refers to Scotch and Canadian whisky. Some exceptions to this rule do exist, however. For example, Maker's Mark and Old Forester bourbon both use the Scotch and Canadian spelling.

Scotch

Scotch is made in Scotland. In Scotland the proper spelling for this alcoholic spirit is *whisky*. There are two main categories of Scotch: single malt and blended. This whisky is made from malted barley that is smoked and dried over peat, which is

Figure 15.12   A bottle of Scotch. [Dorling Kindersley Images]

Figure 15.13 Three bottles of Irish whiskey.
[Dorling Kindersley Images]

compost that has been compressed and aged. Peat is a soft carbon fuel made from vegetable matter that occurs naturally and is harvested from the land. When peat is burned, it has a very pungent aroma. The smoke imparts this aroma to the malted barley. Corn, wheat, and other cereal grains can be used for blended Scotch, but only barley can be used for single malts. Regardless of whether or not the Scotch is blended or single malt, the law requires Scotch to be aged for at least three years in either a used American white oak bourbon barrel or a used sherry barrel.

Single malt scotch can come from five different areas: (1) Lowland, (2) Highland, (3) Campbeltown, (4) Islay, and (5) Speyside. In comparing the five different single malt Scotches, one might find that Lowland Scotch is mild, gentle, and sweet with a little smoke. Highland Scotch, on the other hand, is more full-bodied. It is full of smoke flavors, but it is balanced. Campbeltown is similar to Highland Scotch, but it is more peat-flavored. Islay also is full-bodied, but it has a salty flavor due to the area's proximity to the ocean. Speyside is quite similar to Lowland Scotch, but it has a quality similar to sherry. Different Scotches made in the same region can be very dissimilar because distilleries have different production methods that always will affect the taste.

Blended Scotch was first made to get away from the heavy, smoky flavor that people get from single malt Scotch. As its name suggests, blended Scotch does not come from a single source. Several grains come together to make this drink.

Irish Whiskey

Irish whiskey and Scotch are similar, but Irish whiskey lacks the smoky flavor of Scotch because its barley is not exposed to smoke as it is being dried. In addition, Irish whiskey is rarely made from a single malt. Many grain combinations are used in the production of Irish whiskey, including corn, rye, wheat, and oats. Irish whiskey usually is triple-distilled and must be aged for a minimum of three years. In most cases, it is not shipped out of the country unless it has been aged five to eight years. Like Scotch, Irish whiskey is aged in used bourbon barrels or sherry casks.

Bourbon

Bourbon and religion are linked, as many other great spirits, wines, and beers are linked, to religion throughout history. Bourbon is named for Bourbon County, Kentucky. Legend has it that Baptist Minister Elijah Craig first made bourbon. According to a resolution passed by the United States Senate, bourbon can be made in any state in the United States, but it cannot be made outside of the United States.

There are 6 things that distinguish bourbon from other whiskeys:

1. Bourbon is made from a mash that is at least 51 percent corn.
2. The distillation does not exceed 160 proof.
3. Charred new white oak barrels are necessary in production.
4. The bourbon enters the barrel at no more than 125 proof.
5. Nothing is added but water.
6. Bourbon must be stored for a minimum of two years.

Technically, bourbon can be made anywhere in the United States as long as these six rules are followed, but the only state that can be listed on the label is Kentucky. Most bourbon is now made in or near Louisville, Lexington, and Bardstown, Kentucky.

Tennessee Whiskey

Geographically, Tennessee is very close to Kentucky; therefore, it makes sense that the whiskey made in the two states would be similar as well. The main difference between the two is that Tennessee whiskey is maple charcoal filtered. Almost every other aspect of its production is similar to bourbon. The maple charcoal filter adds a maple flavor that bourbon does not have. There are only two distillers in Tennessee that make this type of whiskey: Jack Daniel's and George Dickel.

Canadian Whisky

Canadian whisky is made from a blend of grains. The blend can contain any combination as long as no one grain makes up more than 49 percent of each mash. Canadian whisky must be aged in white oak barrels for a minimum of three years.

Canadian whisky is known as the lightest and mildest of all of the classic whiskies. Unlike any other whiskey, Canadian whisky may be finished or blended with Sherry or another wine.

Rye Whiskey

Rye whiskey, or rye malt whiskey, is produced from a minimum of 51 percent rye. Rye whiskey can be made from 100 percent rye, but that is very rare. Like bourbon, rye whiskey must be aged for a minimum of two years by law (four years is more common, however) in new white oak barrels. This whiskey has a flavor of caraway seeds; otherwise it is like smooth, rich bourbon.

Liqueurs

Liqueurs, also known as cordials, are flavorful alcoholic beverages made from distilled spirits. Some taste like fruit, others taste like nuts, and others taste like a combination of fruit and spices. Liqueurs are used in mixed drinks, and they are served alone as after dinner drinks.

The word *liqueur* comes from the Latin word *liquefacere*, which means "to melt or dissolve." Liqueurs are made by one of three methods: maceration, percolation, or distillation. To make liqueur, a variety of selected ingredients are dissolved into a neutral distilled spirit. The maceration method allows the flavoring ingredient to soak into the distilled spirit, bleeding its flavors into the spirit. The percolation method works the same way, but the spirit is sprayed over the flavoring ingredient until the spirit takes on its flavor. In the distillation method, the flavoring components are distilled with the spirit. This method is used for seeds and other ingredients that can withstand high heat.

The sugar content of liqueurs can range from 2.5 to 35 percent of the total weight, and the consistency of the beverage can be a thick, syrup-like substance or it can be like any other distilled spirit. The alcohol level ranges from 34 proof to 100 proof, but most liqueurs do not exceed 60 proof.

Coffee-Flavored Liqueurs

Cream Liqueurs   Coffee and chocolate cream liqueurs are consumed by themselves and used to fortify coffee. They tend to be at the low end of the alcohol range, with levels between 30 and 40 proof. These liqueurs are composed of cream, a spirit, and the main flavoring agent. An example of a cream liqueur is Bailey's Irish Cream.

Kahlua®   Kahlua®, a coffee-flavored liqueur, is the pride of Mexico. Kahlua® has an alcohol level of 53 proof and is used in baking and in making candies. It is served in coffee beverages and on its own as well.

Tia Maria®   Tia Maria® is a coffee liqueur made in Jamaica. It is very similar to Kahlua®, and some would argue that they can be used interchangeably. Tia Maria® is sweeter than Kahlua®, and it has an alcohol level of 53 proof.

Fruit-Flavored Liqueurs

Chambord   This French raspberry liqueur has an alcohol level of 33 proof.

Brandy Liqueur   This class of liqueurs includes mostly fruit-flavored grape spirits. Generally, they come in three flavors: apricot, cherry, and peach. They have an alcohol level of about 40 proof.

Malibu   Malibu is a clear, coconut-flavored liqueur. It has an alcohol level of 56 proof.

Maraschino   This is a clear liqueur that is flavored with cherries. Maraschino is aged for several years in ash wood barrels or glass after it is sweetened with simple syrup. The alcohol level can range from 50 to 100 proof.

Midori   Midori is one of the youngest liqueurs discussed in this chapter. This liqueur comes from Japan, where it was invented in the early 1980s. The name means "green" in its native language, which properly describes the color. Midori has a melon flavor and an alcohol level of 46 proof.

Poire William   Poire Williams is a clear liqueur made in Switzerland and eastern France. It is made from the William Pear and has an alcohol level of about 60 proof.

Sloe Gin   Sloe gin is made from the tart sloe plum, so it is not really gin at all. Sloe gin is red and has an alcohol level that ranges from 42 to 60 proof.

Southern Comfort   Southern Comfort, a liqueur with two different proof levels, 70 proof and 100 proof, has an amber color and a peach flavor. It is very popular in the United States. On its label, this liqueur claims creation in the Big Easy (New Orleans, Louisiana) in 1874. This liqueur was created by bartender M. W. Meran.

Orange-Flavored Liqueurs

Aurum   Aurum is an orange liqueur with a brandy base. It is triple-distilled in a special way such that the orange flavor is not added until the last distillation. This Italian liqueur boasts an alcohol content of 80 proof.

Cointreau   Cointreau is a French orange liqueur. It is double-distilled and infused with orange peel and some secret ingredients. Cointreau's alcohol level is 80 proof.

Curaçao   Curaçao is a rum-based, orange-flavored liqueur that is available in three colors: clear, blue, and orange. The clear version is also known as *triple sec.* The alcohol ranges from 50 and 80 proof.

Grand Marnier   Grand Marnier has the reputation of being the king of the orange liqueur. This reputation is only fitting because the base of the liqueur is top-quality cognac. Grand Marnier has an amber color and its aroma hints at the cognac, oranges, and barrel aging that make up this famous liqueur. It has an alcohol level of 80 proof and should be served in a brandy snifter.

Mandarine Napoleon   This is an orange-colored liqueur with the flavor of tangerines. Mandarine Napoleon is made from a base of French brandy. It takes its name from Napoleon I, who liked to drink a similar beverage. It has an alcohol level of 76 proof.

Pimm's   Pimm's is the British equivalent of an orange-flavored liqueur. However, it is based on London gin, so it also has a flavor of assorted herbs. It has an alcohol level of 50 proof.

Van der Hum   This is South Africa's answer to an orange-flavored liqueur. It is made with a special orange that is indigenous to South Africa, the *naartjie,* which is like a tangerine. It has a low alcohol level of only 50 proof.

Licorice-Flavored Liqueurs

Anis/Anisette   Anis is a clear, licorice-flavored cordial. A similar liqueur known as anisette is French in origin. Anisette is very sweet and has an alcohol level higher than anis, which ranges from 42 to 96 proof.

Galliano   Galliano is a yellow liqueur with licorice and vanilla flavors. Galliano is Italian and has an alcohol level of about 70 proof.

Goldwasser   This liqueur has gold flakes floating in a clear spirit. The spirit has been flavored with aniseed, caraway seed, and oranges. With an alcohol level of 60 to 80 proof, Goldwasser stands alone most of the time so the gold flakes are not hidden.

Pastis   Patis is the French version of anis. It is a licorice-flavored liqueur and has an alcohol level of 90 proof.

Sambuca   Sambuca is a clear Italian liqueur that is similar to anis, but it has a flavor of elderberries. The alcohol level is at about 80 proof.

Nut-Flavored Liqueurs

Amaretto Amaretto has the flavors of almonds and apricots. One of the base ingredients of the liqueur is apricot stones, the seed from inside the apricot. Amaretto is served with coffee and chocolate desserts. The alcohol proof range is in the mid-50s and its color is a deep orange brown.

Nut Liqueurs This is a general term used to describe liqueurs with nut flavors such as almonds, walnuts or hazelnuts. The most famous of these is Frangelico, a hazelnut liqueur. The alcohol levels of Frangelico range from the high 40s to about 80 proof.

Herb- and Spice-Flavored Liqueurs

Benedictine Benedictine is an herbal liqueur with a Cognac base. It is named for an order of Christian monks. After being invented in the 1500s, Benedictine was not made for almost eighty years (between 1789 and the 1860s) because the French Revolution banned its production. Benedictine started being produced by a descendant of the monk's lawyer. The liqueur has an alcohol level of 80 proof.

Drambuie Drambuie is an amber liqueur made from Scotch whiskey, honey and herbs. Drambuie has an alcohol level of 70 proof and it is one of the components in a drink called a Rusty Nail. (The other component is Scotch.)

Glayva Glayva is an amber liqueur made with Scotch whiskey, honey and herbs, but unlike Drambuie, the producer also uses oranges. Glayva has an alcohol content of 80 proof.

Kummel Kummel holds the distinction of being one of the oldest liqueurs. Its major flavoring component is caraway seed. Kummel has a vodka base and is produced in Germany, as well as many other eastern European countries. It has an alcohol level ranging between 54 and 70 proof.

Strega Strega is an Italian herb and spice liqueur with a yellow color. It has an alcohol level of about 80 proof.

Other Liqueurs

Advocaat Advocaat is basically Dutch eggnog that can be added to coffee or enjoyed alone. This creamy, yellow-orange liqueur is used as both an aperitif and a digestive; the alcohol level ranges between 30 and 40 proof.

Chartreuse Chartreuse is an herb liqueur that comes in two colors: green and yellow. The production method for chartreuse is highly guarded by the silent Carthusian Order of Monks. Chartreuse has ties to both France and Spain; the production has bounced between the two countries during the two centuries because of political unrest in the two countries. Yellow chartreuse has an alcohol level of 80 proof, while its green sibling touts an alcohol level of 110 proof.

Crème Liqueurs   This class of liqueurs should not be confused with cream liqueurs. Crème liqueurs have no cream and are very sweet. They have many fruit flavors such as banana, raspberry, plum, and strawberry. These liqueurs also have nut flavors such as almond and hazelnut, as well as flavors such as rose petal, mint, celery, tea, coffee, and violet. They usually feature a picture on the label indicating their taste. The alcohol levels range from the high 40s to about 80 proof.

Parfait Amour   This liqueur gets its vivid bluish-purple color from a vegetable dye. Parfait amour gets its flavor from violets, cinnamon, cloves, coriander seeds, and citrus fruit. The name means "perfect love" in French, but it is Dutch in origin.

Key Terms

Distillation	Cognac
Double Distillation	VSOP
Triple Distillation	Armagnac
Still	Calvados
Low Wine	Whiskey
High Wine	Whisky
Eau de Vie	Scotch
Gin	Irish Whiskey
Rum	Bourbon
Tequila	Tennessee Whiskey
Mescal	Canadian Whisky
Vodka	Liqueurs
Brandy	

Study Questions

1. Explain the distillation process.
2. Why do distillers distill?
3. What is a still and how does it work?
4. What is the difference between whiskey and whisky?
5. What is the difference between brandy and cognac?
6. How do bourbon and Tennessee whiskey differ?
7. What does the term *eau de vie* mean and what is the derivation of the phrase?
8. Compare and contrast tequila and mescal.

Chapter

16 *Mixology*

After reading this chapter, you will be able to:

❑ Demonstrate how to properly measure alcohol for drink creation and replication.
❑ Explain the bar set-up for easy drink creation.
❑ Apply drink-mixing techniques.
❑ Discuss why different drinks call for different glasses and select the proper glass for the proper drink.
❑ Explain and be able to apply techniques for garnishing drinks.
❑ Discuss the basic components of commonly ordered drinks.

> *Here's mud in your eye.*
> *Here's how.*
>
> —All-American toasts

This chapter is dedicated to the memory of the late Max Allen, Bartender Emeritus of the Seelbach Hilton in Louisville, Kentucky. Mr. Allen was the 1997 International Bartender of the Year, a title that he won in Switzerland in head-to-head competition with top bartenders from all over the world. Mr. Allen was originally going to be asked to write this chapter before he passed.

Mixology, the mixing of liquids to create cocktails, can be classified as both an art and a science. The act of combining specific amounts of alcohol and mixers, such as water, soda, juice, or milk products, is a science that allows a bartender or a restaurant owner to maintain consistency in their drinks. Using standard amounts also allows the bartender to come up with new drinks that can be reproduced easily by others. The art of mixology is expressed in the drink's presentation and the bartender's flair at showmanship and entertainment.

When a professional bartender makes a drink, it may appear that the bartender starts pouring mixers and alcohol at will. However, the bartender is a highly trained professional who is following a recipe that has been costed out by the proprietor. The bartender must follow the recipes developed by the establishment's management in order for the establishment to make a profit. If the bartender does not follow the recipes, or if the establishment does not have standardized drink recipes, quality, consistency, and profit cannot be assured.

Measuring the Alcohol

The amount of alcohol in a drink can be measured using several methods. The first method requires the bartender to use a small measuring cup called a *jigger*. A standard jigger has two sides: the small side holds a one-half ounce portion and the larger side holds a two-ounce portion. Another way to measure alcohol is to "free-pour." As a bartender pours a drink, he or she silently counts in order to

Figure 16.1   A bartender stirs a drink.
[Pearson Education/Prentice Hall]

Figure 16.2 Different sizes of jiggers. [Pearson Education/Prentice Hall]

pour the correct amount. This allows a bartender to pour without measuring the drink in a jigger. This method works well only if the bartender practices pouring and counting at the same time to develop a good sense of timing and consistency.

Another method is the automatic pouring system. This system uses an automatic machine to pour the correct amount of alcohol. Some systems can pour the amount of alcohol for specific drinks, such as a Long Island Ice Tea. This system is very expensive, but it can save money in the long run and help with the overall consistency of drinks. It also eliminates any guesswork on the part of the bartender and helps eliminate accidental over pours and dishonest bartenders who try to increase their tip, or over pour, for friends.

How to Set Up a Bar

The work area of a bar should be arranged so that every ingredient is easily accessible to the bartender. If the bar is set up correctly, the bartender can quickly and efficiently produce any drink the customer orders. A bartender also should know the bar so that he or she can reach for something and find it without necessarily looking. A bartender needs to stay organized so drink production keeps pace with the customer demand. A good strategy to use to keep up with drink orders is to place the most frequently used items nearest to the bartender.

A pour station should be created in the bar where most or all of the drinks are poured. This station should be used as the central place for drink production. Glasses should be located above the counter of the station or in a nearby place where they are easily accessible. In addition, the pour station should have a clear

Figure 16.3 Bottles of alcohol in the well. [Pearson Education/Prentice Hall]

space on the counter for the glasses to sit while the drinks are prepared. The pour station also can be a place where servers come to pick up drinks.

Under the bar in the pour station distilled spirits should be set up in the following order from left to right: Bourbon, Scotch, gin, vodka, rum, tequila, and triple sec. These spirits are the most frequently used distilled drinks. Garnishes such as sliced lemons, limes, oranges, and cherries should be placed beside this area. Additionally, an ice bin should be nearby with ice, and orange juice and Bloody Mary mix should be kept at hand and chilled.

Figure 16.4 A blender. [Pearson Education/Prentice Hall]

Mixing Techniques

To mix a drink, a bartender pours all of the liquids (and ice if the recipe calls for it) into one container and agitates the ingredients until they are thoroughly combined. There are three methods of agitation: stirring, shaking, and blending. The debonair movie character James Bond made two of these methods household terms when he insisted on ordering his Martinis "shaken, not stirred."

Stirring

Stirring a drink simply means to add all of the components to a glass with ice and stir with a spoon. One of the benefits of stirring is that a carbonated beverage can be added to the drink before the mixing. Carbonated beverages cannot be added to cocktails that are shaken because the shaking will cause the drink to lose its carbonation. Cocktails such as the Kentucky Colonel Cocktail (bourbon and Benedictine), a Rob Roy (sweet vermouth and Scotch) and a Manhattan (sweet vermouth and blended whiskey) are stirred. The bartender, who simply adds a straw, may not even stir the drinks before it is served to the customer. Many drinks served in a cocktail glass are stirred.

Shaking

Shaking a drink is a chance for the bartender to entertain the customer while quickly producing the cocktail. The process starts with ice being placed in a shaker. The other drink components are poured over the ice. A cover is added to the glass and the bartender shakes it for about ten seconds or until frost forms on the outside of the glass. The lid is removed, a strainer tops the container, and the resulting liquid is strained out into the appropriate glass. Shaking the beverage with ice cubes also helps chill the ingredients, which produces a colder drink. Drinks such as Tom Collins (lemon juice, sugar, and gin with club soda added after the shake), Daiquiris (lime juice, sugar, and rum), and Margaritas (tequila, Curaçao, and lime juice) are usually shaken, but these drinks also can be blended. Most drinks are shaken.

Blending

To blend a drink, the bartender combines all of the ingredients and ice in a blender. Blenders are essential for frozen drinks such as Daiquiris, Margaritas, and Piña Coladas.

About Vermouth and Bitters

Vermouth is a spicy, fortified wine that is used in many cocktails, especially the Martini. The flavors of vermouth can come from allspice, anise, bitter almond, bitter orange, cinnamon, clove, fennel, ginger, nutmeg, saffron, thyme, and

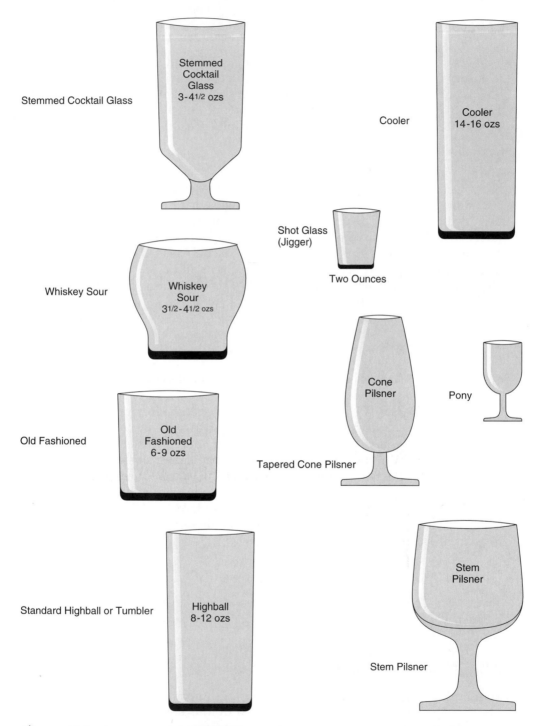

Figure 16.5 An assortment of bar glasses. [Pearson Education/Prentice Hall]

vanilla. Vermouth adds sweetness to a Martini. (If someone orders a dry Martini, he or she is asking for the drink to be made with little or no vermouth.)

Bitters are a distilled spirit that are used the same ways as vermouth. Bitters gain their spicy, bitter flavor from herbs and spices. Sometimes bitters also have oranges or dried orange peel added to them. Vermouth and bitters are used in small amounts and both have secret recipes.

The Right Glass for the Right Drink

A bartender needs to be sure the correct glass is used for the cocktail being served. Some drinks are served in cocktail glasses and others served in Collins glasses or Highball glasses. Other drinks have specific glasses that best suit the drink.

Once the glass is chosen, the bartender must decide whether or not a chilled or frosted glass would be appropriate for the drink. Glasses can be kept chilled in the bar's refrigerator for drinks such as Margaritas or Piña Coladas.

Garnishing Drinks

Most drinks have a specific garnish used as a finishing touch to the presentation. Cocktail garnishes began in the United States during the late 1700s when Betsy Flanagan first used feathers from rooster tails to garnish drinks. Thus the "cock tail" came into existence for the first time in Yorktown, New York.

Figure 16.6 Beverage garnishes. [Pearson Education/Prentice Hall]

Obviously, rooster feathers are not used in bars these days, but the use of garnishes continues. Sometimes the garnish is as simple as a slice of orange, a wedge of lemon, a green olive or a cherry; however, garnishes also can be very ornate and complicated.

One of the most common garnishes is a twist. A twist is a slice of citrus fruit zest and pith. Most drinks with twists will come with a lemon twist, but any citrus fruit can be used. The twist gives the drink a little taste of the citrus fruit.

Other simple garnishes can be a slice or wedge of a fruit. (A *slice* is a round cross-section of the whole fruit, whereas a *wedge* is a chunk of a section of the fruit.) For example, a Tom Collins is served with a cherry and an orange slice. These slices and wedges can be put together in a drink for more complicated garnishes. A bartender might serve a Bloody Mary with a celery stick that includes a piece of cheese or meat, for example.

The most complicated garnishes are those that include setting a drink on fire or a presentation in which the alcohol is layered (*floated*) so that the customer can see the different layers of alcohol through the glass.

How to Flame

Most flaming drinks are served to customers celebrating a birthday or other special event. The key to flaming a drink is to heat both the glass and the alcohol until both are very warm. The alcohol is then ignited with a lighter or a Sterno fuel container. Flaming a beverage can be an impressive way to spark conversation among guests, but it should be done with the utmost care so that nothing but the alcohol catches on fire. [Note: Some jurisdictions outlaw tableside flambé entirely.]

How to Float

Learning to master the art of floating alcohol can lead to amazing rainbow-colored drinks. A bartender must master two skills to float one alcohol on top of another to layer a drink. First, the bartender must be able to pour the alcohol over the back of a spoon so that it flows down into the drink evenly; a large flow in any single area destroys the effect. Second, the bartender must know the specific gravity of an alcohol. The densest alcohol should go on the bottom of the glass so that it can support everything on top. Very talented bartenders can layers drinks with more than eleven layers. The late Max Allen, Bartender Emeritus of the Seelbach Hilton in Louisville, Kentucky, talked about layering a drink thirty-two to thirty-three layers deep.

Drink Formulas

Included below are the names and ingredients of drinks that are popular today. Some of these drinks are traditional ones with a long heritage, but some are relatively new concoctions. The exact formula for each drink can vary from bar to bar depending on local customer preference, glassware sizes, and cost considerations; therefore, only the typical ingredients are listed along with recommendations for glassware and garnishes.

Alabama Slammer—Equal parts of Amaretto, sloe gin, and Southern Comfort mixed with a small amount of lemon juice.

B-52—Grand Marnier, Kahlua®, and Bailey's Irish Cream, either mixed or layered.

Fuzzy Navel—Ice, peach schnapps, and orange juice.

Long Island Iced Tea—Vodka, rum, gin, triple sec, and tequila with a splash of cola.

Margarita—Equal parts of tequila, triple sec, and lime juice served on ice or blended with ice. Salt and a slice of lime are served on the rim of the glass.

Mimosa—Equal parts orange juice, and sparkling wine.

Brandy Drinks

Brandy Alexander—Brandy with dark crème de cacao and heavy cream.

Brandy Sour—Brandy with lemon juice, and powdered sugar.

Metropolitan—Brandy with sweet vermouth, simple syrup, and Angostura bitters served over ice cubes.

Cordials

Grasshopper—Crème de menthe (green), crème de cacao (white) and light cream. This drink also can be served frozen by adding vanilla ice cream to the recipe above.

Kir and Kir Royale—White wine with a splash of crème de cassis. The Kir Royale is made with sparkling wine.

Orgasm—Amaretto, Kahlua®, and Bailey's Irish Cream.

Pousse-Cafe'—A classic example of a layered drink. There are many different recipes involving many different cordials. The final presentation of this drink shows off each ingredient in a clear rainbow in the glass.

Screaming Orgasm—Amaretto, Kahlua®, Bailey's Irish Cream and vodka.

Sex on the Beach—Raspberry liqueur, melon liqueur, vodka, pineapple juice, and cranberry juice.

Gin Drinks

Belmont Cocktail—Gin, raspberry syrup, and cream.

Bennett Cocktail—Gin, lime juice, bitters, and powdered sugar. The drink is shaken with ice and strained.

Gin Martini—Gin and a small amount of vermouth. This drink can be shaken or stirred and garnished with green olives or a twist.

Gin and Tonic—Gin served with tonic water on ice and garnished with a lime.

Gibson—Same as the Gin Martini, but the Gibson is garnished with several cocktail onions.

Tom Collins—Gin with lemon juice and club soda. It is sweetened sometimes and served over ice.

Rum Drinks

Bahama Mama—Several different rums, including a high-proof rum (such as 151), coconut and coffee liqueurs, and lemon and pineapple juices.

Daiquiri—Rum, lime juice, and a little powdered sugar. A Daiquiri can be a frozen drink.

Eggnog—Rum, brandy or whiskey, egg, sugar, milk and/or cream and nutmeg. This drink is blended.

Hurricane—Dark rum, pineapple juice, orange juice, and grenadine served over ice and garnished with a wedge of pineapple.

Mai Tai—A mixture of rums including 151-proof rum, orange curaçao, lime juice, and simple syrup. This drink is garnished with mint, cherry, and pineapple.

Rum and Coke—Rum and cola served over ice.

Vodka Drinks

Vodka Martini—Vodka and a little vermouth. It usually is garnished with several green olives or a twist.

Black Russian—Vodka with a coffee liqueur served over ice. If cream is added, it is a White Russian.

Bloody Mary—Vodka and a spicy tomato juice that includes Worcestershire sauce and Tabasco sauce. The traditional garnish is a celery stalk.

Cape Cod—Vodka with cranberry juice. If grapefruit juice is added to the mixture, the drink becomes a Seabreeze.

Kamikazi—Vodka, lime juice, and orange liqueur.

Cosmopolitan—Vodka with orange liqueur, lime juice, and cranberry juice. It is shaken with ice and served strained.

Gimlet—Vodka and lime juice.

Harvey Wallbanger—Vodka, orange juice, and Galliano served with ice. The real trick to this drink is floating the Galliano on the top of the drink once it has been prepared.

Screwdriver—(Sloe Comfortable Screw)—Vodka and orange juice. The addition of sloe gin and Southern Comfort makes the drink a Sloe Comfortable Screw.

Whiskey Drinks

Boilermaker—A whiskey shot with a beer chaser.
Bourbon on the Rocks—Bourbon whiskey poured over ice. Almost any drink can be served "on the rocks," which means it is served on ice.
Highball—Whiskey and ginger ale served over ice.
Jack and Coke—Jack Daniel's whiskey and cola served over ice.
John Collins—Whiskey, lime juice, simple syrup and club soda served with ice.
Manhattan—Whiskey, vermouth, and Angostura bitters, garnished with a cherry. First made to honor Winston Churchill's mother almost seventy-five years before the former Prime Minister of England came to fame.
Mint Julep—Bourbon whiskey, sprigs of mint, simple syrup or powdered sugar, water, and ice. This is the classic drink of the Kentucky Derby.
Old Fashioned—Bourbon whiskey, sugar, Angostura bitters, and, sometimes, club soda. It is garnished with a cherry and an orange slice. Sometimes this drink is made with other American and Canadian whiskeys.
Preakness Cocktail—Blended whiskey, sweet vermouth, bitters, and Benedictine.
Presbyterian—Bourbon whiskey with ginger ale and club soda.
Rob Roy—Scotch whisky and vermouth. This drink can be served on ice or strained into a glass. The Rob Roy is named for a Scottish hero.
Rusty Nail—Scotch whisky and Drambuie, another Scottish beverage.
7 and 7—Seagram's Seven whiskey and 7-Up served over ice.

Mocktails

Fruit Smoothie—Many fruits mixed together. Yogurt and orange juice may be added.
Fuzzy Lemon Fizz—Peach nectar topped off with lemon-lime soda.
Lemonade—Sweetened lemon juice.
Shirley Temple—Ginger ale that has been sweetened and colored with grenadine.
Virgin Drinks—Many drinks can be made without alcohol simply by replacing the alcoholic drink with something nonalcoholic, such as ginger ale or sparkling water.

Key Terms

Cocktail	Mixology
Free pouring	Shaking
Jigger	Blending
Stirring	Collins
Flaming	Highball
Floating	Twist
Vermouth	Mocktail

Study Questions

1. What is the origin of the term *cocktail*?
2. What is the difference between stirring and shaking a drink?
3. What are bitters?
4. What is vermouth?
5. Explain the process of floating alcohol.
6. Explain how to flame a drink.

Chapter 17

Professional Alcohol Service

After reading this chapter, you will be able to:

- ❑ Describe how sales histories and job descriptions can help determine bar staffing needs.
- ❑ Describe the duties of a sommelier.
- ❑ Describe the duties of a bartender.
- ❑ Discuss proper serving temperatures for wine.
- ❑ Explain and demonstrate how to present and open wine.
- ❑ Explain and demonstrate how to decant wine.
- ❑ Explain and demonstrate how to open champagne and sparkling wine.
- ❑ Explain and demonstrate how to open and pour beer.
- ❑ Discuss the proper glassware used for different drinks.

Lady Astor: "Sir, if you were my husband, I would poison your drink."
Sir Winston Churchill: "Madam, if you were my wife, I would drink it."

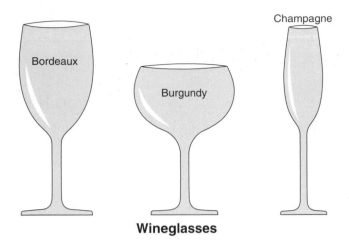

Wineglasses

Figure 17.1 Different wineglass sizes. [Pearson Education/Prentice Hall]

Drink service is one of the most important components of food service because almost every bar or restaurant patron will order a drink; therefore, drinks can be a very profitable part of a business. In some cases, a drink's final price can be from two to ten times the cost of the components of the drink. Every food service manager should have a basic knowledge of bar service, including how to determine staffing requirements, the duties of the bartenders and sommeliers, and the proper glassware for drinks.

Staffing a Bar

In order to realize the maximum amount of profits from beverage service, a food service manager needs to control staffing costs. Every food service establishment will have different needs when it comes to staffing; these needs partially will be determined by the way that the establishment is organized, its customer profile, and its core business hours.

One way to control staffing costs is to develop and use job descriptions. If an establishment has job descriptions in place, it is easier for a manager to determine how many staff members will be needed to perform the necessary tasks for a shift. Managers should analyze each job that is performed at their establishments on a regular basis. A great deal of information for this analysis can be gathered from the employees. Once this information is gathered, it can be used to develop job descriptions and determine staffing needs. For example, your bartending staff may list the following tasks as duties they perform during a shift:

1. Fill the ice bin.
2. Set up the bar.

3. Set up the cash register.
4. Prepare and garnish drinks.
5. Wash glasses.
6. Stock the bar.
7. Count sales revenues and zero out the register.

All these tasks would be included in a written job description. How and how well those tasks are to be carried out are performance standards. For example, the standard garnish for a martini might be two green olives; therefore, in order to perform the task of garnishing this drink properly, a bartender would use two green olives.

A manager should look at employee wages when determining staffing requirements as well. There are two different types of employees:

1. Fixed-cost employees (exempt).
2. Variable-cost employees (nonexempt).

A fixed-cost employee makes the same amount of money no matter how many hours he or she works. A general manager and the bar manager are examples of fixed-cost, or exempt, employees. Each of these people might work between fifty and seventy hours a week, but no matter how many hours they work, they are paid the same amount. In addition, no matter what the sales volume is, fixed-cost employees work at the same rate.

In contrast, a variable-cost employee, such as a server or bartender, makes an hourly wage. A variable cost, or nonexempt, employee might work between thirty and forty hours per week. Their weekly pay is determined by how many hours they work. If sales are high, this employee might work more hours and thus bring home more pay. If sales are low, this employee might work fewer hours and bring home less pay.

In the food service industry, sales are measured in terms of *covers*, or how many plates or drinks are sold. The more covers an establishment sells, the more that establishment needs to rely on variable-cost employees. The less covers the establishment sells, the more the establishment should rely on fixed-cost employees. If business is slow, for example, the manager is likely to send variable-cost employees home earlier to save labor costs. The fixed-cost employee will make the same wage whether he or she works forty hours or fifty hours; if the manager keeps the variable-cost employee working the extra ten hours, the additional cost will be the employee's hourly wage multiplied by 10. If business is good, however, the pay of these employees can be covered by the higher revenues. The additional staff also enables the establishment to better serve the customer, which will help create repeat business and higher revenues.

The best way to look at the staffing needs of an establishment is to chart or log how many covers are sold in a single day, a week, a month, and a full year. Managers should note what time during the day the sales were the highest and lowest on this chart or log. This will allow patterns to emerge. Perhaps Friday and Saturday nights are very busy and/or Monday and Tuesday nights are very slow. This pattern would tell the manager to schedule more of the variable cost employees during the Friday and Saturday night shifts. This sales history, in combination with job descriptions, will help determine minimum and maximum staffing needs. Understanding sales patterns and appropriate staffing needs is important in controlling bar costs and maximizing drink service profits.

Bartenders and Sommeliers

Bartenders and sommeliers are both beverage professionals. The *bartender* creates all alcoholic drinks, especially mixed drinks, and has a general knowledge of all alcoholic beverages. A *sommelier* handles only wine. While the sommelier may have a general knowledge of all alcoholic drinks, he or she has an in-depth knowledge of wines. A sommelier usually does not work behind a bar . A sommelier works on the floor of the restaurant.

Duties of a Bartender

A bartender is the person in charge of the operation of a bar. His or her job duties generally include the following:

1. Preparing the bar for service.
2. Maintaining the bar.
3. Greeting the guests.
4. Mixing drinks and pouring beer and wine for customers.
5. Maintaining the customers' drinks.
6. Keeping the customers safe with regards to alcohol consumption.

Tools of a Bartender

The bartender has several special tools to perform the required tasks. The following is a list of some of these tools.

Corkscrew—This is used for opening bottles of wine.
Bottle opener—This is used for opening bottles of beer.
Cocktail shaker—Both the Boston shaker and the standard shaker fall into this category. The Boston shaker consists of two glasses; usually at least one is stainless steel, and this glass overlaps the other. A pint glass can be used as the second glass. The standard shaker is a glass that has a removable strainer at the top.
Bar spoon—This long spoon is used for stirring drinks.
Jigger—A jigger is a small, two-sided, cone-shaped glass that is used for measuring alcohol for drinks. A jigger usually holds 1½ ounces of alcohol on the large side and some fraction of that on the small side.

Figure 17.2   A cork screw. [Dorling Kindersley Images]

Muddler—This is a small bat used to crush ice, fruit, and herbs.
Blender—This machine is used to blend drinks and crush ice.
Knife and cutting board—The knife and cutting board are used to cut fruit and other garnishes for drinks.
Hawthorn strainer—This is a plate with a spring attachment used to strain drinks.

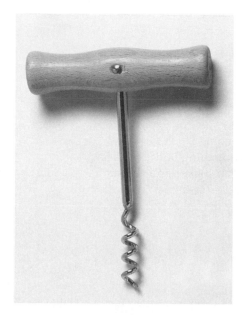

Figure 17.3   A cork screw. [Dorling Kindersley Images]

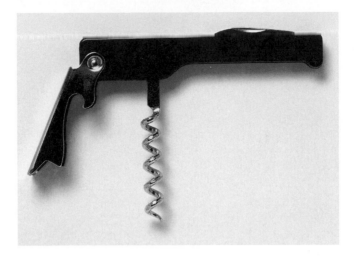

Figure 17.4 A server's cork screw. [Dorling Kindersley Images]

A Sommelier's Duties, Responsibilities, and Tools

The sommelier is also known as a wine steward at a restaurant or hotel. The sommelier is in charge of the wine cellar and helps customers make decisions concerning wine selections for meals. The sommelier also is in charge of serving the wine that a customer picks. He or she has two main tools: the corkscrew and the tastevin.

Figure 17.5 A muddler. [Pearson Education/Prentice Hall]

Figure 17.6 A sommelier serves wines. [Dorling Kindersley Images]

The *corkscrew* comes in several shapes and sizes, with its main purpose being to remove a cork from a bottle. The *tastevin* is a silver cup that hangs by a chain around the sommelier's neck. The sommelier uses this cup to inspect and taste wine for customers.

Wine Service

While a sommelier's job may sound simple, wine service consists of more than just pouring the wine into a glass and placing the bottle on the table. Wine service is a complex piece of bar service. Many factors need to be taken into account, including what wine to serve with what food, the characteristics of particular wines, and the conditions under which each wine should be served.

Serving Temperature for Wine

Before wine reaches the customer's table, the sommelier must be sure the wine is at the correct serving temperature. In general, wines of the same color or type are served at the same temperature. Sparkling wines, for instance, should be served at approximately 45°F. When white wine is presented to the customer, it also should be lightly chilled to about 45° to 55°F. If white wine comes directly from the refrigerator, many of the flavors are lost or masked because refrigeration temperatures are usually lower than 45°F. Allowing the wine to warm up to the high 40° to 55° range allows the features of finer wines to be unmasked for the drinker

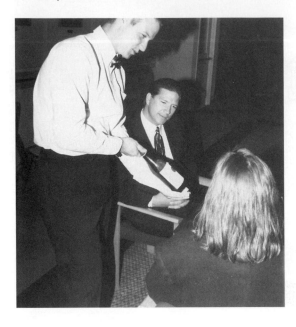

Figure 17.7 A sommelier presents a bottle of wine to a customer. [Pearson Education/Prentice Hall]

to enjoy. Conversely, lesser-quality white wine can be served very cold to mask undesirable flavors and aromas.

Red wines should be served at room temperature. When speaking of red wine, however, room temperature refers to the room temperature in the large houses and castles of 100 years ago, which was about 60° to 65°F. There are some red wines, however, that should be treated like white wines by being chilled to a lower temperature before they are presented to the customer. Beaujolais Nouveau is an example of a red wine that should be served chilled to 45°F.

Presenting Wine

After a customer has ordered a bottle of wine, the sommelier or a server should bring the wine to the table and present it to the customer who ordered the wine. The server should hold the wine up so that the customer easily can read the label and confirm that it is the wine he or she ordered. Once the customer does confirm the order, the server should open the wine.

Opening Wine

Opening a bottle of wine should begin with cutting the top ring off of the *lead*, or plastic capsule, which encloses the top of the bottle. Once this top ring is removed and the cork is exposed, a corkscrew can be inserted lightly into the cork and twisted until the last ring of the corkscrew disappears into the cork. The cork should then be pulled out of the bottle and presented to the customer for inspection. The customer inspects the cork to ensure it is not damaged or old. The cork

Figure 17.8 The label is presented to a customer. [Pearson Education/ Prentice Hall]

Figure 17.9 The cork is pulled from a bottle. [Pearson Education/Prentice Hall]

Figure 17.10 A cork is presented to a customer for inspection. [Pearson Education/Prentice Hall]

Figure 17.11 Wine is poured for the customer to taste. [Pearson Education/Prentice Hall]

should be moist, tough, and a little spongy. (Some customers will smell the cork, even though the smell of a cork will tell little about the quality of the wine inside the bottle.)

Pouring Wine

After the cork has been inspected, it is the time for the customer to inspect the wine itself. The server should start by pouring a little wine into the glass of the person ordering the wine. The server should allow the customer a chance to examine the wine. The customer might look at the wine against a white background, or swirl, smell, and/or sip the wine. Once the customer is satisfied, the server should finish pouring about four ounces into each guest's wine glass, filling the host's glass last.

Decanting Wine

Sometimes an older wine, such as an old bottle of Bordeaux, has sediment in the bottle. Removing the sediment from the wine will increase the customer's enjoyment. The server or sommelier should light a candle and place the candle and a *decanter*, a glass vessel designed to hold and pour wine, on the table. The candle is used to help illuminate the bottle so that the sommelier can see the wine and the sediment.

The bottle should be held between the candle and the decanter and the server should slowly pour the wine into the decanter until the sediment appears near the bottom of the neck of the bottle. At this point the server should follow the general principles of serving wine, using the decanter in place of the bottle.

Figure 17.12 A bottle of wine is decanted. [Dorling Kindersley Images]

Figure 17.13 A bottle of sparkling wine begins to be opened. Note that the server holds his thumb over the cork to hold it in place. [Dorling Kindersley Images]

A wine that is young and needs to breathe also can be decanted. In this case the wine is poured so that it can be exposed to air. The air will allow the wine to mellow a little before drinking. There should be little, if any, sediment in a young wine, so the server does not need to worry about stopping the pour as he or she does with an old bottle of wine.

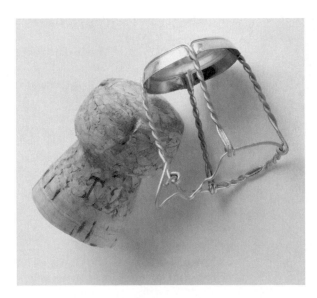

Figure 17.14 A sparkling wine cork and cage. [Dorling Kindersley Images]

Opening Champagne or Sparkling Wine

The pressure inside a bottle of sparkling wine makes opening the bottle very easy as well as dangerous. The bottle and the cork should be controlled at all times by the server.

After presenting the bottle to the customer, the server should remove some of the foil over the top of the bottle. At this point the server should rest the bottle on one leg at a 45-degree (which should be maintained throughout the process of opening the bottle), hold the neck of the bottle with one hand, place the thumb over the cork, and untwist the cage covering the cork until it can be easily removed. The server should make sure that the cork is pointed away from all customers. Covering the cork with a towel, the server should hold the cork in one hand while slowly twisting the bottle with the other hand until the cork begins to creep out of the bottle. The twisting of the bottle should continue until the cork is liberated. There should not be a big "pop" when the cork comes out, just a gasp.

Pouring Champagne or Sparkling Wine

Pouring sparkling wine can be tricky. As the server pours the wine, carbonation will foam up in the glass. In order to pour the wine so the glass is not overcome with foam, the server should pour straight to the bottom of the glass. As the foam begins to build, the server should stop pouring and continue after the foam has subsided. The server will repeat this process until the glass is filled to the level desired.

Opening and Serving Fortified Wines

In fortified wine bottles, the cork usually is attached to a top. This makes pulling the cork out of the bottle fairly easy. Depending on the age of the fortified wine, the server may need to decant the wine. Fortified wines should be served in smaller amounts than other wines because the alcohol levels are higher because of the addition of brandy. Usually, fortified wines are served at the end of the meal or with a dessert.

Beer Service

Serving Temperature for Ale and Lager

The temperature at which beer should be served depends on whether the beer is an ale or a lager. Ale should be served at 45° to 55°F., whereas larger should be served at 38° to 45°F.

How to Pour a Beer

The trick to pouring beer is to hold the glass at an angle. Whether pouring beer from a bottle or the tap on a keg, the angle of the glass will help minimize the head of the beer because it will minimize the loss of carbon dioxide or carbonation in the beer. This pouring process will also maximize the possibility that the beer will stay foamy while the patron drinks it.

When a Pint Must Be a Pint by Law

When a pint of beer is ordered in the United Kingdom, an *imperial pint* of beer must be served. An imperial pint contains 20 ounces, which is different from the American 16-ounce pint. Glasses for imperial pints are clearly marked with a fill line of 20 ounces. In the United Kingdom, if beer is not poured to this line, it cannot be served.

Spirit Service

Mixing and serving spirits is more complex than serving beer. Mixing different liquids to achieve the perfect drink takes study and experimentation.

How to Serve Spirits with Flair or a Flame

Even though most spirits are served at room temperature or cooler, some of these drinks are served with a flame. The nature of distilled alcohol allows the liquid to be lit easily. With the proper safety measures, lighting a drink can be a very dramatic way for a bartender to present a drink. Lighting a drink also can sell more beverages since the tables sitting around the customers receiving a flaming drink are likely to order the same.

Glassware

Proper glassware is an important ingredient of a drink for various reasons. Some drinks are served in particular glasses because the shape of the glass plays a role in the drink's integrity. Sparkling wines served in flutes, for example, retain their carbonation. Other drinks may be identified with a particular type of glass. A Martini, for instance, should be served in a very distinct glass. If served in any glass, the drink is still a Martini, but a knowledgeable customer will know that it is being served in the wrong glass.

Wine Glasses

Wine glass shapes are tailored to the specific wine being served. Wine glasses are divided into white wine glasses, red wine glasses, Port glasses, sherry glasses, and champagne glasses and flutes. There are also special glasses for Bordeaux and Burgundy wines.

White Wine Glass   A basic white wine glass is shaped like a water goblet, but the bowl of the glass is a little smaller and it has a stem. The stem allows the drinker to hold the glass without warming the wine. This is important because white wine should be drunk somewhat chilled.

Red Wine Glass   A basic red wine glass has a larger bowl than a white wine glass. Again, the stem allows the drinker to hold the glass without warming the wine in the bowl. Even though red wine should be served at room temperature, body temperature is well above comfortable room temperature.

Bordeaux Glass   This glass is made specifically for red Bordeaux-style wines such as Merlot and Cabernet Sauvignon. The shape of the glass catches and holds aromas, helping the drinker maximize the enjoyment of the beverage.

Burgundy Glass   The Burgundy glass also is made for red wine. It is made specifically for Burgundy-style wine made from the Pinot Noir grape. This glass works in much the same way as the Bordeaux glass.

Port Glass   A Port glass is smaller than an average wine glass. Port is a fortified beverage, and its alcohol content is double that of some other wines; therefore, Port is served in small portions.

Sherry Glass   Sherry is a fortified wine as well; therefore, the sherry glass is also small. Sherry can be served at the end of the meal, but it also can be served with the soup course, especially if the soup is shellfish-based.

Champagne Glass (Coupe)   The traditional champagne glass has a wide, flat bowl with a thin stem and base. According to legend, the first champagne glass was designed for Helen of Troy. For the Greeks, drinking was a sensual and erotic experience; therefore, they fashioned the glass after Helen's breasts. The same was done later in honor of the Queen of France, Marie Antoinette.

Champagne Flute   The tall, narrow Champagne flute is more common today. The appeal of using a flute is its ability to retain bubbles. The long, slender design allows the bubbles to stay in the glass longer. In a traditional Champagne glass, the bubbles quickly disappear, leaving still wine.

Beer Glasses

Some customers prefer drinking beer from a bottle, but others prefer a glass. For those who do want a glass, there are two choices: (1) the beer stein or mug and (2) the pilsner glass. The glasses are interchangeable and many times the use of a specific glass depends on which type the establishment prefers. Beer also can be served in a goblet or in a yard glass, but these are less common.

Beer Stein   This glass is essentially a beer mug. It can be very ornate and can come with or without a lid.

Pilsner Glass   This is a tall glass that is shaped somewhat like a funnel, with a larger top than bottom. This allows the beer to "show off" its bubbles.

Goblet   A goblet is a bowl-shaped glass with a stem.

Yard Glass   This very tall, thin glass is about a yard in length. The traditional yard glass holds 42 ounces. Today the glass can be found in a half yard as well. One of the benefits of drinking beer from a glass is that the beer is not as damaged in a glass from the act of drinking. A glass allows the beer to slide back and forth from the glass to the mouth of the drinker with little disruption or damage to the beer itself. In a bottle, on the other hand, the beer is thrown from one side of the bottle to the other as the drinker drinks. This damages the beer, allowing the carbonation to dissipate faster than it would if the beer were in a glass.

Spirit Glasses

Spirit glasses come in all shapes and sizes. Each glass is used for a special purpose or a specific drink.

Shot Glass   A shot glass is used for customers who want straight alcohol; however, there are some mixed drinks that call for shot glasses as the preferred glass of service. Alcohol served in a shot glass is usually room temperature. The glass holds between 1 and 1½ ounces of spirit.

Cordial Glass   This glass resembles a stemmed shot glass and can be used as a shot glass or for cordials.

Rocks Glass   This glass is for serving alcohol with cubed ice (rocks) and for some mixed drinks. It is also known as an Old-Fashioned glass.

Whiskey Sour Glass   This glass looks like a wine glass and is used specifically for Whiskey Sours.

Cocktail or Martini Glass   This cone-shaped cocktail glass is made for a drink that is shaken or stirred together with ice in another container and strained into the glass.

Margarita Glass   This is an oversized champagne glass. It is for Margaritas on the rocks or with crushed ice.

Brandy Glass or Brandy Snifter   This glass has a large bowl and a short, stubby stem, which encourages the drinker to hold the bowl of the glass cradled in his or her hand. The cradling action allows the brandy to be warmed and enhances the aromas enjoyed by the drinker.

Pousse-Café Glass   This is a straight, narrow glass used for layered drinks.

Parfait Glass   This glass is very similar to the Pousse-Café glass, but it flares at the top.

Coffee Glass   This glass looks similar to the Parfait glass or the Pousse-Café glass, but it has a handle. It is used for mixed coffee drinks.

Collins Glass   This glass is tall, thin, and used for Collins drinks such as the Tom Collins.

Highball Glass   The Highball glass looks like the Collins glass, but it is for larger mixed drinks such as the screwdriver.

Key Terms

Bartender	Flute
Sommelier	Coupe
Stein	Shot Glass
Pilsner Glass	Rocks Glass
Yard Glass	Martini Glass
Wine Glass	Snifter
Red Wine Glass	Job description
White Wine Glass	Fixed-cost employee
Port Glass	Variable-cost employee

Study Questions

1. When serving red wine, what is meant by "room temperature?"
2. At what temperatures should white wine be served?
3. At what temperatures should red wine be served?
4. What are the differences between a sommelier and a bartender?
5. Is all wine served in the same type of glass? Why or why not?
6. Give examples of three mixed-drink glasses. Give your opinion on the three glasses that would be most important to a bar and why.
7. What are a bartender's tools?

Chapter

18 Purchasing, Receiving, Storing, and Issuing

After reading this chapter, you will be able to:

❏ Describe a wine list in terms of its depth and breadth.
❏ Identify factors to consider when choosing wines, beers, and spirits.
❏ Explain proper storage techniques for wines, beers, and spirits.
❏ Identify factors affecting choice of purveyors.
❏ Describe purchase orders and outline their use.
❏ Identify control concerns during the issuing process.

Work is the curse of the drinking class.

—Oscar Wilde

The proper selection, purchasing, storing, and issuing of wines, beers, and spirits are the cornerstones of any successful beverage operation. While these tasks can seem daunting, it is important to adhere to certain control procedures in order to maximize profits. Establishing and following sound purchasing, receiving, storing, and issuing procedures will help the beverage manager increase profits and ensure quality of product. Because beverage profit margins are generally more favorable than food profit margins, losing alcoholic beverages to employee theft, product spoilage, and breakage can have a significant impact on the bottom line. To eliminate these potential problems, it is essential that the operator have a system of procedures in place for controlling the entire beverage production process.

Purchasing

Alcoholic beverage sales account for more than 22 percent of profits in most foodservice establishments. Not all alcoholic beverages are appropriate for all establishments, however. For example, certain imported Belgian beers might not sell as well at the local sports bar as they would at a restaurant bar. Management first needs to determine what kind of alcoholic beverages the establishment should sell. This decision will depend upon the type of operation being managed as well as the market the manager is trying to attract.

What to Buy: Wine

Any establishment should consider the recent explosion in the popularity of wines when considering which and how many different types of products to offer for sale. Upscale, full-service establishments will want to offer a larger and more varied wine menu than smaller establishments. This is primarily because the larger establishment will be more able and willing to purchase and store more expensive wines. When purchasing wines, a manager should consider the breadth and depth of the beverage menu. The number of different wines offered on an establishment's beverage menu is referred to as *breadth*. The number of wines offered in a certain category (e.g., Chardonnay or Cabernet Sauvignon) is referred to as *depth.*

The actual number of wines offered and the quantity in which wine is ordered are decisions that are left to the individual establishment and the managers. Each establishment will have its own beverage menu just like each establishment will have its own food menu. Wines can be purchased by the bottle or by the case, depending on how quickly the product will rotate out of the storeroom. Generally speaking, each bottle costs less when purchased by the case, but the establishment needs to have the space to store the wine properly if managers are going to buy in that quantity.

When purchasing wine, a primary consideration should be what products will sell. This will depend upon the tastes of your guests and their degree of wine sophistication. Just because a manager is able to get a deal on a certain type of wine does not mean that it will sell at his or her establishment. It is important to remember that a properly developed wine list serves as an important sales tool that not only allows management to increase profit margins, but enhances the overall dining experience in an establishment.

What to Buy: Beer

Beer is the most popular alcoholic drink served with dinner, and it accounts for almost 40 percent of total alcoholic beverage sales. Almost all establishments will want to have some type of beer on the drink menu. Because of its increased popularity and the myriad number of brands—both domestic and import—available, deciding exactly which beers to offer is somewhat more complex than in days past. Beer is still primarily purchased in bottles, cans, and kegs. Each receptacle has its own advantages and disadvantages, and much of the decision making with respect to what type of container to purchase will be based on customer preferences and the operation's available refrigerated and nonrefrigerated storage space. Some of the advantages to offering draft beer include the relatively small space required to store it and the ease and quickness with which it can be served. One disadvantage of serving draft beer is that, once tapped, the beer has a short shelf life (about three weeks). In addition, draft beer lines must be kept clean, and the product can be messy and easily wasted if the bartender is not trained in proper drawing techniques.

Bottled beer has a longer shelf life, but it requires more storage space. Buying beer in bottles is appropriate for establishments that do not forecast large sales of certain types of beers but would still like to offer them to their customers. Buying these beers in bottles will allow the establishment to keep small amounts of many different types of beer for longer periods of time.

Beer can come from many countries and almost every continent. The vast array of beers available to consumers today includes one for almost every palate. With the rise in popularity of *microbrewed beers,* the hospitality manager should decide whether offering some of these beers would be profitable for the establishment. In addition, low-alcohol or non-alcoholic beers also should be considered. With the public's increased awareness of the hazards of drinking and driving, stocking alcoholic alternatives is a must.

What to Buy: Spirits

Purchasing decisions for spirits will not depend upon whether or not to sell vodka or gin, but on which brands and how many varieties of each should be offered. Spirits are widely consumed, and they have an extremely long shelf-life. Like beer and wine, the popularity of distilled spirits and the variety available to consumers has increased dramatically. Most spirits are sold in bottles called *fifths.* A fifth has 25.4 ounces, or twenty-five 1-ounce servings. They can also be sold in

1.75-liter or 59.2-ounce containers. The larger bottles tend to be more cost effective but are more difficult for bar employees to manipulate.

In deciding what brands of liquors to carry, operations first must determine which brands will make up the *well* and which brands will constitute the *call* and *premium* brand categories. *Well brands* are those that the bartender pours when the customer does not specify a particular brand. For example, if a customer orders a vodka and tonic, the bartender would prepare the drink using well stock. *Call brands* are those that the customer *names* or *calls* when ordering a drink, such as a Bombay Sapphire Martini, specifying a particular brand. The decision of which brands to carry in the well is an important one because of price and customer expectations. Well products are poured most frequently, so they are purchased frequently and often in large quantities. The availability and price of brands chosen for well stock will determine overall profit margins as well as customers' perceived quality of your operation. Because most operations today continue to adhere to a two-tier, and, in some cases, a three-tier pricing structure, the choice of which premium or call brands to carry is an important one as well. Like the well stock, call brands significantly reflect on the overall quality of the establishment, and choosing which brands to offer is an important matter from the perspective of your customers.

Purchasing Procedures

The choice of which distilled spirit, beer, and wine purveyors to use primarily will be determined by product availability and price, but it is important to remember that many states and locales have strict laws with respect to purchasing beverages on the wholesale market. Some factors that should be considered when choosing a purveyor are:

- Price
- Products available
- Delivery schedules
- Bulk buying discounts
- Payment policies
- Minimum order requirements

The purchasing of beverages also may be complicated by what type of state in which your establishment is located: a *license state* or a *control state*. *License states* are those which allow beverage operations to choose which wholesalers or distributors with which they will work. *Control states* require that all liquor be purchased from state-owned stores (see Table 18.1). While this may prevent price wars, it does tend to limit the operator's options with respect to brand selection, delivery options, and supplier stock outages.

Determining when and in what quantities to purchase distilled spirits is primarily based on the operation's sales history and its customers' selection prefer-

Table 18.1   Control States

Alabama	Montana	Utah
Idaho	New Hampshire	Vermont
Iowa	North Carolina	Virginia
Maine	Ohio	Washington
Michigan	Oregon	West Virginia
Mississippi	Pennsylvania	Wyoming

ences. Inventory levels and *par stock* should be carefully developed so as to avoid stock outages and ensure good customer service. *Par stock* is the amount of product needed to be on hand in order to support daily operations. A good rule of thumb is to stock just enough product in the storeroom to prevent running out between deliveries. At the bar, sufficient product should be on hand to prevent running out between shifts or in one day, depending on the operation. Management also must remember that there is no value in tying up capital in a beverage inventory that does not "move," or sell.

Most businesses will develop strict control procedures with respect to purchasing, storing, and issuing alcoholic beverages. *Purchase orders* should be utilized throughout this process in order to create an audit trail that will track the product from the time it is ordered to the time it is received and stored. Some operations stamp or specially mark product as it is delivered before putting it in inventory in the storeroom. An *empty-for-full* system can then be implemented in order to exchange used, empty bottles from the bar for full, fresh product from the liquor storeroom. Because guests' preferences will frequently change, it is important to note that your operation's par levels should be monitored closely and adjusted in response to this. Products with slow movement or no movement at all should be replaced with products that consumers demand.

Receiving

During the receiving process, beverages are generally delivered by the case or by the bottle, so it is not difficult to determine whether a case or a bottle is partially empty or whether beer being delivered is past its expiration date for freshness. Managers should have procedures in place to monitor incoming inventory, verify that they are receiving the proper items, and ensure that items are undamaged and fresh. Managers should make sure that all orders are immediately checked and stored; the person responsible for taking incoming orders should check the items received against the items on the purchase order, check freshness dates, and open cases to be sure all bottles are accounted for and undamaged.

Storing

There are several industry guidelines regarding beverage storage that a foodservice manager should be aware of to minimize loss of product and to ensure freshness and quality. These rules may be somewhat different for each kind of wine, beer, and spirit being offered.

When a manager considers where to store wine, there are several important points to remember, including light, heat, vibration, and oxygen. Wine should be stored in a dark place with a moderate temperature (about 55°F.) that is free of vibrations. In addition, the bottles of wine should be stored on their sides, and the storeroom should be maintained at 70 percent relative humidity whenever possible. Adhering to these last two points will ensure that corks are kept moist and plump; this will prevent oxygen from getting to the wine. (Oxygen spoils the wine, turning it into vinegar.) In the proper environment, some wine can be stored for years and even decades.

Beer, like wine, is perishable when exposed to the wrong environmental elements. Beer is damaged by light and heat and should be stored in a dark place with a moderate temperature. Beer in kegs should be refrigerated. Most bottled beer is sealed with a metal cap that keeps the carbon dioxide from escaping, and it keeps oxygen from spoiling the beer. Some beer bottles are sealed with a cork, not too unlike sparkling wine.

Spirits are the most stable of all alcoholic beverages in that they will last for years. However, caution should be taken when storing these beverages because they are very flammable. They should be stored away from heat and flame to avoid a fire hazard. Keeping spirits away from heat sources also helps avoid a flavor change in the beverages. Certain cordials and cream-based liqueurs present challenges with respect to storage, especially once the product has been opened. Operators should take care to constantly monitor the quality of these products.

Issuing

Issuing product from the storeroom to the production area—in most cases the bar—is an important part of the checks-and-balance system necessary to control product theft and, consequently, profit margins and cost percent. Alcoholic beverages are a target for employee theft because the product is easily concealed and is highly desirable. It is essential to implement procedures during the purchasing, storing, and issuing processes that will ensure product quality as well as eliminate all opportunities for theft. Managers can discourage theft by keeping alcohol storage areas locked at all times and by implementing strict issuing procedures.

Issuing is defined as the process of the bar acquiring alcoholic beverages and other food items from the storeroom. Larger establishments may have full-time storeroom staff that take care of issuing product from the storeroom to the bar.

This process might include formal requisitions that require management's signature. Issuing creates an audit trail so that management can track where products, especially alcoholic beverages, are going. In smaller establishments, the issuing process may be as simple as asking the manager to unlock the cabinet or room in which the product is stored. The manager can take note of what is being removed from the cabinet and for what reason.

Key Terms

Breadth

Call brand

Control state

Depth

Empty-for-full

Fifth

Issuing

License state

Microbrewed beers

Par stock

Premium brand

Purchase orders

Well brand

Study Questions

1. What are some of the factors that affect the depth and breadth of a wine list?
2. What factors must be considered when choosing purveyors of wines, beers, and spirits?
3. How should wine be stored properly?
4. How should beer be stored properly?
5. Describe the proper methods for storing the following:
   a. bottled wine
   b. bottled or canned beer
   c. beer in kegs
6. What factors should be considered in the storage of distilled spirits and liqueurs?
7. What control techniques are necessary in the storing and issuing process to prevent theft?

Chapter

19

Beverage Cost Control: Managing for Profit

After reading this chapter, you will be able to:

❏ Compute the cost of beverages sold.
❏ Determine prices using product cost percentage and contribution margin methods.
❏ Understand the variables that influence beverage menu pricing and their effects on profits.
❏ Understand beverage pricing methods for banquets and other catered events.
❏ Understand the importance of standardized recipes and how they influence profits.
❏ Understand the difference between keeping a physical and a perpetual inventory.
❏ Employ techniques to track and control beverage costs.

Onion soup sustains. The process of making it is somewhat like the process of learning to love. It requires commitment, extraordinary effort, time, and will make you cry.
—Ronni Lundy in "The seasoned cook," *Esquire* (March 1984)

Figure 19.1   A well-stocked bar. [Dorling Kindersley Images]

Alcoholic beverages account for nearly 22 percent of restaurant sales. The majority of the money generated from these sales goes to profit because of the high markup on beverages. In fine restaurants, for example, a markup of 100 percent for a bottle of inexpensive wine is not unusual. Most drinks are easy to pour or mix, and the labor and beverage costs combined represent a small portion of the selling price.

   In the previous chapter, we discussed purchasing, receiving, storing, and issuing procedures for alcoholic beverages. While these procedures are similar to those used for food products, one should not necessarily assume that the process for controlling beverage costs will be the same as that for controlling food costs. In this chapter, we will focus on the procedures for tracking alcoholic beverage costs, determining prices, and controlling inventory.

Calculating Beverage Cost As a Percent of Sales

The percentage of cost spent on beverages is one of the primary benchmarks by which an operation gauges its overall performance. The formula for calculating beverage cost percentage is:

Cost of Beverages Sold ÷ Beverage Sales = Beverage Cost Percentage

The cost of beverages sold is calculated on the basis of the value of the entire beverage inventory:

Beginning Inventory (last period's ending inventory)		$_____
Plus this period's purchases	+	$_____
Equals goods available for sale	=	$_____
Less Ending Inventory (next period's beginning inventory)	−	$_____
Equals Cost of Beverages Sold	=	$_____

Determine the cost of beverages sold for a given month, and divide this number into the beverage sales. The result will be the *beverage cost percentage*.

When performing these calculations, it is important to note that if the bar transfers any beverage products to the kitchen for cooking purposes, those transfers need to be tracked and their value subtracted before totaling the cost of beverages sold. On the other hand, if the kitchen transfers product such as mixers and fruit to the bar, those transfers must be tracked and their value added before totaling the cost of beverages sold.

Because of the relative ease with which a dishonest employee can manipulate inventory records, and, therefore, beverage cost percentage, most experts recommend that the duties of receiving, storing, issuing, and inventorying be separated. This is known as *separation of duties*. In other words, the individual who receives the product should not be the same individual who stores and issues the product. In addition, a different individual should be responsible for month-end inventories. While separating these duties is relatively easy for larger operations, it may be next to impossible for the smaller owner-operator who must rely on a limited staff. In cases such as these, it is wise to assign all of these duties to the owner or manager of the operation.

Determining Prices to Ensure Profitability

In the restaurant industry, *cost of sales* refers to the restaurant's cost for products that are sold to its customers. Some operations may use the term *cost of goods sold*. Most foodservice operations break down food sales and beverage sales separately. Costs for each category also are shown separately on most operations' profit and loss statements (P&Ls). Beverage costs include the purchase price of the alcoholic beverages and other ingredients, such as juices, carbonated mixers, and fruit used to make drinks. These (and all other) costs are customarily stated both in dollar amounts and as a percentage of sales. Determining what prices to charge for beverage products is related to cost control and to an operation's overall profits. Charging too little for products can result in lowered profits; charging too much can result in lowered customer counts. Menu pricing for beverage sales is affected significantly by many factors, including local competition, customer demographics, product quality, and portion size. While a manager may not have an effect on all of these factors, he or she can exercise control in determining the amount to charge customers for drinks. In general, foodservice managers use one of the two following concepts to determine what price to charge:

1. Product cost percentage
2. Contribution margin

The *product cost percentage* method of pricing is based on the idea that an item's cost should be a predetermined percentage of its selling price. In other words, if a manager knows how much of a cost percent he or she wants to achieve on a drink, he or she can determine the price. Let's say, for example, an operator wishes to achieve a 20 percent beverage cost on a Martini that costs $1.50 to produce. The Martini's selling price can be determined by using the following formula:

$$\text{Product Cost} \div \text{Desired Product Profit} = \text{Selling Price}$$
$$\$1.50 \div .20 = \$7.50$$

If the Martini is sold at $7.50, a 20 percent beverage profit will be achieved. This across-the-board approach to pricing has its flaws. It often results in some items being priced too low and some items being priced too high.

In general, pricing bottled wine only by the product cost percentage method is a strategy that may result in overall decreased bottled wine sales. It is important to price bottled wine so that the *price spread*—the range between the lowest- and highest-priced bottles—is not excessive. Reducing the price spread may assist the operator in not only selling more wine, but in selling more high-priced wine. One goal of establishing selling prices is to create a good price-value relationship in the mind of the customer. If a customer does not believe he or she is receiving good value for the money spent, he or she will not make the purchase; therefore, beverage pricing usually is not based on a mathematical equation alone. Managers must keep the notion of *perceived value* in mind when creating prices.

Another method of product pricing is to focus not on the item's cost percentage but rather on its *contribution margin*—the difference between the item's product cost and its selling price, expressed as follows:

$$\text{Selling price} - \text{Product cost} = \text{Contribution margin}$$

Contribution margin is defined as the profit or the amount that remains after product cost is subtracted from an item's selling price. When using this pricing approach, operators often establish different contribution margins for various beverage items or groups of items. For example, draft beer may be priced with a contribution margin of $2.00 each, cocktails with a contribution margin of $3.00,

Figure 19.2 Bottles of wine marked with bin numbers. [Pearson Education/Prentice Hall]

and bottled wines with various other contribution margins. Therefore, in this case, if draft beer costs $1.75 per serving, its selling price would be $3:

$$\text{Cost} + \text{contribution margin} = \text{selling price}$$
$$\$1.75 + \$2.00 = \$3.75$$

Pricing and Inventory Control for Parties and Receptions

Beverage pricing for parties and receptions can seem daunting, but it need not be. Clients often have the choice of arranging for a *cash bar* or a *host bar*. When a *cash bar* is requested, guests attending the function are expected to pay for their alcoholic beverages as they are consumed. For a *host bar*, the host is charged at the end of the function.

Cash Bar Procedures

Standard pricing procedures will suffice for a cash bar. It is important, however, to institute strict control procedures in order to prevent bartender theft. Many operations now use a ticket system rather than having cash exchange hands between bartenders and the customers attending the event. This method requires that guests purchase drink tickets that can be exchanged at any of the satellite bars set up for the function. Some operations color code tickets. For example, they may use blue for beer, pink for wine, and green for mixed drinks. Other operators simply assign a set dollar value to each ticket. When the guest "buys" a beverage, beer might cost one ticket and a mixed drink might require two, depending on the cost of the drink.

Host Bar Procedures

Many banquet clients prefer to pick up the entire beverage tab of their function. If this is the case, a host bar is generally arranged. If a *host bar* (sometimes called an *open bar*) is called for, guests do not pay for beverages as they are consumed. Instead, the host is presented with the bill at the end of the function.

There are numerous methods for setting prices and controlling inventory for such functions. Two of the most common methods are:

1. Charging the host on a per-person, per-hour basis
2. Charging the host for the actual amount of beverages consumed

If the per-person, per-hour basis is used, the operator must estimate how much the average guest will consume during the function to establish a per-person charge. Clearly, various consumer groups will behave differently when attending a hosted bar function; therefore, this pricing method is somewhat risky. Some operators, however, have had success by keeping meticulous beverage consumption records that detail the average consumption of a wide variety of groups. These records are used to establish pricing guidelines.

One of the most tried and true methods for controlling a host bar is to charge the client for the actual amount of beverages consumed. This method requires that a beginning and ending inventory be taken at all satellite bars operating at the function. If there are any additions to inventory during the course of the function, these must be recorded as well. A simple form such as the one in Table 19.1 can be devised for this process. Note that if assorted brands of each wine, spirit, and beer are to be offered, the form should be designed to reflect varying product costs.

If this control method is used, it is customary for the host or his or her designee to be present to verify the beginning and ending inventory. In addition, some hosts will insist that the operator provide empty bottles as proof of product consumed. If a product has been opened but not entirely consumed, some state liquor authorities allow the host to purchase the entire bottle and carry out what remains in the bottle. Other state liquor laws prohibit this practice. If the latter is the case, the operator must employ a system of *weighing* or *measuring* to determine quantities consumed from partially used bottles.

Table 19.1   Sample Host Bar Inventory Control Form

Beverage Type	Beginning Inventory	Plus (+) Additions	Equal (=) Total Available	Minus (−) Ending Inventory	Equal (=) Total Usage	Unit Cost	Total Cost
Liquor A							
Liquor B							
Beer A							
Beer B							
Wine A							
Wine B							
Total Product Cost							

Controlling Costs at the Bar

One system used to control bar costs is portion control. Portion control is necessary to achieve desired profit margins. It is also important for the operator to have solid systems of control in place because incidents of employee theft and misuse can be a frequent problem at the bar. It is recommended that mixed drinks conform to standardized recipes with standardized portions in order to achieve desired costs. An example of a standardized recipe is shown in below.

Developing and using standardized recipes in beverage operations also has a major impact on the overall consistency of products being served. A customer's drink should look and taste the same each time it is ordered. Achieving proper

Sample Standardized Recipe

Vodka Martini $4.25

In a cocktail shaker with ice:
2 oz vodka
A splash of sweet Vermouth.
Shake and strain into martini glass. Garnish with olive.

portion control when producing mixed drinks can be done in a variety of ways. Three of the most common are using jiggers, using special bottle pour spouts, and using liquor computer systems.

As explained in Chapter 16, a *jigger* is a device used to measure spirits; it typically measures in ounces or portions of an ounce. It is uncomplicated and inexpensive, and it is the tried and true choice of many operators today. Other operators use specially designed pour spouts that allow only a predetermined measure of liquor to flow from bottle to glass when the bartender prepares a mixed drink. These devices have become much more common in recent years as manufacturers have fine-tuned the measuring mechanisms located in the spouts. Computerized beverage management systems are more extreme. These allow a bartender to dispense a predetermined measure of liquor from a beverage gun only after the sale has been rung up or pre-checked. These sophisticated systems offer a high level of control, and they are popular in large hotel and casino operations. Their relatively high cost puts them out of reach for most smaller, independent operators, however.

Whatever system is in place, operators must enforce its use through constant monitoring, training, and positive reinforcement. Because there are so many ways for a dishonest bartender, or a dishonest bartender and cocktail server working in collusion, to steal, an entire cottage industry of professional restaurant and bar mystery shoppers has developed. These professionals can be hired by upper management to visit the establishment anonymously. Posing as customers, they may sit at the bar for an hour or more observing bartender and server transactions. Well-trained mystery shoppers can often spot irregularities that may indicate employee theft. These irregularities may include:

1. Orders filled but not rung up and the bartender pocketing cash.
2. Bartenders bringing in extra product and pocketing cash.
3. Bartenders under- and over-pouring.
4. Bartenders making incorrect change to cover theft of cash.
5. Bartenders substituting less expensive product and pocketing cash.
6. Bartenders providing drinks to servers without drinks being rung up.
7. Bartenders giving away product to friends.

Because most states' dram shop laws (see Chapter 2) create immense liability for the operator, mystery shoppers also are trained to observe alcohol awareness and safety issues. Mystery shoppers write very detailed and thorough reports to management based on their observations.

Controlling Inventory

A proper system of inventory management helps ensure beverage cost control and is essential if the operator desires to achieve profitability. Commonly, two types of inventory may be kept: *physical* and *perpetual*. A *physical inventory* refers

to the actual number of each item that is on hand, either in storage or in the bar production area. Physical inventory generally is taken at regularly scheduled intervals, such as the last day of each month after the bar has closed for business, and it requires that all items on hand be accounted for and assigned a value. While this may seem like a tedious process, there is no substitution for a regular physical inventory. *Perpetual inventories* are continuous records of what has been purchased and what has been issued from storage to the beverage production area. Just as you balance your checkbook each time you write a check or make a deposit, operators who employ a perpetual inventory system account for *additions to* (deposits) and *deletions from* (withdrawals) inventory as they occur.

Operators must prove the actual value of their inventory on hand by doing a physical count. Why do operators bother with a perpetual inventory if they must then do a physical inventory anyway? Some don't. Other operators employ both methods but only monitor high-cost items on a perpetual inventory basis. This allows the operator to know if there is a problem with possible theft or beverage cost control before it is too late to make necessary changes or adjustments to procedures and systems.

Key Terms

Cost of Beverages Sold	Host Bar
Cost of Goods Sold	Open Bar
Cost of Sales	Standardized Recipe
Contribution Margin	Jigger
Price Spread	Mystery Shopper
Cash Bar	

Study Questions

1. Refer to the information below to compute the Kon-Tiki Bar's cost of beverages sold:

Beginning Inventory	$26,000.00
Purchases	$34,256.00
Goods Available	$_____
Ending Inventory	$22,849.00
Cost of Beverages Sold	$_____

2. The Kon-Tiki Bar's beverages sales totaled $178,129.00. Based on your answer to Question #2 above, calculate the bar's beverage cost percentage.

3. List and discuss at least three variables that will influence beverage pricing.

4. A restaurant operator desires a 24 percent beverage cost on a bottle of wine that costs the operator $12.00. What is the most appropriate selling price for the bottle of wine?

5. A restaurant operator desires a $10.00 contribution margin on a bottle of wine that costs the operator $8.00. What is the most appropriate selling price for the bottle of wine?

6. List and discuss two beverage pricing methods for an open bar (host bar).

Chapter

20 Marketing and Selling

After reading this chapter, you will be able to:

❐ Develop a business plan.
❐ Distinguish between the terms *marketing* and *selling*.
❐ Define the term *organization*.
❐ Explain how suggestive selling can increase profitability.
❐ Explain the relationship between customer mix and target markets.

Successful individuals have game plans and purposes that are clearly defined to which they constantly refer.
—*Seeds of Greatness*, Denis Waitley

Marketing a successful beverage operation entails much more than advertising and sales promotion. Marketing encompasses everything from developing the operation's concept and product/service to pricing, promoting, and making the product available to consumers. Marketing should be guest-oriented, but an operation's main goal should be to have a happy marriage between financial concerns of management and consumers' preferences. Because marketing is such an integral part of an operation's overall business plan, this chapter will begin with a discussion of strategic management plan goals and the written business plan.

Strategic Management Plan

In the foodservice and beverage industry, everything starts with the customer. Finding and holding onto this elusive creature is the most important factor in the success of any operation. In order to find and keep customers, management must first identify who these customers are. Then they must determine strategies for fulfilling these customers' needs and wants. A business must have a strategic plan in place in order to accomplish these goals.

An organization's strategic plan should consist of a mission statement, short-term and long-term goals, and actions for achieving these goals. In addition, strategic management is important for the organization to process, identify, and develop a competitive advantage and to remain profitable. It also provides a sense of direction so members of the organization can strive to excel in the day-to-day activities as well as keep the organization's long-term plan in focus. By providing employees with measurable and achievable goals, managers increase motivation and employees will have a clear idea of the major outcomes that they are expected to achieve.

Strategic Management Plan Principles

One of the main principles upon which all foodservice/beverage operations are based is *customer value.* If customers do not feel they are receiving value for their money, they will not return and the business will not survive. It is difficult to be all things to all people; therefore, the owner(s) must create a specific kind of value in a specific way. Management must decide what it can offer, and it must create the organization accordingly. This value will be reflected in more than the types of liquor the establishment chooses to sell; it will be inherent in the establishment's atmosphere and its working environment.

Another strategic plan principle is *organization.* Organization refers to how management structures its departments, employees, products, services, accounting procedures, and work procedures and methods. The nature of the business will determine how a company selects its preferred leadership organization and style. Management may be tightly or loosely structured; however, managers must keep the establishment organized and focused to accomplish the organization's goals.

All operations need to develop a *competitive advantage* in order to remain profitable. Simply stated, a competitive advantage means providing better products and services than other businesses in your target market. If successful, a business will be able to develop customer loyalty and maintain greater success than its competitors during the organization's life cycle.

Another important business principle involves establishing *controls.* Managers are responsible for controls that are developed by looking at company goals and assigning tasks that will motivate everyone toward those goals. Controls will be "processed" by budgets: labor costs, beverage costs, the selection and hiring process, and purchasing, each representing important management decisions. Controls must be in place for accounting, operations, marketing, sales, information systems, and the support functions of each department.

The last principle is *profitability*—the establishment's ability to make money for the business owner(s). Success can be measured in a variety of ways, but to remain in business, to grow, compete, and continue with long-term plans, profit must exist. There are many types of establishments serving alcohol, each with its own personality and potential. The common goal of these businesses is to develop the maximum flow of sales into the operation and serve the consumer most effectively for the highest profit.

The Business Plan

All foodservice and beverage operation owners should have a business plan in place. This plan is a written statement of an operation's business strategy; it provides the operation with goals for all aspects of the business, including marketing. A business plan is most useful when the original business concept is in the early planning stages. The importance of the business plan as an ongoing management tool, however, should not be overlooked. A well-written business plan not only will help convince investors of the viability of the original idea; it also will allow management to remain on track, following the plan as the business grows and develops.

A written *business plan* provides information and details on the nature of the business, the customers, the products and services, the marketing strategies, the management team, the competition, and the financing. A simple format can be developed for each subject with organizational charts and projections to reflect potential revenues and expenses.

Business plans serve many important purposes. For example, lending institutions will require a complete business plan if the future owner(s) wish to obtain a mortgage. This requirement forces the owner to think carefully about every aspect of the proposed business. Many business owners are anxious to offer their products and services, but most do not understand all of the laws, licenses, capital, labor costs, and inventory requirements. The high failure rate of establishments in the foodservice industry partially is due to owners starting a business without prior knowledge of these requirements and costs.

A well-conceived business plan also provides a basis for measuring progress. Since revenue projections are assumptions, it is important for the owner(s) to monitor business transactions and to be able to apply modifications and corrections for establishing a successful business. Business plans also will establish professionalism and credibility with future vendors, employees, and the community and assist in the business's growth and maturity in the marketplace.

If adequate financing and human resources are well planned, the major stepping-stones have been accomplished. With capital and labor, the process of developing new ventures will be comprised of five major stages of growth: existence, survival, success, takeoff, and maturity. These stages represent the life cycle of a business. Strong companies will develop new methods to extend their success by offering new products and services during the success of the company.

The parts of a business plan are included in the following:

Summary Statement: An Overview of the Business
1. Summarize the business plan—its purpose and promise. State the reasons why the business should exist.
2. Analyze the strengths and weaknesses, the owner's business education, the owner's experience, and the owner's desires.
3. Develop a legal plan that focuses on whether to form a sole proprietorship, a partnership, or a corporation and understand the advantages and disadvantages of each.

Market Analysis: Defining the Business's Niche
1. Determine who the prospective customers are and find out exactly what these customers need and desire. Every hospitality business has more than one prime market; usually, one or two principal sources of business dominate the prospective markets.
2. Once the customers have been defined, the owner or manager must conduct research in order to find the service level, products and facilities that will meet the market's needs.
3. Prepare a plan for conducting a market analysis every year because customers change, and the owner or manager must translate his or her knowledge of the market into current market conditions. (A market may be defined as business people, traveling customers, college students, social events, and/or professional organizations, either individually or in-groups.)

Management Plan: Organizational Chart and Staffing
1. Develop an organizational plan which outlines the talents, skills and specialized individuals that will comprise the organization. If the com-

pany is developed with a partner, each person should complement the other individual and be an asset to the operation.
2. Develop a selection and hiring process of all employees that "fit" the organization's short-term and long-term goals to grow and mature as a business.
3. Develop protocols for assigning authority, responsibility, accountability, and reporting. These are other important parts of the organizational format and staffing process.

Products/Services of the Business
1. Select the products and services that best fit the business's strengths and desires.
2. Research customer income and age, competitive prices, benefits of use, growth potential, and what the business's products and services cannot do.
3. Consider such external forces as economic, social, environmental, and legal conditions that will affect the business's products and services.

Marketing Strategy
1. Develop a sound marketing strategy that focuses on a particular group of customers and their buying behaviors.

Financial Data
1. Consult with a certified accountant to learn important laws, accounting formulas, and how to establish a correct business structure (i.e., sole proprietor, partnership, etc.).
2. Develop a financial plan.
3. Work with accountants on insurance planning and the development of an information system plan to assist daily operations.

Projections: The Future of the Business
1. Determine a method to forecast revenues and expenses and list these projections. Forecasting revenues and expenses is critical to all operations. Is the forecast believable? Is it realistic? If not, develop the forecast accurately so the flow of cash in and out of the business can be anticipated. Projections will assist the manager or owners with many present and future decisions, as well as prepare the business for future growth. Forecasts normally are determined over a three-year period.
2. Include information on how revenues and expenses will be recorded monthly for the first year; quarterly systems can be applied for the second and third year.
3. Use a balance sheet and a profit graph. These will be valuable tools to evaluate the profit (or lack of) and adjust the organizational goals and business plan as needed.

Marketing

Management's marketing objectives are (1) to develop potential products, (2) to identify the consumer's needs and wants, (3) to provide service, and (4) to convince customers to return. The first step in meeting these goals is to identify the potential customer, or market. A *market* is a group of customers made up of individuals or organizations with certain characteristics. Many factors must be looked at when determining the target market for a business. An owner must determine the buying behavior, customer satisfaction level, attitudes, and lifestyles of his or her customers. The study of psychographics is relatively new for many marketers; however, it is critical in understanding these variables (i.e., personality traits, marital status, number of children, sexual orientation, political leaning, religion, work environment, hobbies, television-watching habits, participation in sports and arts, vacation plans, and frequency of socializing). A combination of geographic data and demographic characteristics is used to segment and target specific markets. This information is referred to as *geodemographics.*

The physical location of the establishment is another critical factor that must be kept in mind when developing a marketing strategy. High-traffic areas obviously are good locations for bars and restaurants; if an owner is trying to determine a good location for a new establishment, these types of venues should be given preference. How management and owners use their existing space is a component of marketing strategies as well. For example, today, hospitality organizations place their bars on the first floor with an outside entrance to generate sales so they do not have to rely solely on their primary customer base, their hotel guests. Bars connected to dining rooms will serve several purposes. These locations make it possible for customers to get a drink before dining. They also provide a gathering place for socializing, conducting business, and, if applicable, entertainment.

Marketing is a long-term system of planning that allows a business to be successful, and it makes it possible for the entire business to be seen from the point of view of the customer. By identifying the target customer and figuring out how to market the product to that customer, an owner can create, design, and operate a successful, profit-making business.

General Beverage Marketing Trends

Identifying and keeping current with trends are important aspects of developing and implementing any marketing plan. Additionally, customer attitudes and desires change continually, therefore, it is important for operators to keep their fingers on the pulse of society. Just as in the world of fashion, beverage products come in and out of vogue. In the 1970s and early 1980s, wine bars were the rage from coast to coast. The late 1980s and early 1990s saw a marked increase in the consumption of the so-called white liquors—gin, vodka, tequila and some rums. Martinis, Manhattans, Old-Fashioneds and other such retro cocktails that were popular in the 1950s were once again in style during this period. The mid- to late-

1990s ushered in a return of the popularity of the dark liquors. No serious beverage operation could be without a variety of fine, aged Kentucky bourbons and imported single malt Scotches in the 1990s.

Consumers today expect a wide variety of imported and domestic wines, and operators who offer beer have discovered that one or two domestic brands in bottles and on tap no longer satisfy today's sophisticated consumer. Microbrews and a wide variety of imported beers are the norm today.

One should be aware, however, that while trends will often seem to be taking hold or losing ground, this is not necessarily a good reason to make dramatic changes in the business's methods of operation. Different regions of the country have different values, and what is true of one coast may not be true of the other or of the Midwest. Studies and guides are useful, but whether the information they contain applies to your city or your operation can only be determined by asking your customers.

A Tale of Two Bars

The methods used for marketing and selling beverage products is dependent on what type of establishment is trying to sell the drink. Consider two different bar concepts: *The Library* and *The Office.* These bars are in the same town. The Library is located next to a large university, whereas The Office is located in a downtown business district.

The Library's target market will be very different from that of The Office. The Library should expect to draw most of its customers from the university, whereas The Office draws its customers from the downtown business area. (See Table 20.1.)

Referring to the customer demographic information, consider the following questions:

1. What types of drinks would The Library sell?
2. What types of drinks would The Office sell?

The Library probably would sell very little wine but a good deal of draft beer such as Budweiser, Miller, and Coors. They also would most likely sell mixed drinks with suggestive names such as *Sex on the Beach* or *Sloe Comfortable Screw.* The Library food menu might include traditional American pub grub such as hot wings, potato skins, or personal pan pizzas.

Table 20.1   Customer demographics of two bars' target markets.

The library	The office
Under 25	Over 25
Single	Most single but some married
Limited income	More disposable income
"Looking to party"	"Looking to unwind"

The Office, on the other hand, would sell more wine and microbrews, such as Sam Adams Anchor, or Yuengling. In addition, The Office probably would sell classic mixed drinks such as Martinis or Whiskey Sours. The Office food menu might include American bistro cuisine such as light pasta dishes, soup and sandwich combinations, or grilled pizzas.

The Library and The Office also might choose different strategies to attract their respective customers during different holidays. Review the chart below and consider how the two establishments might target their customers during these times of celebration.

Month	Name of holiday	The library's selling strategies	The office's selling strategies
January	New Year's Day		
	The Super Bowl		
February	Valentine's Day		
	Mardi Gras (Fat Tuesday)		
	American Wine Appreciation Month		
March	St. Patrick's Day		
April	April Fool's Day		
	Easter		
	Passover		
	National Secretary Day		
May	May Day		
	Kentucky Derby or The Triple Crown		
	Memorial Day		
	Mother's Day		
	Cinco de Mayo		
June	Father's Day		
	Flag Day		
July	Independence Day		
August	Football tailgating parties		
September	Labor Day		
October	Oktoberfest		
	World Series		
	Halloween		
November	Election Day		
	Thanksgiving		
	Beaujolais Nouveau		
December	Christmas Season		
	New Year's Eve		

The Library and The Office may emphasize different days to attract their customers, and if they did celebrate the same holiday, they probably would celebrate in different fashions. For example, each one of these establishments most likely would celebrate or acknowledge Halloween, but they would do it very differently. The Library might have a live band and a "wild" costume party. The Office might have something less outrageous but just as enticing to its customers. In addition, some days The Library would celebrate would not be celebrated by The Office, such as football tailgating parties. On the other hand, The Office might celebrate National Secretaries Day but The Library would not.

Internal Marketing

Marketing is a precise, carefully measured and coordinated detailed plan of action. One should think of marketing as a blueprint for the future. In general, marketing is divided into two categories: *internal marketing* and *external marketing. External marketing* refers to activities undertaken to bring the customer into the establishment, such as television advertising or coupons. *Internal marketing* refers to in-house promotions. Internal sales can be boosted by conducting promotions with table tents, mailings, and guest databases. As with external marketing, bar promotions are effective and lasting only with planning. The "one-shot specials" may only create a temporary impression unless management develops methods to keep the product alive.

Many operators turn to their suppliers for merchandising ideas and assistance, and suppliers are only too glad to help. Today it is not uncommon to see suppliers and operators working hand-in-hand to offer promotions geared around the exquisite pairing of a special menu with two or three varieties of the supplier's wines. Microbreweries also are anxious to get their products into the hands of consumers. They do this by joining forces with bar operators interested in co-promoting products and events.

Internal marketing also includes *suggestive selling.* Suggestive selling refers to the practice of wait staff offering purchasing ideas to the customer. For instance, if a customer orders a Martini, the server might ask, "Would you like that made with Tangueray or Beefeaters?" Suggestive selling may help sales because the suggestions may lead the customer to trade up on his or her order or to order something in addition to the original purchase. In order for suggestive selling to be effective, however, employees must be knowledgeable about the operation's products and services, and they must be willing to engage the customer. In general, the employees who will be best at this maintain a team spirit and enjoy the hospitality service industry. In the end, however, to make this type of internal marketing successful, managers must commit to teaching, developing, training, and retraining employees.

Customer Mix

Management will generally attempt to create a certain type of establishment in order to attract a certain type of clientele. Atmosphere, decor, entertainment, scenery, and image all serve to attract the type of clientele that management has targeted as its core customer base. A bar will have the "no-nonsense drinkers" who know their beverage and brand and will judge the glass, the quality of

Figure 20.1   A busy bar. [Dorling Kindersley Images]

liquor and service, and their surroundings. They either will or will not develop a comfort zone in the bar.

Service Styles

Service transactions are electronic, indirect and/or direct (face-to-face), and the employees representing the business are a large part of the guest's experience. Face-to-face service by each employee and the delivery of personal interaction between the guest and the employee is critical. Without friendly interaction in the bar business, repeat business will not develop.

Key Terms

Customer Value
Organization
Competitive Advantage
Control
Profitability
Geodemographics

External Sales
Internal Sales
Suggestive Selling
Customer Mix
Target Markets

Study Questions

1. Use the list of holidays in this chapter to create a plan for The Library and for The Office. Compare and contrast what the two establishments might do for the holidays.
2. Identify the major components of a business plan and outline their importance to the overall success of a beverage operation.
3. Define *strategic management* and identify methods for employing strategic management techniques.
4. Explain the difference between sales and marketing and give examples of techniques used to employ each.
5. Define *internal marketing* and give examples of how to successfully implement techniques for a successful beverage operation.

Glossary

Acetic: A descriptive word for a wine that has an excess of acetic acid or vinegar flavors.

Aftertaste: Also known as the finish, aftertaste is found in complex wines and is the flavor left in the mouth after the taster has swallowed the wine.

Aggressive: A descriptive word for a wine that has slightly high tannin or acid.

Alcohol: (C_2H_5OH) Ethanol.

Alcohol content by volume: The alcohol content of a liquid expressed as a percent of total volume. It can legally vary by up to $\pm 1\ 1/2\%$.

Ale: A beer made with a top fermenting yeast.

Ampelographer: An individual who practices ampelography, the study of the identification of grapevine botany.

Appellation d'Origine Contrôlée (AOC): An agency created by French authorities in 1935 that establishes the rules for French wine production in specific growing regions of France.

Armagnac: The oldest brandy; made in the area of Armagnac, southeast of Bordeaux in France.

Aromatic: A descriptive word used to characterize wine in which the aromas and/or flavors of the wine have a spicy or herb quality.

Astringent: A descriptive word used to characterize wine that has very high tannin or acid.

Atmospheres (atms): A term used to describe a unit of pressure equal to 14.69 pounds of force per square inch; often used in the production of sparkling wine, where it describes bottle pressure which can range anywhere from 5 to 7 atms.

Auslese: A descriptive term used to describe a usually sweet German wine made from "late-picked" grapes that have achieved a higher sugar level.

Austere: A term used to describe a young wine with a high tannic and/or acidic level that might soften with aging.

A.V.A.: American Viticultural Area, a wine-growing region located within the United States.

Bacchanalia: A Roman celebration of Bacchus, the Roman god of wine.

Bacchus: The Roman god of wine.

Baked or burned: Describes a burned caramel flavor in wine caused by overexposure to heat.

Balanced: A wine-tasting term that refers to a wine that has the perfect combination of flavors: acid, alcohol, fruit, tannin, and sugar; in other words, none overpowers the others.

Balthazar: A 12-liter bottle of wine.

Barbaresco: A dry red Italian wine from the area of Barbaresco, located in Italy's Piedmont region, that is made with 100 percent Nebbiolo grapes.

Barbera d'Alba: A red grape varietal from the town of Alba, located in Italy's Piedmont region.

Barbera d'Asti: A red grape varietal from the town of Asti, located in Italy's Piedmont region.

Barnyard: A descriptive word for a wine that has an aroma similar to animal fecal matter.

Barolo: A dry red wine from the area of Barolo, located in Italy's Piedmont region, that is made with 100 percent Nebbiolo grapes.

Baron Rothschild: Baron Philippe de Rothschild, who died in 1988, owned some of Bordeaux's most premier estates, including Château Mouton-Rothschild. He is best known for upgrading Château Mouton-Rothschild from a second-growth to a first-growth wine, which was the only change ever made to the 1855 classification.

Barsac: A small wine-growing region in Bordeaux France known for its sweet wines.

Bartender: An individual who works behind a bar preparing drink orders for customers and/or waitstaff.

Beaujolais Nouveau: New wine from the Beaujolais region of France, made with Gamay grapes. The wine is released for sale in November and is the first wine available in the Northern Hemisphere.

Beefy: A descriptive word used to characterize a full-bodied wine.

Beerenauslese (BA): An intensely sweet German wine made from hand-picked grapes in order to ensure the quality and sweetness of the wine. This wine is usually very expensive; the grapes are sometimes infected with Noble Rot and left on the vine in order to heighten their sugar content.

Big-Full-Heavy: A descriptive term used to characterize a full-bodied wine that is high in alcohol content and that has good balance.

Bitter: A word used to describe a wine with high tannin levels or another element that makes the wine bitter.

Black Rot: A fungus rot of grapevines caused by a black fungus. This condition is always viewed as unfavorable.

Blanc de Blanc: A term to describe a sparkling wine that is made from white grapes, usually the Chardonnay grape.

Blanc de Noir: A term used to describe a white sparkling wine that is made from red grapes, usually the Pinot Noir and Pinot Meunier grapes.

Blending: The process of mixing two wines together in order to achieve a single outcome or product.

Blood Alcohol Content (BAC): The most common system for measuring and reporting Blood Alcohol Content (BAC) uses the weight of alcohol (milligrams) and the volume of blood (deciliter). This yields a Blood Alcohol Concentration that can be expressed as a percentage (e.g., 0.10% alcohol by volume).

Bodega: A Spanish term used to describe a wine storage or cellar facility.

Bordeaux: A wine-growing region in southwestern France that produces both red and white wines. The red wines consist of mostly Cabernet Sauvignon and Merlot blends, whereas the white wines consist mostly of Sauvignon Blanc and Sémillon blends.

Bordeaux Blanc: A white wine from the Bordeaux region of France.

Bottle fermented: A term used to describe a fermenting process for both sparkling wine and beer in which the second fermentation occurs in the bottle.

Bottom fermenting: A beer fermentation process associated with lagers in which the fermentation occurs at the bottom of the tank.

Bourbon: A whiskey, mostly associated with the state of Kentucky, produced from at least 51 percent—but not more than 79 percent—corn. Bourbon must be aged for a minimum of two years, but most distillers age for at least four years. It also must be aged in a new, charred, white oak barrel.

Brandy: A generic term used to describe distilled wine.

Bright: A descriptive term used to characterize a young wine with fresh and fruity aromas and flavors.

Brix: The name of a system used to measure the sugar content of grapes. The brix multiplied by 0.55 equals the potential alcohol by volume content of the wine being produced.

Brut: A term used to describe one of the driest French champagnes. Only Extra Brut would be drier.

Bual: A red grape varietal used to make a semi-sweet style of Madeira.

Burgundy: A wine-growing region in eastern France known for the production of red and white wines. The red wines are chiefly made from Pinot Noir grapes, and the white wines are made primarily from Chardonnay grapes.

C.A.R.E.:   (Controlling Alcohol Risks Effectively)—A professional certification course in alcohol awareness for employees who serve and sell alcoholic beverages. The course is offered by the Educational Institute of the American Hotel and Lodging Association.

C_2H_5OH: The chemical formula for alcohol.

Calvados: The brand name for apple brandy produced in Calvados, a region in northern France.

Canadian whiskey: A whiskey produced in Canada made from a blend of grains such that no single grain contained in the mix can exceed 49 percent of the total.

Carbonation: The amount of carbon dioxide in a given amount of liquid.

Carbon dioxide (CO_2):   A by-product of the fermentation process that gives beer and sparkling wine their effervescence.

Cash bar: A term associated with banquets and other catered functions at which attendees pay for their own drinks.

Chablis: A small area located in northern Burgundy in France that produces dry, high-quality white wines made from Chardonnay grapes. Also, a term used to describe inexpensive California white wines that are usually not made from Chardonnay grapes.

Champagne: A sparkling wine produced in the Champagne region of France using the champagne method, or **méthode champenoise,** in which the second fermentation process takes place in the bottle in which it is sold.

Character: A word to describe a wine with specific qualities related to its style or variety.

Charmat method: A method used for making sparkling wines; named for Frenchman Eugène Charmat, the developer of the method.

Châteauneuf-du-Pape: Literally, "new castle of the pope." This appellation is located in the southern part of France's Rhône region. This area was the first in France to adopt strict rules for grape growing and winemaking.

Chewy: A descriptive term used to characterize a very rich and intense full-bodied wine.

Chianti: A sturdy, dry red wine produced in Chianti, a wine-producing area in Tuscany in central Italy.

Classic champagne: Also referred to as nonvintage (NV) Champagne. The product has no vintage year, and is a blend of the three Champagne grapes: Chardonnay, Pinot Noir, and Pinot Meunier.

CO_2:   Carbon dioxide, a by-product of fermentation which when captured, causes the bubbles in beer and sparkling wine.

Coarse: A term used to describe a poor-quality wine with body.

Cocktail: A generic name for a mixed drink.

Cognac: A fine French brandy produced in the town of Cognac and the areas surrounding it in western France, north of the Bordeaux region.

Collins: A mixed drink that may contain either gin or vodka, lemon juice, sugar, and carbonated water; usually served on ice in a tall, narrow glass.

Common law: A system of unwritten law not evidenced by statute but by traditions and the opinions and judgments of courts of law. It is generally agreed that the Law of England, as it existed at the time of the North American colonial settlements, is the basis of common law in the United States today, with the exception of Louisiana, which found its influence in the Napoleonic Code.

Contribution margin: The difference between a menu item's cost and its selling price. The profit, or margin, that remains contributes to covering fixed costs and providing for a profit.

Control state: A state in which the sale of alcoholic beverage products is directly controlled by the state.

Cork: A device commonly used to stopper a bottle. Real cork is derived from the bark of the evergreen oak tree.

Corky or corked: Descriptive words for a wine that has spoiled.

Cost of beverages sold: The dollar amount of all alcoholic beverages actually sold, thrown away, wasted, or stolen, plus or minus the value of transfers to or from other units within a foodservice operation.

Cost of goods sold: The actual dollar value of all goods used, or consumed, by a business operation in the process of selling a product or products to consumers. Foodservice operations generally break this cost into two distinct categories: **Cost of food sold** and **cost of beverages sold.**

Cost of sales: See **Cost of goods sold.**

Côte de Beaune: An area in the Burgundy region of France known for its outstanding white wines.

Coupe: A small, short-stemmed champagne glass with a wide, shallow bowl.

Crisp: A word used to describe a noticeably acidic wine, but one in which the acid does not overpower the wine.

Cru: Translated from the French as "growth," a term used to signify a potentially high-quality vineyard based on the prices that the wine has sold for in the past.

Delicate: Describes a quality wine that is light and well balanced.

Demi-Sec: Literally, "half-dry." A French term used to describe a sweet, sparkling wine.

Denominazione de Origine Controllata (DOC):   Italy's equivalent of the AOC in France. Established in 1963 and instituted in 1966, the DOC establishes the rules for wine production in Italy.

Dense: A descriptive term used to characterize a full-flavored wine or a wine with a deep color.

Deuxièmes Cru: Literally, "second growth." The second-highest category of wine rankings in the Bordeaux region of France, according to the 1855 classification.

Dionysus: The Greek god of wine, fertility, and drama.

Disgorging: A term used to describe the removal of sediment from a bottle of sparkling wine during the *méthode champenoise.*

Distillation: A process whereby the alcohol is removed from a beer or a wine.

Dom Pierre Perignon: The French monk who is credited with perfecting the technique for making champagne by blending grapes and wines from various vineyards to achieve a harmonious balance in the wine.

Dosage: A term used to describe a process that determines the level of sweetness in the final champagne product.

Double distillation: After the initial distillation, a process whereby the alcohol is removed from a beer or a wine a second time. Most distilled spirits are double distilled.

Doux: A term used to describe the sweetest level of champagne.

Dramshop laws: State laws that create a statutory cause of action against businesses and, in some cases, its employees, shifting the liability for acts committed by an individual under the influence of alcohol *from* that individual *to* the server or the establishment that supplied the intoxicating beverage.

Dried out: A descriptive term used to characterize a wine that has lost its fruitiness.

Earthy: A term used to describe a wine in which there is the aroma of dirt or earth in the wine.

Eau de vie: Literally, "water of life"; an unaged brandy.

Eighteenth Amendment: The Eighteenth Amendment to the U.S. Constitution, also known as the Volstead Act, that outlawed the production, transportation, and sale of alcoholic beverages.

Eiswein: A German term used for wine that is made from grapes that are harvested when frozen; literally, "ice wine."

Elegant: A descriptive word for a high-quality wine.

Empty-for-full system: An inventory control system in which alcoholic beverage stock is replenished by trading an empty container for a full container. The system is useful in combating pilferage.

Enzyme: An organic substance that acts as a catalyst during the fermentation process.

Extra Brut: A term used to describe the driest of all champagnes.

Extra Sec: A term used to characterize a sparkling wine that has been slightly sweetened.

Fat: A term used to describe a full-bodied sweet wine.

Fermentation: The process whereby yeast converts sugar into alcohol and carbon dioxide.

Finesse: A term used to describe a high-quality, well-balanced wine.

Fino: A major classification of sherry that is dry, light, and pale in color. The Fino classification is a result of the development of **flor** during the aging process.

Firm: A term used to describe a well-balanced, high-tannin, or acidic wine.

Flabby: A descriptive word for a wine that does not contain enough acidity.

Flat: A term used to describe a wine that lacks flavor because of its lack of acidity.

Fleshy: A descriptive word used to characterize a full-bodied, high-alcohol, smooth wine.

Flor: A white yeast crust that forms on the surface of fino sherry during the aging process. Flor does not form on Oloroso sherry.

Flute: A short-stemmed, tall glass with a conical bowl used to drink sparkling wine and champagne.

Fortified wine: A wine to which brandy has been added.

Forward: A term used to describe an early-maturing wine.

Fragrant: A descriptive word used to characterize a wine with a floral aroma or bouquet.

Free pouring: A method of measuring a pour of alcohol in which no actual measuring device is used. Rather, some operations train bartenders to silently count a pour; a four-count pour equals 1 fluid ounce.

French-American hybrids: The botanical mating of French grapevines and American grapevines.

Fresh: A descriptive word for a simple, well-balanced, fruity wine.

Fruity: A descriptive word for a wine that contains the aroma and flavor of fruit.

Full-bodied: A descriptive term used to characterize a wine or a beer that is rich, powerful, and intensely flavored and that normally has high sugar and alcohol content.

Fumé Blanc: A term coined by Robert Mondavi for California wines made from the Sauvignon Blanc grape in the style of those made of Pouilly Fumé in the Loire valley of France.

Gin: A distilled spirit flavored primarily with juniper berries and other seeds, roots, and barks.

Glucose: ($C_6H_{12}O_6$) A fermentable sugar found in grapes and in malt.

Grand Cru: Literally, "great growth"; a term used to signify the best wines of Bordeaux, Burgundy, and Alsace.

Grand Premier Cru: Literally, "great first growth"; a wine term specific to one house: Château d'Yquem in the Sauternes area of the Bordeaux region in France.

Grapey: A descriptive term for a wine with the flavors and aromas of grapes.

Grassy: A term used to describe a wine with the aroma of freshly cut grass.

Green: A descriptive term for a young, underdeveloped wine.

Grip: A young tannic or acidic wine with a firm texture that needs more time to develop.

Hammurabi's Code: An ancient code of law associated with Hammurabi, sixth king of the Amorite Dynasty of Old Babylon. It encodes many laws that probably evolved over a long period of time and is interesting to scholars because of what it tells them about the attitudes and daily lives of the ancient Babylonians.

Hard: A descriptive term for a wine with too much tannin or acid.

Heavy: A term used to describe a full-bodied, highly alcoholic wine.

Herbaceous: A term used to describe a wine with the aroma of herbs.

Hermitage: A winemaking area in the Rhône region in France in which the wines are made with the Syrah grape.

High wine: Also known as new whiskey, it is the unaged, second distillation.

Highball: A cocktail containing whiskey and some kind of carbonated mixer.

Hollow: A descriptive term for a wine with very little flavor or a disappointing flavor.

Hops: A dried, cone-shaped flower that is found on the catkin vine; related to the cannabis family. Hops adds the bitterness to beer and antiseptic qualities to prevent the growth of bacteria.

Host bar: A term associated with a banquet or other catered event at which the client, or host, pays for all beverages consumed. The term is synonymous with **open bar.**

Hot: A descriptive word for a wine out of balance and with a high alcohol content.

Hydrometer: An instrument used to measure the specific gravity of a liquid.

Intoxicated: The state or condition of being drunk or inebriated.

Irish Whiskey: A triple-distilled whiskey from Ireland that is made mostly with barley.

Jammy: A descriptive word for a wine with a concentrated fruit flavor.

Jeroboam: A term that refers to a bottle that is equal to four bottles, or 3 liters of wine; also known as a *double magnum*.

Jigger: A device used at a bar to measure specific quantities of alcoholic beverages. Jiggers are usually marked in ounces and portions of an ounce.

Lager: A bottom fermented beer; most macrobrewed American beers fall into this category of beer.

LBV: Late Bottled Vintage; a kind of port wine that is first aged in wood and then bottled after a vintage is declared.

Lean: A descriptive word for a wine with very little flavor.

License state: A state in which the state's liquor authority or alcoholic beverage control board licenses the establishments that are allowed to sell alcoholic beverages.

Light-bodied: A term used to describe a wine or beer that is lacking in body and or alcohol content.

LIP: The Australian equivalent of the AOC in France.

Liqueur d'Expedition: Also known as dosage.

Liqueur de tirage: The sugar or sweetener added to a still wine to begin a secondary fermentation which will produce a sparkling wine.

Liqueurs: Also known as cordials; a term generally used to describe a spirit to which some sort of sugar and flavoring have been added. Most liqueurs range between 34 and 60 proof, or between 16 percent and 30 percent alcohol by volume.

Low wine: A term used to describe a whiskey after its first distillation.

Mâconnaise: A town in Burgundy, France, known for its white wine production.

Magnum: A bottle equal to two bottles or 1 ½ liters.

Malmsey: The sweetest of Madeira wines.

Malolactic fermentation: A bacterial fermentation where the bacteria convert the malic acid into lactic acid. It is most associated with the production of Chardonnay wines in the United States and in red wines.

Malt: The germinated and roasted grain used to make beer and distilled spirits.

Martini glass: A stemmed, triangular shaped glass used to serve a martini.

Meaty: A term used to describe a full-bodied wine with rich flavors.

Medium-bodied: A term used to describe a wine or a beer that is somewhere between light- and full-bodied.

Meritage: A term used in California winemaking to describe a Bordeaux-style wine that employs a blend of the five Bordeaux red grapes: Cabernet Sauvignon, Merlot, Petit Verdot, Malbac, and Cabernet Franc.

Mescal: A distilled spirit similar to Tequila. It is made from the green agave plant as opposed to Tequila's blue agave. Sometimes Mescal is only distilled once; Tequila is always distilled twice. Mescal can be produced anywhere in Mexico. Tequila can only be produced in the Tequila region of Mexico.

Metallic: A wine with a tin-like flavor.

Méthode champenoise: A method for producing champagne in which the second fermentation process takes place in the bottle in which it is sold.

Methuselah: An oversized bottle equal to eight bottles or 6 liters.

Microbrewery: A small brewery.

Mocktail: A mixed drink made with no alcohol; many times made to mimic alcoholic drinks.

Moldy: A term used to describe a wine with a mold-like aroma or flavor.

Mousseux: A term used for sparkling wines produced outside the Champagne region in France.

Mouth-filling: A term used to describe a wine with a rich, full-bodied flavor.

Mystery shopper: A trained individual hired by management to pose as a restaurant or bar customer; the mystery shopper observes for service-related issues, theft, product quality and alcohol awareness issues, and then provides management with a detailed, written report.

Nebbiolo: An Italian red grape varietal used in the production of Barolo and Barbaresco.

Nebuchadnezzar: An oversized bottle equal in size to 15 liters or twenty bottles.

Neutral: A term used to describe a wine with very little flavor or aroma.

Noble Rot: Also known as Botrytis; it is employed in the production of dessert wines.

Nonvintage: A term used to describe sparkling wines that do not come from a single vintage.

Nutty: A descriptive word used to characterize a wine with a flavor or aroma of nuts.

Off: A term used to describe a wine that is flawed or spoiled.

Off-dry: A term used to describe a semi-dry wine.

Oily: A term used to describe a wine with an oily character in the flavor or in the aroma.

Oloroso: One of the two types of sherry produced without **flor;** usually full-bodied, sometimes sweet.

Open bar: A term associated with a banquet or other catered event at which the client, or host, pays for all beverages consumed. The term is synonymous with **host bar.**

Overdeveloped: A term used to describe a wine that has passed its prime.

Oxidized: A term used to describe a wine that has been exposed to air. This exposure has changed the quality of the wine from good to bad.

Penetrating: Describes a wine with an intense nose usually with a high alcohol content.

Peppery: Describes a wine with a spicy, black-pepper flavor.

Perfumed: A term used to describe a wine with a fragrant aroma.

Perpetual inventory: A method of monitoring inventory whereby additions to and deletions from the inventory are recorded as they occur. The method is normally reserved for high-cost food or beverage products.

Phylloxera: An abbreviated term used to describe *Phylloxera vastatrix.*

Phylloxera vastatrix: A louse that eats the rootstock of grapevines, thus destroying the vine. In the late 1800s, it devastated most of France's vineyards.

Physical inventory: An inventory control system in which an actual physical count and valuation of all inventory on hand is taken at the close of each accounting period.

Pilsner glass: A tall beer glass with a short stem and full, funnel-shaped bowl.

Pitching yeast: The process of adding yeast to a wort to help begin a controlled fermentation.

Port glass: A small short-stemmed wineglass that holds from 2 to 3 ounces. Used for drinking Port.

Pouilly-Fumé: A town in the Loire valley of France known for its production of white wines, made from the Sauvignon Blanc grape, which carry the same name.

Premier Cru: Literally, "first growth"; a term used to describe the highest-ranking wines of the Bordeaux region's 1855 classification; included only for houses Château Haut-Brion, Château Lafite-Rothschild, Château Latour, and Château Margeaux. Château Mouton-Rothschild was added in 1973.

Price spread: The difference in price of similar menu items between the highest- and lowest-priced items.

Prohibition: The period in the United States from 1920 to 1933 during which the manufacture, sale, and transportation of alcoholic beverages was prohibited. The period was marked by the Eighteenth Amendment to the U.S. Constitution which went into effect on January 16, 1920, and was repealed on December 5, 1933, by the Twenty-first Amendment.

Proof: A scale used to measure the alcohol in distilled spirits. One degree of proof equals one-half percent of alcohol.

QbA: *Qualitätswein Bestimmter Anbaugebiete;* The lower-level quality of wine produced in Germany.

QmP: *Qualitätswein mit Prädikat.* The higher-level quality of wine produced in Germany, subdivided into six subcategories: Kabinett, Spätlese, Auslese, Beerenauslese, Trockenbeerenauslese, and Eiswein.

Quinta: In Portugal, a wine estate equivalent to that of a French château.

Rainwater: A type of Madeira that is a blend of the Tinta Negra Mole grape and the Verdelho grape; very light.

Raw: A term to describe a wine with a young and underdeveloped flavor.

Reasonable care: A legal concept associated with a restaurant or bar owner's common law duty to protect customers from harm or injury. To provide reasonable care is to do or not do what any other sane and reasonable person would or would not do under same or similar circumstances.

Refractometer: A device used to measure the sugar content of grapes in the field in order to determine when the grapes are ready to harvest.

Rich: A term used to describe a wine with a balanced, full flavor.

Riddling: The quarter-turn of a bottle when using the *méthode champenoise.*

Robert Mondavi: A famous winemaker from California, owner of Robert Mondavi vineyards, which includes Byron vineyards and Opus One, among others.

Robust: A term used to describe a wine with a full flavor.

Rocks glass: A short, stemless, 6-to-8 ounce glass.

Rough: A term used to describe a wine that is overly tannic or acidic.

Round: A term used to describe a wine with a well-balanced, mellow, and full-bodied flavor.

Ruby Port: A younger port which takes its name from it color.

Ruländer: The German name for Pinot Gris.

Rum: A distilled spirit made from fermented sugar cane juice.

Sake: An alcoholic beverage made from rice. Even though often labeled as a wine, it is more correctly labeled a rice beer even though it lacks carbonation.

Salmanazar: A very large bottle equal to twelve bottles or 9 liters.

Sancerre: A town in the Loire valley of France known for its production of white wines, made from the Sauvignon Blanc grape, which carry the same name.

Sauternes: A small area in the Bordeaux region of France known for its production of sweet, white dessert wines.

Scented: A term used to describe a wine with a fragrant aroma.

Scotch: A whiskey made in Scotland from barley. Old bourbon or sherry barrels are used for aging scotch. It gets its smoky taste from the peat over which the barley is dried.

Sec: Literally, "dry"; a French word used to describe sparkling wines that are semi-dry.

Secondary fermentation: The addition of sugar and yeast to an already fermented wine to encourage carbonation.

Sercial: A kind of Madeira that is very dry, similar to fino sherry.

Sharp: A term used to describe a wine with too much acid.

Short: A term used to describe a wine with very little flavor in the finish.

Shot glass: A small glass used to measure a specific amount of distilled spirit.

Silky: A term used to describe a wine with a smooth texture and flavor.

Simple: A term used to describe a wine that is not complex.

Smoky: A term used to describe a wine that has a smoky flavor.

Smooth: A term used to describe a wine that has a smooth texture and finish.

Snifter: A round, bulbous, short-stemmed glass used for drinking brandy.

Soft: A term used to describe a wine that is mellow and well balanced.

Solid: A term used to describe a wine that is full-bodied from high levels of acidity, alcohol, fruit, and tannin.

Sommelier: A wine expert usually employed by upscale restaurants.

Sour: A term used to describe a wine with a lot of acidity.

Sparklers: The Australian term for sparkling wine.

Sparkling wine: A wine that contains a carbon dioxide effervesence.

Spätburgunder: The German word for Pinot Noir.

Spätlese: Literally, "late picked"; the German word for the second level of QmP wines.

Specific gravity: The relative thickness of a liquid based on water.

Spumante: The Italian word for sparkling wine.

Stalky or stemmy: Terms used to describe wine with a green flavor.

Steely: A term used to describe a white wine that is high in acidity and well balanced but that is otherwise lean.

Stein: A large German beer glass, usually with a handle.

Stewed: A term used to describe a wine that has been exposed to heat and tastes cooked.

Super Tuscans: Wines made in the Tuscan region of Italy; made specifically with the Merlot and the Cabernet Sauvignon grapes, not from Italian varietals.

Supple: A term that describes a wine that is soft but well-structured.

Süssereserve: In German winemaking, this refers to a reserve of juice that is held back from the fermentation so that it can be added later to the wine in order to sweeten it. This is a necessary process in German winemaking because the grapes are so acidic.

Tannin: The astringent, mouth-drying qualities in certain red wines that comes from the skins, the seeds, and the stems of the grapes.

Tart: A term used to describe a wine that is high in acid and leaves a sharp, sour note in the mouth.

Tawny Port: A wood-aged port whose name is derived from its characteristic orange color.

Tennessee whiskey: Whiskey made in Tennessee from a special process that uses a charcoal, maple filter. Only two houses currently produce Tennessee Whiskey: Jack Daniels and George Dickel.

Tequila: A distilled spirit made from the blue agave plant found only in the Tequila region of Mexico.

Terroir: A French word with no literal translation; generally used to describe all of the environmental factors which are unique to a particular location.

The 1855 Classification: A classification of wines in the Bordeaux region of France, which was developed at the request of the Emperor Napoleon III. It breaks down sixty of the top châteaus into five crus.

TIPS (Training for Intervention Procedures): A professional certification program, offered by Health Communications, Inc., that teaches sellers, servers, and consumers of alcohol how to prevent intoxication, drunk driving, and underage drinking.

Tired: A term used to describe a wine that has been overaged.

Top fermenting: A fermentation process associated with ale.

Tough: A term used to describe a full-bodied wine with lots of tannin.

Transfer method: A method of making sparkling wines that was developed in Germany.

Triple distillation: The process of distilling a spirit three times.

Trockenbeerenauslese: Literally, "dry berry out-picked," one of the German classifications of wine quality, generally the sweetest, rarest, and most expensive.

Twenty-first Amendment: The amendment that repealed the Eighteenth Amendment.

Vanilla: An aroma in wine caused by aging the wine in new oak barrels.

VDQS: The second-quality tier of French wine.

Vegetal: An aroma in wine of a vegetable character in the nose.

Vintage Port: A vintage dated port of a very high quality; bottled directly and usually aged for fifteen to twenty years; normally requires decanting.

Vitis labrusca: Grapes indigenous to the Americas.

Vitis vinifera: Grapes indigenous to Europe.

VML (Very Large Machine): Used to riddle bottles in sparkling wine production outside of Champagne, France.

Vodka: A neutral distilled spirit that can legally be made from anything but is most often made from potatoes or grain.

Volstead Act: Another name for the Eighteenth Amendment to the U.S. Constitution.

VSOP (Very Special Old Pale): Four-star brandy.

Warren Winiarski: A winemaker in Napa Valley, California, best known for winning the top prize at a 1976 international wine competition for Cabernet Sauvignons.

Watery: Describes a wine with a watered-down flavor.

Whiskey: A distilled beverage made from grain in the United States or Ireland.

Whisky: A distilled beverage made from grain in Scotland or Canada.

White Burgundy: A Chardonnay wine made in Burgundy, France.

White Zinfandel: A white wine made from the red Zinfandel grape.

Woody: A term used to describe a wine that has been aged too long in oak barrels.

Yeast: A nonchlorophyll plant that converts sugar into alcohol and carbon dioxide.

Yeasty: A term that describes a wine with a yeast aroma.

Zesty: A term used to describe a white wine with a fresh crisp flavor and aroma.

Index